The Puritans Thomas & Stephen Tracy: A Personal Quest for Family Lineage

MARTIN BOOTH TRACY PH.D.

ISBN: 1542853699
ISBN 13: 9781542853699
Library of Congress Control Number: 2017901605
CreateSpace Independent Publishing Platform
North Charleston, South Carolina

TABLE OF CONTENTS

1

INTRODUCTION

I didn't know it at the time, but I had been bitten by the notoriously infectious *Cognatio Genealogia Indagatio Insectum*. It is a particularly insidious pest that languidly lies in waiting until the victim reaches their late 60's or early 70's before pouncing without warning or mercy. In some cases, it strikes at an even earlier age. It is a member of the phylum *Family Genealogy* which was designated specifically to identify the irrational quest for knowledge *information* of family ancestors who lived long ago and far away. Okay, so I'm making all this up, including the Latin. It's a tribute to my high school Latin teacher, Mrs. Lorraine Swann. She'd be so proud.

It all began the summer of 1995 at one of the first gatherings of many of the members of the far-flung Tracy-Booth family. Held in the San Francisco Bay area, folks came from as far away as Australia and Hawaii, but most were from Oregon, Washington, California, Arizona, Colorado, New Mexico, and Michigan. I was the lone representative from southern Illinois a stone's throw from Western Kentucky where I spent my childhood near picturesque Kentucky Lake. *LBL*

At the conclusion of a fun-filled couple of days sampling wine and cheese in beautiful Sonoma County enjoying the company of cousins, aunts, and uncles, our host gave each of us a surprise gift. It was a large chart of our family tree, along with a detailed chart book entitled: *A Genealogy of the Tracy & Booth Families.* It was the gift of Bonnie Aloma Seto, my paternal 1st cousin once removed. "Once removed" is genealogy-speak for the child of a 1st cousin. In this case it happens to have been a daughter of my delightful and engaging 1st cousin Muriel Elizabeth Bloxom Seto. Paternal, of course, just refers to near and distant relatives born in the father's family line. Incidentally, the Booth family is my father's maternal line. No, they are not closely related to that Booth! My Booth line originated in Manchester, England, not London. My Booths settled in the Ohio River town of Marietta, Ohio in 1810.

But I digress (I apologize up front, I'll do that often in this narrative); the important point is that Cousin Bonnie had hired a professional genealogical research company, *Lineages, Inc., of Salt Lake City*, to undertake an exhaustive examination of our family lines. Let me assure you, such a task is a major undertaking, especially when the family is not particularly historically well known. Obtaining records and documents with even basic information on dates and places of births and deaths, much less marriages and parentages can be a real challenge, even for the best genealogist. Of course, the further back in time an ancestor lived, the harder it becomes. I didn't fully appreciate the difficulties involved until I started doing my own research. My admiration for the painstaking investigation reflected in Bonnie's seminal work continues to grow.

Her splendid gift that keeps on giving took everyone at the reunion by surprise. And, I, being the wanna-be-historian that I am, was simply blown away! I couldn't wait to get home, put aside that academic paper on income programs for the elderly in Malaysia that needed my attention, and delve into the backgrounds of some of the more beguiling family ancestors. I especially wanted to investigate my ancestors who lived in the Puritan era in New England. However, reality soon sunk in that any serious research would have to take a back seat to my teaching, administrative, and research duties, as well as family obligations. There was, though, no doubt that the damage had been done – I was infected! I had contracted that tedious pest the *Cognatio Genealogia Indagatio Insectum*. The only cure was to cautiously forge ahead, keeping in mind, as Faulkner put it, *The past isn't dead, it isn't even past.* Or, in the case of my affliction, "The *pest* isn't dead." If you can't stand puns and slightly snarky humor you may want to put the book down now. I'll forgive you. My wife, son and forbearing friends will fully understand!

As much excitement as the family chart generated, it was, after all, only a chart with bare bone details of names, dates and places of births, deaths, and marriages. Critical information, to be sure, but, now that I had the names I wanted to put some flesh on the bones so I could see more than a mere skeleton. WHO WERE THESE PEOPLE? Where did they come from; where did they live; what did they do to earn a living; how were they involved in their communities; what public offices did they hold; what were their religious views; what existential angst did they face; were they criminals; were they famous; and, most importantly; why should you and I care!? To begin with, I love history and I find it very enlightening, not to mention more interesting, when I look at ancestors within an historical context. As President Harry Truman once observed, *"The only new things in the world is the history you do not know."*

It didn't take me long to find out that what many amateur family genealogists, and make no mistake the vast majority of us are amateurs, look for most often is for relationships to famous people. In the case of families with English ancestry, they want to establish a blood connection to nobility and royalty. I plead guilty as charged, your honor! I fell for this early on. I should have known better. After all, I like to think of myself as a serious research analyst and I've been known to produce a scholarly work or two. But, my training failed me in this instance and I succumbed to the temptation to jump on the bandwagon with numerous Tracy family faithful anxious to establish that aristocratic blue blood flows through our veins. I wanted to believe that the DNA in my Tracy line is composed of patrician nucleotides.

A Surprise While Hiking in the English Cotswolds

I might not have been so gullible to readily accept the notion of a direct connection to British Tracy aristocracy, if it had not been for a casual trip to England with our son, Morgan. My wife, Patsy, Morgan, and I had made enjoyable visits to England previously when I worked in Geneva, Switzerland in the late 1970s. Morgan was age 6 and 7 when we took those trips. Flash forward to 1993 when he graduated from college. His graduation gift was a hiking trip in England. With his travel-loving dad, of course! Mind you, this was two years before the California family reunion. So, this was a pure pleasure trip with no genealogical distractions that, much to the chagrin of my long suffering yet somehow understanding spouse, have come to be the norm. Morgan and I were simply out for a bonding father and son outing hiking off and on the enchanting Cotswold Way about 90 miles west of London.

As Gilbert of Gilbert and Sullivan would have expressed our outing we were *"tripping hither tripping thither, nobody knows why or whither."* You're all big Gilbert and Sullivan fans, right? I mean, who among us with even a smidgen of English DNA isn't? We backpacked and stayed in charming (read inexpensive and rustic) Beds & Breakfasts in villages with names indicative of a J. K. Rawlings tall tale only found in England like Stow-on-the-Wold, Moreton-in-Marsh, Chipping Camden, and Snowshill. Each day we would work off the cholesterol ingested from the previous night's pub food. We had chosen from such delicacies as toad-in-the-hole, bangers and mash, shepherd's pie, or my all-time favorite; ploughman's lunch (a serious hunk of stilton cheese, pickle, and bread). Naturally, all this English *haute cuisine* was washed down with a pint of a local brew.

Of course, each morning we were infused with a calorie-loaded full English breakfast. For those of you unfortunate not to have indulged in this tasty tradition, any basic B&B worth its salt will serve you ample amounts of bacon (traditionally back bacon), fried, poached or scrambled eggs, fried or grilled tomatoes, fried mushrooms, fried bread or toast with butter, sausages, and baked beans. Black pudding, bubble and squeak and hash browns are often also included. Bubble and squeak is a serving of fried left-overs from last night's roast dinner with added vegetables. In England, the highest compliment of a delicious food is to describe it as "lovely." We both still dream about the lovely Cumberland sausages. Thus fortified with fried foods, we had plenty of energy to get us over hill and dale to carry us to our next destination and well-earned evening meal.

Somewhere along the line of the third or fourth day out, we happened to pick up a brochure on Stanway House located near the small Cotswold town of Winchombe. Stanway House, AKA Stanway Manor, is a striking Jacobean manor with baroque gardens that is a big tourist attraction. A no less dignitary than J. M. Barrie of Peter Pan fame was a regular guest at the manor in the 1940s, as were such other English luminaries including Arthur Conan Doyle, A. A. Milne, and H. G. Wells. But, what got our attention was a reference in the brochure to the Tracy family. It seems that for 800 years Stanway House was owned by Tewkesbury Abbey, a Benedictine Monastery. Following a political upheaval that I'll get to in more detail later; it fell into the hands of the Tracy family where it remained for 500 years until 1798 when the family ran out of male heirs. The last unadulterated Tracy male in this particular line was the 8th Viscount Henry Leigh Tracy who was born in 1732 and died in 1797.

The only child and heiress of the 8th Viscount was Henrietta Susanna Tracy. She married her cousin Charles Hanbury of Pontypool. This is not to be confused with *Pontypool* the 2008 Canadian horror film! Cousin Charles was from Pontypool, Monmouthshire in Wales. In a gesture way ahead of today's hyphenated family names, he added the family name of Tracy to his own surname. By Royal License the family became Hanbury-Tracy. Charles Hanbury-Tracy was the 1st Baron Sudeley. The current and 7th Baron Sudeley is Merlin Charles Sainthill Hanbury-Tracy born in 1939. He was in the House of Lords for 39 years. You might be familiar with his well-known political leanings. I couldn't possibly comment.

The curiosity that this whole scenario aroused in me was just too intriguing to ignore. My inner tourist-historian wanted answers. So, on an almost sunny Sunday morning (this was, after all, England in late spring) we trekked through fields, pastures, and woods along the Cotswold Way. When we reached Stanway we saw some locals, about eight of them, heading into a lovely Norman church conveniently located next to the manor. Needless to say, we followed along, and also needless to say, we attracted a good deal of attention. However, the locals did wait until the service ended before approaching us to inquire as to what did they owe the honor of our presence. I quickly uttered that we were hiking the Cotswold Way, and, by the way (no pun intended) our family name is Tracy. Well, that definitely broke the ice with hardy heartfelt handshakes all around. They were so excited they neglected to offer us a spot of tea and scones! Nevertheless, those assembled knew a whole lot more about the Tracys than we.

One older gentleman gave us a short history of the family which whetted my interest. He turned out to be Martin Michael Charles Charteris. His title was the Baron Charteris of Amisfield. He had recently retired as a private secretary to Queen Elizabeth II. He was the uncle of the 7th Baron Sudeley, the previously mentioned Merlin Charles Sainthill Hanbury-Tracy. I have a framed photo of the Baron taken with me with Stanway Manor as a backdrop. *Wikipedia* has a biography on him. He could have been a wonderful resource on family history after I became hooked on genealogy. Unfortunately, he died in 1999. A missed opportunity there! It is truly said "he who hesitates is lost."

Spurred on by our conversation with the Baron Charteris, I later learned that the Stanway branch of the Tracy family is replete with aristocracy of various stripes. They were particularly known for their important roles in the development of Protestantism in England. But, was this family line my family line? I'm going to leave you sitting on the edge of your seat in anticipation and delay answering that question until much later. Suffice it to say that the appeal of having highborn blood came to the fore when I first laid eyes on Cousin Bonnie's genealogical chart.

At first blush, the chart seemed to confirm an association with the Tracy family of Stanway House through my 7th Great Grandfather, Lt. Thomas Tracy. With chart in hand I thought what fun it was going to be confirming the link between my ancestor and the Tracys of Stanway Manor. Alas, only in the past year or so have I discovered that this isn't likely to be true. Thomas Tracy is unquestionably from England, but his birth place may not be Gloucestershire County where Stanway is located. By the by, while Stanway Manor was the home of a distinguished line of Tracys, that family line was also prominent in nearby Toddington and Tewkesbury. To simplify the mentions of that family line, future discussions of Stanway are generally also a reference to these other sites. I should hasten to point out that while it is doubtful that Thomas was of nobility or aristocracy, he was an honorable man.

This doesn't mean that Lt. Thomas Tracy and I aren't related to the Stanway Barons. We are linked in as much as people who carry the surname Tracy in England and Ireland are related. However, the connection is undoubtedly very distant dating back to the first person to carry that moniker who graced the shores of England. One widely held notion is that our common Tracy ancestor is probably Hugh de Trasi who came to England with William the Conqueror in 1066. Hugh is also known as Rufus (Red). He took his surname from the village of Tracy-Bocage in Normandy, France. The Tracy family had a castle in the French commune of Caen in the prefecture of Calvados. In addition, there is a Tracy-sur-Mer on the coast of Normandy.

There were also Tracys who at some point crossed the English Channel and ended up in Suffolk County, England. Apparently, that batch of Tracys hailed from Tracy-le-Mont and Tracy-le-Val in France. These are two villages located about 60 miles northeast of Paris in the Oise Department. Normandy or Oise (pronounced *waz*), all you Tracys out there are of French origin, *mes cousins et mes amies*! For you wine connoisseurs who like to mix pleasure with family history, there is an outstanding Château de Tracy vineyard 125 miles south of Paris in Tracy sur Loire. If you are an oenophile (look it up, I had to), try the *Château de Tracy Pouilly Fumé* to complement your hors d'oeuvres.

Hugh de Trasi was probably the father of Sir Turgis de Traci (note the change of spelling) was the Baron of Barnstaple. Sir Traci had one daughter who was bestowed in marriage to William, illegitimate son of King Henry I, also known as Henry Beauclerc. He was the fourth son of William the Conqueror. William was born at Bradninch Manor in Devon County. When he married Sir Traci's daughter, William adopted his wife's surname and became William de Tracy (1090-1136). He was the grandfather of William de Tracy (d. 1189) who was one of the assassins of Thomas Beckett, Archbishop of Canterbury. I'll have more to relate about this much later in this narrative. If you want to explore the early stages of all the Tracy lines in England, I suggest reading a book written in 1796 by John Kent Tracy titled *A Short Memoir, Critically Illustrating the Histories of the Noble Families of Tracy, and Courtenay, Exhibiting Likewise, the Ancient Usage, or Variation, of Coat Armour, in That of Tracy.* It was reprinted by Eighteen Century Collections Online Print Editions. It is a fascinating read.

Stephen Tracy, Jr. & Lt. Thomas Tracy

Over time, of course, the off springs of Hugh de Trasi and Turgis de Traci diverged into all manner of social and economic standings all around the English Isle. My narrative follows the lives of two "commoner" descendants of the first Norman/English Tracys who were early colonial New England settlers. These are Stephen Tracy, Jr. and Lt. Thomas Tracy. They were primogenitors of numerous Tracy family lines in the United States and Canada. Stephen Tracy, Jr. was an English Pilgrim and Puritan, who arrived at Plymouth, Massachusetts in July, 1623. He was also a founder of Duxbury, Massachusetts in the Plymouth Colony. Thomas Tracy (commonly known as Lt. Thomas Tracy) came from England to the Watertown settlement in the Massachusetts Bay Colony in 1636. He also lived briefly in Salem followed by several years' residence in Wethersfield and Saybrook, Connecticut Colony before becoming a founder of Norwich, Connecticut.

One of his sons was also a founding father of Norwich. Two other sons were founders of Preston City, Connecticut.

Stephen Tracy, Jr. is not included in Cousin Bonnie's family chart because no direct ancestry to him has been established with my Tracy line. Thomas is indisputably my ancestor and before all is said and done I will make the case that he is quite possibly a cousin of Stephen, but I can't prove it. Even if I'm mistaken and they aren't closely related, I'm going to explore the life of Stephen because it epitomizes the life of a Puritan who left England for Holland and later left Holland for New England as a Pilgrim. And, of course, because he was a TRACY, what possible better reason could there be?

If you don't object, since I refer to these two ancestors so often, I'm going to streamline my references to them, for the most part, as Thomas and Stephen. I'll let you know when I'm talking about a different Thomas or Stephen of whom there were legions in the early 1600s.

Conducting Research

Before going any further the educator in me insists that despite my own misadventures in gathering data on my ancestors, I should say a few words about my research process, flawed as it may be. Now pay close attention all you budding family genealogists! No, there will not be a follow-up test. This is knowledge for its own sake. Perhaps you are familiar with the legend of a beginning student of geometry who asked Euclid, "*What shall I get by learning these things?*" Euclid responded by sarcastically calling to a slave; saying come and "*Give him* [the student] *a coin, since he must make gain out of what he learns.*" There is no coin at the end of this tale, only the joy of discovery.

I should add the caveat that my references to historical events are intended merely to give a hint of historical context to the times in which Stephen and Thomas lived. It is, you might say, "history light." If my favorite college history professor, Dr. Frank Steely, was still with us, I'd ask his forgiveness. So if any of you out there are real historians, don't get after me if I've inadvertently misinterpreted an historical event or left out some important historical aspect. There are no intentional "alternate facts" in the text. If you feel compelled to further explore or "fact check" any of the history I mention, and I hope you do. Go for it!

Ut is realized that - ~   but, the explain
*   is*

I realize that for many folks genealogical research doesn't hold the fascination that it does for the likes of me. The feeling of "oh no, not family genealogy again" whenever the subject is raised is well expressed in a quote from William V. Havens of Joliet, Illinois in a letter written to Dr. Dwight Tracy, M.D., D.D.S. in 1905. Mr. Havens was responding to a family genealogical inquiry from Dr. Tracy. Havens concluded his response with a post script, as follows: *"P. S. My experience is that the average citizen takes to collecting genealogical data with about the same zest and relish they would have if on occasion they found they were breaking out with the measles."*

Undaunted by such cynicism, I began my research on Stephen and Thomas by delving into a serious review of a vast array of books and articles that made specific references to these two fellows. You'd probably be surprised, as I was, as to how many historians and genealogists have written about them. The problem, as I eventually found out from the experts, is that there are many more flawed genealogies of them and their acquaintances than there are accurate ones. Incorrect genealogies tend to take on a life of their own. Someone makes a speculation about a family line without basing it on trustworthy and primary documentation. Someone else reads it and takes it for gospel. Then, of course, someone else continues to disseminate the mistakes.

The progression is like the old *game of telephone* (it works the same with Facebook, Tweeter, Instagram, and any other social media) where one person whispers to another and so on through a line of people until the last player announces a totally distorted message to the entire group. The alteration is really akin to the phenomenon of "fake news" that emerged in social media in the election of 2016, but the effect of a malicious or unintentional spin is pretty much the same. It is hard to break the cycle. You can't put the genie back in the bottle. And, as you know, it is frustrating as heck to decipher what is true and what isn't. Add the dimension of misinformation that has circulated for, in many cases, hundreds of years; being passed down in book after book, article after article, and family genealogy after family genealogy and the extent of the problem becomes more palpable.

Apropos to this quandary is an astute sign to the entrance of the Waterfield Library at Murray State University. It beckons entry to the library *"Because employers want employees who know the difference between websearch and research."* This is good advice for both budding students and garden variety genealogists. It doesn't mean that the web isn't a good tool; it's just that its limitations should be recognized and factored into the equation when making assumptions. Ditto that for offline documents that aren't based on empirical research. Primary records are difficult to obtain and I'm as guilty as the next person who has grabbed onto data that have little by the way of viable documentation to back them up. I'm working on doing better!

Pitfall   *(Good verbage*

Because of the large quantity of erroneous information floating about in cyberspace, I try as much as possible to acquire hard copies of primary documents and records. I then attempt to corroborate the kernels of information found therein with data from books and journals written by reputable genealogists and researchers. This usually means using sources other than a family genealogist like me! Although family genealogists are sometimes the only source of otherwise impossible to find information, such as family bibles and wills. Nevertheless, I generally rely on the observations of genealogists who have drawn their documentation from primary records such as court records, census records, marriage and birth records, obituaries (although they are not always reliable), wills, correspondence, and personal papers. The prevailing rule is that primary records are always better than secondary records.

A huge advantage in conducting research is to have a relative or good friend who is a librarian who can put their fingers on materials that it would take you and me hours, days, weeks or even months to find and maybe not even then. Fortunately, my son, Morgan, just happens to be a librarian's librarian who knows how to access the most elusive of materials! Morgan, Director of Library Services at Asbury University in Wilmore, Kentucky, has been an invaluable resource! In addition to tracking down books and documents for me that are near impossible to find by dolts such as dear old dad, he has led me to several online resources, including the marvelous *HathiTrust Digital Library*. Other great online book resources are *books.google.com*, *Heritage Quest Online*, and *archives.org*. Many books on these sites are available in their entirety online and are searchable. All you have to do is search for a person or event and let the *find* button do the work.

Alas, one often finds a book online that only tantalizes. A promising title is provided with a hint that what you are looking for is actually in the book, but it turns out not to have been scanned into any accessible online services. Sometimes the website will provide information on where the book is housed in a library by linking you to the *OCLC World Catalogue*. Or you can go directly to the World Catalogue website. Unhappily, for those of us who live in a rural Kentucky town such repositories are frequently quite distant.

Fortunately if you aren't able to conveniently get to the library where the book is housed there are a couple of options. One is to request a library loan from your local public library. Occasionally this works and is worth the effort. Most often, however, many old and limited edition genealogical books that are housed in public and private libraries are not loaned out willy-nilly. There are good reasons for this as every librarian is all too familiar with getting loaned books back with missing pages, highlighted text, underscored text, or "sad sams." For those of you who read only from Nooks and Kindles, that's an allusion to a turned down corner on a paper page to mark it for later use. Don't do that!

The good news is that most public libraries will make copies of specific materials and even look up an explicit request. This covers more than books. A public library may also have vertical files of families, and, of course, newspaper items, including obituaries. Many public libraries will do a search for free, charging only for copies and postage. Others charge a reasonable search fee or ask for a contribution. If the library doesn't conduct searches, librarians are usually very good about steering you in the right direction. Tickity boo!

Speaking of public libraries, my long-suffering wife is altogether too familiar with my insistence that we stop to visit community libraries along the paths of where my far-flung family resided over the generations. Many of these wonderful edifices have information on Tracy and associated families. It is difficult to identify a chapter in American history that had more of an impact on our democratic and literary legacy than the public 1,689 libraries built by the Scottish-American steel magnate Andrew Carnegie from 1899 to 1919. The architecture alone, ranging from Beaux-Arts and Italian Renaissance to Baroque, is enough reason to stop and go into these marvels. Carnegie believed libraries gave to the *"industrious and ambitious; not those who need everything done for them, but those who, being most anxious and able to help themselves, deserve and will be benefited by help from others."* Trust me, the largely absent equivalent in developing nations and the former Soviet Union has greatly inhibited the nurturing of democratic values and principles.

Historical societies in a locality of interest are also an excellent source for documents and related references. I've obtained numerous documents from the staff of historical societies. One that I've used is the *Norfolk (England) History Society*. I've acquired some valuable help from the *Watertown (Massachusetts) Historical Society* and the *Watertown Historical Commission*. Most recently Archivist and Historian Carolyn Ravenscroft of the *Duxbury Rural and Historical Society* in Duxbury, Massachusetts furnished me with appreciated materials related to Stephen Tracy.

In May, 2016 the Archivist at the *Kingston Public Library*, Kingston, Massachusetts, Susan Aprill, sent me email attachments on Stephen's land grants in Duxbury. Genealogist Louise Leake of *The Society of the Founders of Norwich*, Connecticut has been very helpful in obtaining information on Thomas Tracy. Another useful resource for Thomas has been Diane Hoyt of the *Old Saybrook Historical Society in Saybrook*, Connecticut. And Lorna K. Kirwan at the *Bancroft Library at the University of California at Berkeley* tracked down an elusive family collection for me. I'm indebted to all of these nice folks and others who are mentioned in the acknowledgements at the end.

Establishing contact with historical societies can also have positive spinoff effects that link you to folks who are informally or formally connected to a society. One very recent example is from my contact with the *Duxbury Rural and Historical Society* who linked me with a professional land surveyor, Lamont (Monty) R. Healy, who shared a copy of his worksheets on ownership of land grants in Duxbury, including Stephen Tracy. This information is extremely helpful in identifying exactly where Stephen lived when he moved from Plymouth to nearby Duxbury. It's gratifying how complete strangers who have a passion for history will help you in your quest for information that would otherwise not be available to you.

There are also national resource libraries with extensive genealogical materials that frequently will have the obscure book you are looking for. One major institution is the *Chicago Newberry Library*. Another Midwestern library with extensive genealogical holdings is the *Fort Wayne, Indiana Allen County Public Library*. I have no idea how or why it became a national genealogical resource center, but there it is.

It is also beneficial to establish correspondence with friends and acquaintances as wacky as yourself when it comes to learning about ancestors. I've been fortunate to have a friend from childhood who is a consummate genealogist. He has been a huge help in leading me to resources that I would not have thought of on my own, especially resources regarding 17th Century New England, DNA, and research methods. One very useful publication he recently called my attention to is the award winning Ebook *Finding Family: My Search for Roots and the Secrets of My DNA* by Richard Hill. This engaging and informative book reads like a mystery novel. Indeed, I got the idea for my own humble attempt to write this narrative from Hill's book. Thank you Vernon Brian Anderson, old and faithful friend and fellow genealogy geek.

My 1st cousin, Tracy Allen, gave much time and effort to help enlighten me by doing some valuable library research for me on material available only in his home state of California. I've made a number of new "virtual" friends whom I've found online who are also interested in the same Tracy lineage. This includes multiple distant cousins. The exchanges we're had have been mutually beneficial in filling in gaps. A certain amount of common sense caution is advised when initiating contact with folks at the other end of the cyber highway. Don't give snail mail or email addresses until you are reasonably sure that the folks on the receiving end are legitimate. Fortunately, it is possible to engage in conversations related to ancestors on *Ancestry.com, LegacyFamilyTree.com, FamilySearch.org*, etc. without divulging who you are or where you live until you are ready to do so.

When I began looking for my roots in 1995 I utilized the limited online genealogical services available at the time, including *rootsweb.org* message boards and other now archaic services. I also spent a copious amount of time browsing through genealogical materials housed in the *Pogue Library* at Murray State University and the *Martin E. Schmidt Research Library* in the *Thomas D. Clark Center for Kentucky History in Frankfort, Kentucky*. Although both of these fine facilities highlight Kentucky history they also house genealogical journals and documents covering the nation. The *Murray State University Waterfield Library* holds numerous history books on the 1600s that were of great use in my research.

The *McCracken County Public Library* in nearby Paducah, Kentucky also proved to be a valuable resource. The McCracken Library is also one of the many repositories for *Family History Centers* that provide

Great place to check out

access to microfiche data from the *Family History Library* in Salt Lake City, Utah. Of course, I'm also grateful to the wonderful *Calloway County Public Library* in my hometown of Murray, Kentucky for all the help the staff have been in acquiring books for me through the library loan program. I've also been able to access books and articles on *HeritageQuest Online* from the comfort of my own home work room through the library's website.

An ongoing outstanding resource is the *New England Historic Genealogical Historic Society (NEHGS)* in Boston, Massachusetts. It has both a great library and an online subscription service. Historian Henry Louis Gates, Jr., Harvard Professor and host of the PBS TV series *Finding Your Roots* relies a great deal on NEHGS for his research on celebrities of all sorts. NEHGS' portal on the web is available at AmericanAncestors.org. One of the many useful resources available from NEHGS is *The New England Genealogical Historical Register*. Another is *The Great Migration Newsletter* edited by Robert Charles Anderson. The newsletter is wonderful resource for background material on the Great Migration (1620-1640) from England to New England. It is available for a modest subscription price. I'll have much more to say on that seminal period of American history covered by the *Newsletter* as we go along.

In 2007 I had an opportunity to visit the NEHGS library in Boston. I wanted to access the vast resources of the library related to New England history, as well as family genealogy. I had arranged to pay for an hour's assistance with one of the Society's esteemed genealogists. I came prepared with a list of specific questions related to gaps or "brick walls" that I had encountered in my research. My most pressing brick wall was the fate of my paternal Grandfather James Albert Tracy, Sr. who was last seen boarding a ship in the San Francisco harbor in the summer of 1929. Unfortunately, that brick wall remains as solid and impervious as ever, but that is another story. Despite that disappointment, the NEHGS genealogist was able to help me with research issues regarding both Stephen and Thomas. I should point out that, in addition to this one time visit, I've benefited enormously by being a member of NEHGS with online access to ever expanding resources.

Another useful online tool that I use is the *FamilyTree Maker* software which has led to numerous connections to useful documents and other folks who were doing research on the Tracy family. This is no longer functioning as it once did, although there are updates for Mac users one of which I am not. I've used Windows on my PC for ages, and I'm too long in the tooth to change now. I have recently subscribed to *Legacy Family Tree 8.0*. It is an advanced and more comprehensive software tool that allows you to sync with *FamilySearch.org*. I've also found *WikiTree.com, Myheritage.com, WorldVitalRecords.com*, and *GenealogyBank.com* to be helpful resources.

Accessing the information on these sites really only scratches the surface. Anyone who wants to devote even more time than I am willing to commit can sign on to all kinds of informative webinars offered by NEHGS, Legacy, and a host of other genealogical sites. If you want to take things a step further, you can join guided study groups to Salt Lake City, London, Boston, and elsewhere. In other words, it can be equal to a full-time occupation. So far I've restrained myself from going overboard to that extent, although my wife would say: "Seriously?!" Or who do you think you're kidding!?

I would be really remiss not to mention the thousands of times I've relied on *Wikipedia* for fast and, for the most part, accurate information. I've learned that not everything on this publically available and FREE website can be taken at face value, but it sure is convenient for quick answers and explanations. When I'm in doubt about some specific information I've seen on *Wikipedia* or some other online source, I rely on tried and true resources such as primary documents, academic books, and articles. I'll also do this when I want to learn more in-depth about a topic. It's good to doubt, very little is a certainty. Plus, doubting suggests that I'm thinking. You know the oft quoted, but not quite correctly understood saying by René Descartes *"cogito ergo sum"* (I think therefore I am.) A closer examination reveals that the intent of this is better stated as *"dubito, ergo cogito, ergo sum"* (I doubt, therefore I think, therefore I am). Let us doubt together as we work our way through this narrative.

An online source I hesitate to mention, but should because it is often used by others is the *Family Data Collection*. These records were created while gathering genealogical data from 20 million people for use in the study of human genetics and disease. The compilation of data was done by family historians of all levels of experience from the novice to the professional. This certainly gives one pause. More specifically, the problem I have with it is that it doesn't cite the source of information other than itself. For example, when it provides a date of death or birth, I haven't a clue as to where that date came from. Maybe I just don't understand the process, but I am very wary of using the data it provides.

Another useful source is *U.S. and Canada, Passenger and Immigration Lists Index, 1500s-1900s*. This was originally compiled by William P. Filby, but is now available online at *Ancestry.com*. Like the *Family Data Collection*, the list is drawn from thousands of sources ranging from passenger lists to personal diaries. So, it too, is not infallible, but it is a good way to help confirm information from other sources. That is to say confirm as much as anything can be confirmed of data from 400 years ago.

I decided not to include footnotes or endnotes in this narrative because I think they distract from the flow, however weak, of the telling of a story. That doesn't mean I'm making everything up and that I don't have sources. In fact, I've included an annotated bibliography at the end with notations that correspond to material in this account. It isn't actually a full annotation of the works cited. It is more of an abbreviated annotation limited to references I've used for this book. I apologize for the rather large number of works, coming in at a total of more than 200. I went through each reference with a fine tooth comb to try and save you the trouble of finding the ones that you might want to explore in more depth on your own.

Admittedly some sources are a bit suspect, but this is not meant to be a scholarly product or a comprehensive study. Those are not nearly as much fun to write or read! Be warned that there are places in the text that I employ the delicate art of conjecture and supposition, but I will try to make it crystal clear when I do that.

For the skeptics among you I have separately prepared well-documented research on both Stephen and Thomas Tracy with annoying attention to detail. Those papers are written minus the snarky comments, attempts at puns, divergences, and historical context. They are available on request. The paper on Thomas Tracy will be in a forthcoming issue of *The Connecticut Nutmegger* in 2017.

If you want to follow the bouncing ball as I enumerate the litany of information from the documents listed in the bibliography, there are seven books from which I have extensively drawn information on events and activities. They are so important to my research that they merit special recognition. The books that are chock full of the lives of Thomas and Stephen Tracy that I've used, in alphabetical order, are:

> Jeremy Dupertuis Bangs, *Strangers and Pilgrims, Travellers (sic) and Sojourners: Leiden and the Foundations of Plymouth Plantation* (Plymouth, MA: General Society of Mayflower Descendants, 2009).

> Frances Manwaring Caulkins, *History of Norwich, Connecticut: From its possession by the Indians, to the year 1866. Also A Brief Sketch of the Life of the Author, to Which is Added An Appendix Containing Notes and Sketches, Continuing the History to the Close of the Year 1873* (Hartford, CT: The Friends of the Author, 1874). It was first published in 1845.

Donald Lines Jacobus, *The Waterman Family: Descendants of Robert Waterman of Marshfield, Massachusetts Through Seven Generations*, vol. 1 (New Haven, CT: E. F. Waterman, 1896).

Nathanial B. Shurtleff (Ed.), *Records of the Colony of New Plymouth in New England Printed by Order of the Legislature of the Commonwealth of Massachusetts, Court Orders: I. 1633-1640* (Boston, MA: Press of William White, 1855).

Nathanial B. Shurtleff (Ed.), *Records of the Colony of New Plymouth in New England Printed by Order of the Legislature of the Commonwealth of Massachusetts, Judicial Acts 1636-1692* (Boston, MA: Press of William White, 1857).

J. Hammond Trumbull, *The Public Records of the Colony of Connecticut Prior to the Union with New Haven Colony, May 1665; Transcribed and Published, (In Accordance with a Resolution of the General Assembly,)Under the supervision of the Secretary of State, with Occasional Notes, and an Appendix*, vol. 1 (Hartford, CT: Brown and Parsons, 1850).

J. Hammond Trumbull, *The Public Records of the Colony of Connecticut, From 1665 to 1679; With the Journal of the Council of War, 1675-1678; Transcribed and Edited, in Accordance with a Resolution of the General Assembly, with Notes and an Appendix*, vol. 2 (Hartford, CT: F. A. Brown, 1852).

Books like these are wonderful resources, but, it is even better if you can put your hands on a primary source. I was hoping to do just that when I went to the *Norfolk Record Office* in Norwich, England in May, 2013 to see what I could find about Stephen. After getting groggy going through miles of micro films and blurry original handwritten records in archaic English, I began to understand why amateur genealogists seek the help of experts. I usually know when I'm licked, so in June, 2103, a month after returning home, I hired Joanne Penn, a professional genealogist, to see what she could come up with on Stephen. Joanne is affiliated with the *Norfolk Family History Society* and the *Norfolk Record Office* in Norwich. She prepared a document for me on July 11, 2013 that she fittingly entitled *Report on Tracy Family History*. The document has been very helpful in authenticating the life of Stephen as discussed in this narrative.

yDNA Testing

A new source for finding one's roots that has been unavailable until relatively (pun intended) recently is yDNA testing for paternal ancestry. I've been tested by both the *Genographic Project by National Geographic* and by *23andMe*. The test results have been incorporated into the data compiled by *Family Tree DNA* which allows for data comparisons and facilitates connecting to those who have varying degrees of yDNA match. I should say that understanding the many nuances of data from yDNA tests has been a real challenge for me. Thanks, however, to step-by-step manuals written for simpletons, I've been able to use the test results to good advantage, including connecting with contemporary cousins that I otherwise would never have found. These connections have led to some very intriguing information about my ancestors. I'll give some details on what I've learned from my yDNA tests at the end of the story.

Utilizing all these resources in my search for Stephen and Thomas, by 2008 I had accumulated a sizable stack of journal articles, books, and related documents that necessitated the purchase of a four-draw filing cabinet and several smaller containers to hold an overflow of materials. It occurred to me that I just might have enough odds and ends to write a summary of the lives of several of my Colonial ancestors, including, of course, Stephen and Thomas. By that time, I'd been retired from academia for five years and my consulting for the International Labor Organization in Geneva, Budapest, and southeastern Europe had come to an end. I was ready to have some fun and dive into a serious exploration of family history. Having spent so many years doing research and analysis in my professional career, I just couldn't walk away from that ingrained routine cold turkey. It's like an itch that won't go away without lathering it with the salve that comes from the labor of searching and the thrill of discovering.

Shameless Adaptation of Analytical Method
When I was in graduate school working on my masters in Political Science at the University of Illinois it was grilled into my brain, such as it was and is, that the basic questions to good policy research is to ask the question of *"who gets what, when and how."* Now the political scientist who came up with this little dictum, Yale Professor Harold Lasswell, did not have genealogical research in mind. So with sincere apologies to the late Dr. Lasswell, Dr. Richard Merritt and others of my political science professors for appropriating this approach for my own purposes, I proceeded to use this line of inquiry in constructing my family history. The result was a publication with the unwieldy title of *New England Colonial Ancestors of James Albert Tracy, Sr. (Born 1972 in Wood County, WV) Descendant of Lt. Thomas Tracy (1610-1685) & Stephen Tracy (1595-1655).* It was self-published in January 2009 and distributed to NEGHS, the US Library of Congress, the Kentucky Historical Society, and the Wisconsin Historical Society, among others. If you want to have your work out there for all to see, publish it yourself! Thank you Amazon CreateSpace!

I'm going to save you the trouble of going to Boston, Washington, Frankfort, or Milwaukee to read the document about Stephen and Thomas. Because I'm going to cover that material and more! Moreover, I'm afraid that I'm going to correct myself, especially some of what I wrote about Thomas in that earlier publication. Of course, this just proves the point how difficult it is to correct mistakes written in good faith. Once it is in print or online, it is there permanently. There is nothing to do but to try and get it right this time and hope anyone doing research will read subsequent writings, such as this. Although, I can't blame anyone for viewing this narrative with a jaundiced eye! That being said, I'll proceed with caution. Since Stephen was the first Puritan and Pilgrim Tracy in New England, I'll begin with his story. However, his story can't be fully understood without first briefly discussing his father, Stephen Tracy, *families*

Sr. followed by an explanation of the Puritan movement that attracted Stephen Tracy, Jr. in which he became deeply involved in Holland. Finally, I get around to giving details of his life in Plymouth and Duxbury. These topics will be the focus of the next three chapters.

2

STEPHEN TRACY, JR. – PURITAN BACKGROUND

Before delving into the life of Stephen Tracy, Jr, I want to relate a little about his father Stephen Tracy, Sr. Norfolk County Parish records document that he was baptized in East Ruston in 1558 where he was probably born. Most online postings on the branch of the Tracy family list the father of Stephen, Sr. as Christopher Tracy. To be blunt, this is erroneous. His father was Roger Tracy. Roger was born in 1540 in Norwich and died sometime after 1562, probably in East Ruston. I know this because at my request in 2013 Norfolk, England genealogist Joanne Penn examined the *East Ruston Parish Register.* She found this entry: *"Stephen Trace (sic) son of Roger and Margaret was baptized 7 April 1558."* Penn testified that *"There is no doubt the name is definitely Roger, not Christopher."* Consequently, the parents of Stephen Tracy, Sr. were Roger and Margaret Tracy (spelled both as Trace and Trayce in Norfolk records). He had at least two brothers, Thomas born in 1560 and Edward born in 1562, probably in East Ruston. The names of the grandparents of Stephen, Sr. are unknown.

Stephen, Sr. seems to have spent his childhood in East Ruston, but left for the big city in his mid-20s. In the 1600s East Ruston, like now, must not have provided many work opportunities beyond farming for young men, so by age 26 Stephen had gone to seek his fortune in the nearby North Sea port city of Great Yarmouth. Great Yarmouth is only 20 miles southeast from East Ruston, so it wasn't far from home. A harbor city, it was known for its fishing, especially herring, and for ship building. It was there that he met Anne (Agnes) Erdley. She was 17 when they married on February 20, 1586. Great Yarmouth was also a principal port to sail from to cover the approximately 135 miles across the North Sea to Amsterdam as the crow flies or 117 nautical miles as the ship sails.

A year or so ago a search I did looking for Tracy families with very distant DNA connections led me to a website managed by a Tracey (sic) who is Irish. The site is *info@traceyclann.com*. On Facebook it is TraceyClann. I contacted the webmaster because I had seen that he mentioned Stephen, Sr. on the website. The site didn't have much information on Stephen, Sr., but the webmaster did confirm that Stephen was a merchant in Great Yarmouth, although he didn't know what he sold. My Irish contact knew that Stephen had been a merchant because he had a photo of the trade token of Tracey (sic) of Great Yarmouth. I can't blame Stephen, Sr. for the misspelling, but nobody in the 21st Century has an excuse, unless they happen to be Irish. I mean, haven't those who spell it with an "e" ever heard of Dick or Spencer Tracy? Give me a break. Sorry for the emotional outburst!

Back to the trade tokens that were also called barter tokens. Back in the day (to use a new phrase for "historically," "long ago" or "when grandpa was a little boy") trade tokens were issued by merchants of the time when there was a shortage of coins of the state which, apparently, was often. If you are of a certain age, you've heard the expression "not worth a farthing." Well, in this case Stephen Tracy, Sr.'s tokens were worth exactly a farthing which is to say a fourth of a penny. I recently obtained a copy of the photo of Stephen, Sr.'s trade token and posted it on my Ancestry. com site. There are copies of the coin online at *https://norfolktokenproject. wordpress.com/tokens/*. One side of the coin shows a lion rampant with the star mintmark at the tip of the lion's tail. On the other side are the initials S. A. T. which stand for Stephen. Agnes. Tracy. There is an inscription "of

Yarmouth" circling the initials. I found a token dealer *Rare Coins and Tokens* with an online site I checked out the site in September of 2016 and discovered that their last Stephen Tracey (sic) token in stock was sold in July, 2016. I doubt if I could have afforded it!! I can't help but wonder who did.

In case you are like me and not an expert in heraldry, I looked up Lion rampant. It refers to a lion that stands with his forepaws raised. I did a little further research and found that a Lion rampant is the unofficial symbol of Scotland. I couldn't understand why Stephen, Sr. would have used a Scottish emblem, but a little further research paid off by revealing that the Lion rampant is also an historic symbol of prominent Norfolk families. While on the subject, there is also a Lion passant used by many members of nobility. This is when the lion strikes various poses with his forepaws, but is not standing. The things you learn on *Wikipedia*!

Stephen Tracy, Jr.
Stephen Tracy, Jr. was baptized in East Ruston, Norfolk, England in 1596. Given that baptisms were typically soon after birth in those days, his birth date is usually given as 1596. His parents were Stephen and Agnes Erdley Tracy. His grandparents were Roger and Margaret Tracy. I'm racking my brain trying to recall when I first ran across a reference to Stephen. He isn't included in Cousin Bonnie's family genealogical chart, so it had to have been from some other source. A good historian would have kept meticulous notes on when and how such discoveries were made. I'm afraid I've fallen short of this seemingly simple task. My only excuse is that I didn't know I was looking for Stephen and when I did run across his name, I didn't know how significant he was to the Tracy family history. My best guess is that his name first came to my attention following my yDNA test with National Geographic in 1996. When I got the results and matches of the test there were several expected shared links to Thomas, but who was this Stephen to whom I was also apparently related?

Finding Stephen proved to be a lot harder than "Finding Nemo or Finding Dory." It became more intriguing when a quick and dirty search revealed several references to Stephen because of his early arrival at Plymouth. But to be honest, initially I didn't come up with enough evidence to think him worthy of pursuing. In short, I put the little material I had on Stephen on the back burner for about 11 years while concentrating on Thomas and several other related family lines in the Colonies of the 1600s.

I recently resurrected my study of Stephen. In part, this has been because of a mounting personal fascination with the Pilgrims and early settlers of New England. This grew out of research I did on another ancestor of that period, James Travis, who is also a 7th Great Grandfather. James was a fascinating figure because of his involvement in King Phillip's War during the siege of Brookfield, Massachusetts in 1675. Some of you may recall that I wrote a small book about that event hoping to inform the youth of my extended family and to generate interest in family history. Doing the research on the book made me realize how little I knew about this time period in American history.

There is abundant coverage of our nation's history shortly before, during, and after the Revolution. Much less attention is paid to the 150 years of history prior to the winnowing from mother England. This seems remarkable to me, as well as the fact that the Plymouth Colony was composed of several communities for 72 years before becoming a part of the Commonwealth of Massachusetts. The more I delved into our early history, the more I wanted to know. Adding fuel to my interest was that I had learned that I had not one, but two Tracy ancestors who played seminal roles in the development of the early endeavor to establish English communities on these sacred shores.

Stephen got my attention because he was an authentic Puritan who joined the movement as a young man from Norfolk County, England. At a young age he left his home to join other Puritans to live and work in Leiden, Holland for several years. He wasn't with the first group of Pilgrims from Leiden to go to New England, but he joined his fellow travelers at Plymouth only three years after the *Mayflower* arrived at that famous Massachusetts "rock" in 1620. That's all fascinating, to be sure. But exactly what was Stephen so caught up in that he would gamble his life and that of his wife and daughter to travel across an often unforgiving sea in a vessel the size of a modern Wall Street tycoon's luxury yacht crowded with smelly animals and equally malodorous people to an uncertain future in a foreign and hostile land? Diligent research revealed that the answer to this question lay within the development of Puritanism.

Puritan Background

To acquire even an inkling of an understanding of Stephen's motivation, I thought I needed to review what I should have learned or have forgotten from my college history class about life in England in the late 17th century. This proved to be a challenging task. Not because it was hard to find information, but because there was so much material to sift through and try and boil down. As most any high school student in England knows, that period in history was a turbulent time for those who thought that the beliefs and rituals of the Anglican Church of England were too much like those of the Roman Catholic Church.

The reforms that were being advocated were aimed at purifying the established church. This was, of course, a process that had started under Henry VIII. After many machinations involving back and forth Catholic-Protestant domination, the reform measures were given a strong toehold under Queen Elizabeth I with the adoption of the *Thirty-Nine Articles* in 1653. The nickname given to folks who were intent on making further reforms of the English Church was "Puritan". It was not meant to be a compliment. Her Majesty Queen Elizabeth I who ruled supreme for 45 years from 1558 to 1603 was not amused.

Elizabeth I was a strident stay-as-we-are Protestant who had no patience with those who would reform certain church practices that continued despite the official break with Catholicism. Beginning in 1588 many

Puritan leaders were arrested, creating an underground movement. The good Queen further tried to stymie the Puritans with the 1593 *Act Against the Puritans*. This act made it illegal for Puritans who were inclined to hold their own "reformed" church services instead of attending the sanctioned Protestant Church. The penalty for noncompliance was imprisonment without bail until they conformed. Not a cheery prospect even with the proverbial English stiff upper lip.

At the death of Queen Elizabeth I in 1603, a group of Puritans thought they might have better luck with her successor, King James I of Scotland. He was duly petitioned to entertain moderate reforms in the Church of England. It was known as the *Millenary Petition* because it was signed by 1,000 Puritans. The petitioners recognized that the King was a big supporter of Royal Supremacy; after all it made him supreme. They were duly careful not to challenge him on that issue. But, they did ask for his help in making the church less "popish" by eliminating practices leftover from the Catholic Church that the Puritans considered to be superstitious acts. This included making the sign of the cross and bowing when the name of Jesus was uttered at church services. They also asked to eliminate the baptism of infants and the custom of clergy wearing vestments. To his credit the King did convene a conference with Puritan leaders at Hampton Court Palace in 1604. It was made abundantly clear, however, that any reform he thought would even marginally weaken his supremacy was non-negotiable. Off the table, as it were.

While some reform concessions were made, James I made sure to retain control of the church by appointing church bishops who were loyal to him. This ensured that local elders in the villages and towns would have minimal influence. Further, he made it clear that separatism from the Anglican Church would not be tolerated. He upheld the tenants of the 1593 Act, warning the Puritans that if they held their own services he would "*harry them out of the land*." I must say, however, I found it ironic that those who were desperate to be "*harried out*" to Holland were forbidden to leave on their own accord!

A quick search on Google for King James I revealed that he also went out of his way to get under the skin of Puritans. This was evident in 1618 when he released his *"Declaration of Sports"* known better as the *"Book of Sports"*. This was not aimed at improving athletic events in the Kingdom. It was a rebuke of Puritans who were steadfastly opposed to any form of recreation on Sundays. Much to their chagrin, James's decree granted permission for archery, leaping, vaulting, and dancing around the Maypole on Sundays. King James I wasn't totally unmindful of the Puritan requests. He did forbid bear and bull-baiting on the Sabbath.

It wasn't just Queen Elizabeth I and King James I who had a low opinion of the Puritans. Even the bard himself, William Shakespeare, got into the act through his character, Malvolio (which means Ill Will). Malvolio is a Puritan scapegoat in the play *Twelfth Night*. His downfall and humiliation reflects the prevalent public antipathy for hypocrisy, rigid moral values, and egotism that characterized the Puritans.

As it happens, a Cambridge educated Puritan by the name of Reverend John Robinson seized Shakespeare's admonition through the character Malvolio to *"be not afraid of greatness"*. Robinson bravely began endorsing Puritanism during his appointment as a deputy to the minister of St. Andrew's Church in Norwich, Norfolk County. From 1523 to 1662, Norwich, located on the River Winsum, was the 2nd largest city in England with a population of about 15,000. In 1608 it established one of the earliest public libraries anywhere! (Did Andrew Carnegie get his idea of the value of public libraries from Norwich?).

Norwich was also the home of England's most influential Puritan merchants and leaders. And, it was a hotbed of Protestants fueled by a large influx of Dutch Flemish and Walloon who came to escape Catholic persecution in Holland. By the mid-16th Century these two groups of immigrants made up a third of the population of Norwich. They were instrumental in introducing the weaving industry to the county that lasted for centuries. They were referred to by the locals as "Strangers." I ran across this term on several occasions in reference to any group of people that didn't meet the norms of the community.

Curiously, the Dutch weavers who came to Norfolk also brought along their pet domesticated canaries. Yes, canaries, as in the little yellow song birds. By the 18th century Norwich was famous for its canaries. In fact, the team of the Norwich Football Club (soccer to us on this side of the Atlantic) is nicknamed The Canaries. Not the Fighting or Combative Canaries, just The Canaries. Naturally, team colors are green and canary yellow. By the way, English youngsters were playing football in schools in the 15th century. With that long history of playing the world's most popular sport, it's a mystery why they've only won one World Cup. My son and I follow English football a little. We're Cheltenham fans first and foremost because of our fondness for the Cotswolds. Go Robins! But, we also like to see The Canaries have a good season.

Shortly after Rev. Robinson took up his pastoral duties in Norwich, King James I issued a proclamation that all clerics had to conform to a new book of church canons. Although this requirement was soon repealed, when it was issued Rev. Robinson was so opposed to it that he packed his bags and left St. Andrew's Church in Norwich. He departed to preach, illegally of course, to private groups of Puritans 130 miles to the north in Nottinghamshire County. By 1607 he had attached himself to a church pastored by Richard Clyfton near the hamlet of Scrooby. It was a Separatist church that met secretly at Scrooby Manor House which was owned by William Brewster. A member of this church was young William Bradford. Despite a quarter century difference in their ages, Brewster and the younger Bradford became great friends and leaders of the Pilgrims in Holland and Plymouth. Bradford served as the Plymouth Colony's Governor five times over a period of thirty years. Brewster was an influential Puritan elder throughout his life in England, Holland, and the Plymouth Colony. Notably, both were well acquainted with Stephen Tracy in Holland and Plymouth.

Puritan Separatists & Non-Separatists

I relied on various books and articles to try and get a grip on the meaning of Separatism as it applied to Puritans and Pilgrims. I learned that Separatists like Rev. Robinson, Brewster, and Bradford were radical Puritans who initially advocated a thorough reform within the Church of England. Others with a similar agenda had long been unhappy with the slow pace of reform. As early as 1581 the Puritan Robert Browne shifted from advocating for reform to supporting separation from the Anglican Church. Browne established an independent congregational church in Norwich. His vision was for a congregation that would be autonomous. He wanted congregations to be able to elect their own officers and limit membership to "visible saints", i.e., those who could "prove" to the satisfaction of the congregation that they were among God's chosen people. This reflected the doctrine of John Calvin and the Presbyterian Church that individuals had to demonstrate that they were chosen among the "elect" through visible signs of wholesome living and financial success.

For a while, the Separatists were knows as "Brownists". Robert Browne was often arrested and often released for his non-conformist views. In fact, he went through that revolving door 32 times. Following release from his first arrest he and several companions moved to the Netherlands to establish a church. The initiative failed after only two years. He returned to England where he continued to be an outspoken proponent of separatism. He eventually died in prison in 1633 after making the serious mistake of assaulting a constable.

It took a while for me to boil down the essence of Puritan Separatism. I had given an early draft of this narrative to a 2nd cousin, Richard Tracy, to review for clarity. I only recently connected with him, but had communicated enough to value his insight. He pointed out that I wasn't being very clear about the distinction regarding Separatists, Puritans and Pilgrims. I took his comments to heart and made a concerted effort to boil down a complex concept to where I might understand it correctly. What I discovered through additional reading, in simplistic terms, is that over the years Puritans divided into two distinct schools of thought: Separatists and Non-Separatists. The Puritan Separatists believed that every local church of visible saints should be fully independent from outside control. The Puritan Non-Separatist agreed that church membership should be restricted to visible saints, but they did not want to separate from the Church of England. They sought reform from within. Robinson's congregation in Holland was Separatist. The members of his Puritan congregation who went to Plymouth became known as Pilgrims.

I think it might help to sum it up in the following way: all Separatists and non-Separatists were Puritans, but all Puritans were not Separatists. As discussed later, the Puritans who came with the Massachusetts Bay Colony were Puritan Non-Separatists. Their compatriots who had earlier settled the Plymouth Colonies were Puritan Separatists, also known as Pilgrims. Stephen Tracy was a Puritan/Pilgrim Separatist. Thomas Tracy was a Puritan Non-Separatist. It is infinitely more complex than that, but hopefully it gives you a rough idea.

Holland was attractive to the Puritan Separatists because the northern seven provinces (modern day Netherlands) was solidly Calvinistic. However, Holland itself was in political and religious turmoil under the control of the Catholic King of Spain, Phillip IV. As noted above, many Dutch fled to England to avoid persecution from the Spanish. Can you say Spanish Inquisition? There was a close association between Dutch and English Puritan clergy and academicians at Cambridge and Leiden universities in Holland.

The Puritan Separatists knew that they would have to leave England in order to form their own church, but no one could leave the country without permission from the authorities. In the winter of 1607-08 there was an unsuccessful attempt by the Separatists to reach Holland from the town of Boston in Lincolnshire on the coast of the North Sea. However, in the spring of the following year a group of about 100 Separatists was successful in making their escape from Boston on a Dutch ship.

The original port of call was Amsterdam, but a year later the group relocated to Leiden, a university city that offered better work opportunities. The group included many of those who were later to come on the first four ships to Plymouth in the three-year period of 1620-1623; namely, the *Mayflower, Fortune, Anne,* and *Little James.* Incidentally, those of you who really want to explore how the Puritans in Leiden morphed into the Pilgrims of Plymouth read a 2009 publication by Jeremy Dupertuis Bangs entitled *Strangers and Pilgrims, Travellers (sic) and Sojourners: Leiden and the Foundations of Plymouth Plantation.* With 700 pages of text, it will answer most of any questions you may have. Bangs is the Director of the *Leiden American Pilgrim Museum Foundation.*

Another excellent source was one provided to me by Dr. Duane Bolin, Pundit and Professor of History at Murray State University. The book is *Making Haste From Babylon: The Mayflower Pilgrims and Their World: A New History* by Nick Bunker. It was published in 2010. Dr. Bolin has been most gracious in loaning me other works related to religion in the early colonies and beyond. These have been very helpful in answering many of my questions and raising many more. Bunker made the interesting observation that Puritans weren't only interested in Christian liberty. It was *"an amalgam between religious beliefs and secular concepts of virtue, gentility, and heroism."* Puritanism, it seems, offered a more enlightened idea of what it meant to be a Christian gentlemen. It wasn't just about having wealth or being separated from the English Church. It was also about diligence in performing public service. For me, that puts quite a different and more positive spin on Puritanism.

In reading Bangs and other sources I learned that the Puritans who made their way to Holland were from all walks of life and social, education, and economic strata bound together by a shared religious faith. The disregard for distinction of social and economic class was clearly a factor in the development of a preference for a democratic approach to community that is manifested later in New England. The life of hard labor and menial work in the Netherlands also prepared them for a harsh life in the New World with increased capacities for practical, economical, and thrifty living.

From Bangs I also learned that the members of John Robinson's congregation in Leiden were a very close knit community. Indeed, Robinson preached that this was an essential aspect of every "true church". This emphasis played a very important role during the development of Plymouth and the Massachusetts Bay Colony which I'll get to later in more detail. Robinson's Leiden congregation started out in 1609 with about 100 adults plus children. By 1620, there were about 400 English Puritan families in Leiden with numerous members from Norfolk County. Among these were Stephen and his wife Tryphosa Lee.

Trip to the Norfolk Broads: Home of Some of the Tracys
Thanks to the help of the *Norfolk Record Office* I had discovered that in 1558 the year that Elizabeth I became Queen, the father of our subject, Stephen Tracy, Sr., was born in East Ruston, Norfolk. It is a small rural village 17 miles northeast of Norwich and 136 miles northeast of London. So, when I conspired with my wife and son to plan to take our then 13-year old granddaughter, Mary Patsy, to England on her first trip abroad, I naturally suggested exploring London followed by an excursion to the touristic *Norfolk Broads*. We made the trip in May, 2013 and stayed at the Mornington Hotel. After a delightful few days enjoying the museums, galleries, gardens, and shops of London, we took a train to Norwich. (Travel note: If you rush out to get your tickets to replicate our trip, purchase your tickets before going, as we did. You'll save a bundle and can watch the charming English countryside glide by in an inexpensive first class seat). Upon arrival we rented a car and drove to the nearby *Bridge House B&B* in the lovely little village of Coltishall on the *River Bure*. It is located within an easy a drive to East Ruston and environs. There is also a convenient public bus that runs to and fro from Norwich which saved us from negotiating traffic and the dreaded roundabouts.

I generously let my son do the driving so that he could experience the thrill of driving on the left side of the road when, that is, there actually were two lanes. He quickly learned to negotiate rural one-lane roads with high hedges on either side. There was, thankfully, an occasional turnout available when there was oncoming traffic. The fact that he was driving a brand new no-mileage BMW added no pressure. I'm sure he appreciated my giving him the opportunity (although he has yet to express it). He did fine!

During our stay in Coltishall we took a short hike from our B&B to the *Horstead Watermill* on the *River Bure*. The river is the longest of the many *Norfolk Broads* rivers that had been formed by the flooding of ancient peat channels. It wasn't until the 1960s that scientists discovered that the rivers are not a natural marvel. Rather, they are channels of medieval peat excavations that filled with rain water over centuries. Regardless of their origin, the *Norfolk Broads* are beautiful! While we were making our way along the path leading to the mill, we encountered a friendly and inquisitive Englishman and his family. He inquired of our nationality and purpose of visiting the Broads. I explained that East Ruston was a family ancestral home. He asked me my surname. I said Tracy and without missing a beat he waged his finger at me and forcefully said French! Well, that's true, but we came to England in 1066. How long does a family have to have resided in England before being identified as English!! We shared a jolly good laugh.

When we made our short trek to *East Ruston*, we found it to be not unlike numerous Norfolk communities in the area. It is a quaint, quiet place of fewer than 600 English souls. It dates back at least to the 14th Century and probably much longer. It is a pretty little village. Not much remains of historic interest with the exception of a fine example of a Norman Church located on the village outskirts. It was one of hundreds of Norman Churches in the county and one of thousands in the country. In fact, there are so many medieval churches in England that visiting one a week would take 308 years. We didn't have that much time, so we focused on the one in East Ruston, the Parish Church of St. Mary. It was originally constructed in the 1400s and, undoubtedly, was the place of worship for the Tracy family. The church is now only occasionally used for special occasions, such as weddings. Happily, it is under the care of England's *Churches Conservation Trust* which ensures that it will not fall into disrepair anytime soon.

We did not have an opportunity to enter the church. As disappointing as that was, we immensely enjoyed strolling among the luscious tree ferns, succulents, and palms in the 32-acre *East Ruston Old Vicarage Gardens* adjacent to St. Mary. This private garden dates only from 1973, but it makes a visit to East Ruston worthwhile even if you don't have an ancestral connection. Besides the garden, the village's other claim to fame is that it is the site of the hiding place of Abe Slaney. You Sherlock Holmes aficionados will recognize the name from reading *The Adventure of the Dancing Man*. Of course, no self-respecting English village could possible exist without a pub and in East Ruston it is the highly rated *The Butchers Arms* where hungry travelers and locals alike can enjoy a delicious Shepard's pie or leg of lamb roasted to perfection washed down with a local brew. Eat your heart out Ina Garten!

It was great fun was to visit the region where Roger, Stephen, Sr., and Stephen, Jr. had lived long ago. It was ever so much more meaningful to have been there with my wife, our son, and granddaughter. It is a cherished memory. Yet, I was not happy just having a feel for where Stephen came from, I wanted to know why he came to New England. I wanted to know something about the role he had played in the Puritan movement and how it came to pass that he was among the first to settle the Plymouth Colony. It seems quite obvious that Stephen fell under the influence of the teachings of Rev. Robinson and Robert Browne who, by now, you are aware, had a strong presence in Norfolk County.

Stephen was only 12 years old when Rev. Robinson took his first group of Separatist followers to Leiden to escape persecution. I think I might get some agreement here, that at age 12 bright children look for spiritual in-spiration to answer the age-old existential question of every juvenile worth the name – why am I here? Or better yet, why are *we* here? Inquiring minds want to know! I'm assuming he got caught up in the religious rebellion that held sway at the time in Norfolk County. Moreover, the church in Stephen's home of Great Yarmouth was a particularly ardent sympathizer of the Puritans. Further, there may have been a more practical motivation as he had seven siblings, four brothers, and three sisters. Since he was not the eldest, the chance of him inheriting his father's business was remote. He may well have gotten excited about the opportunity to seek his for-tune with an inspiring religious group with work and career prospects in Holland.

As Dr. Bangs noted, many of the Leiden Puritans were from Norfolk. In addition, as I'll discuss later, there were thousands of folks from East Anglia who chose to leave England to fulfill their destiny in the New England Colonies. They mostly came on the ships of the Massachusetts Bay Colony in the 1630s from the counties of Suffolk, Essex, and Norfolk. Norfolk had a long tradition of non-conformity and dissent dating back to AD 60 when *Boudicca* the female leader of the *Iceni* tribe led a revolt against Rome. Centuries later Norfolk rose up during the *Peasants' Revolt of 1381* against poll taxes. Then along came the Pilgrims (I'm skipping over nu-merous other uprisings). A rebellious tradition in Norfolk didn't end with the Pilgrims. Thomas Paine who knew a thing or two about rebellion was a native of Thetford, Norfolk.

3

STEPHEN TRACY, JR. – PURITAN/PILGRIM

Thanks for patiently wadding through the Puritan historical context in England. Bear with me a bit longer as I try to explain the Puritan movement in Holland of which Stephen was a part. Then I'll have a few words as to how he came to Plymouth as a Puritan/Pilgrim in 1623. Stephen Tracy, Jr. was baptized December 28, 1596 in Great Yarmouth, Norfolk, England. This date and place are confirmed by baptismal records at the *Norfolk Record Office* which show that Stephen, Sr. and Agnes were the parents of five sons and three daughters, all born and baptized in Great Yarmouth. Their fourth son was Stephen Tracy, Jr.

The Great Yarmouth baptismal record reads "*Stephen Trayce (sic), son of Stephen and Agnes, baptised (sic) 28th December 1596.*" Since baptisms were typically performed soon after birth, the assumption is that he was born in 1596. Another supporting source is from 1929. In that year the respected publishing firm, Phillimore & Company, Ltd., was commissioned to conduct research on Stephen Tracy of the Plymouth Colony. The company is well-known for its publications on British history and family genealogies. The result of the research was a pedigree for Stephen affirming that he was baptized on December 28, 1596. The pedigree also showed his parents to be Stephen and Agnes Erdley Tracy. This is our boy who later came to New England. For the sake of brevity and to reduce the times I forget to add the "*Jr.*" I'm usually going to refer to him as "Stephen" from here on.

Stephen Tracy – Leiden, Holland
It isn't clear when Stephen left England and joined the Puritans/Pilgrims in Holland. Primary documents show him listed as one of 32 individuals who went to Leiden from Great Yarmouth in the period 1608-1620. We know for certain that he was there in 1620 because he was betrothed to Tryphosa Lee on December 18, 1620 in Leiden. They married January 2, 1621. He was 24 and she was 23. He was described as "*a bachelor serge weaver from England.*" She was labeled "*an English spinster.*"

After literally years of looking for verification of this marriage, lo and behold I found a copy of the marriage document two hours away from my home in Kentucky at the *Tennessee State Library and Archives* in Nashville. It was found under "*Leyden (sic) Documents Relating to the Pilgrim Fathers.*" It was a welcomed and significant find. I scanned a copy of it and posted it online as soon as I could. I have noticed that many others tracking the Lt. Thomas Tracy line have copied it for inclusion on their family lines on *Ancestry.com*. Dr. Bangs also made a reference to the marriage.

The marriage document lists two witnesses to the civil wedding (the Church did not perform wedding ceremonies in those days). They were Anthony Clements for the groom and Rose Lisle Jennings for the bride. Anthony was a native of Middleburg, Holland and was a student of theology in Leiden. Having a theology student as a friend suggests to me that Stephen could possibly have also been studying theology while earning a living as a "saymaker" described below. Rose Lisle Jennings was the wife of John Jennings, both were born in England. They also ended up in the New England Colonies, but not until 1639, some sixteen years after Stephen arrived. They settled in Hartford, Connecticut, joining their son, Francis, who had arrived in 1634.

Hoping to find out something about Tryphosa's origin and parents, I dug around for anything I could find on a Bridget Lee who lived in Leiden at the same time. There is some online speculation that Bridget might have been Tryphosa's sister. It is not certain, but it isn't an implausible idea. I discovered that Bridget married Dr. Samuel Fuller, a native of Norfolk County. She was his third wife, death having claimed his first two. He was a surgeon who arrived on the *Mayflower* in 1620. She came later on the *Anne*, the same vessel that carried Stephen.

It has been ventured by some genealogists that Stephen could have been traveling with his sister-in-law, Bridget, on the *Anne* rather than with his wife. As I'll explain below, Tryphosa apparently came later. Bridget's husband died in 1633, the same year it is believed that Tryphosa died. There is documentation that Bridget continued to live in Plymouth until her death in 1664. I've tried to track down a Lee family genealogist who might know more about this family, but it's been a dead end.

While we're on the subject of Tryphosa, this is not a name with which I was at all familiar. Nor have I run across in any other families that I've researched. A little checking reveals that it is a Greek name meaning "luxurious." A more popular form of the name is Tryphena, although you can't prove it by me. The names derive from a biblical passage in which St. Paul wrote his friends at Rome saying "*Salute Tryphena and Tryphosa, who labour in the Lord*" (Romans 16:12). My Greek brother-in-law, George, will be happy to know there was a Greek name in the Tracy clan.

It was relatively easy to establish that Stephen and Tryphosa were one of 42 families with membership in Rev. John Robinson's congregation (Calvinist) in Leiden. This entourage included such future historic Pilgrim luminaries as William Bradford, Edward Winslow, and William Brewster. It was a tightknit community who lived in the lower income area of town. They resided in one of 21 small houses near Pieterskerk (St. Peter's Church) on Pieterskerkkoosteeg (Peter's Alley) in Zevenhuizen, an area that become known as "English Alley". A 1622 poll tax lists the residence of Stephen and Tryphosa in Zevenhuizen. They shared living quarters with the Fairfield and the Willit families in a house owned by Thomas Brewer. Brewer was a wealthy patron of William Brewster who provided the funds to help him print Puritan pamphlets. The name of the alleyway is now Williem Brewstersteeg.

Multiple sources attest to the fact that most of the Separatists who escaped England for Holland made their living by working with a variety of articles made from cloth. For example, Dr. Samuel Fuller worked as a silk worker, although he was a physician. As best as I can determine a silk worker was a worker who spun raw silk, twisted silk into thread, joined broken threads, or wove silk, etc. Future Plymouth Governor William Bradford was a fustian-maker (cotton cloth) worker.

Most of the references to Stephen's occupation in Leiden indicate that he was a say-weaver or saymaker. Say is a coarse thick material that workers would convert into table cloths and bedding. This differs a little from other references that suggest he was a "serge maker". Serge is a type of twill fabric with ridges on both sides. I suppose there is no reason why he couldn't have done both types of weaving. None of these crafts were particularly useful in preparing for a life of hard scrapple farming in New England. Nor did they pay well. The meager income earned from the long, hard labor of Stephen and his fellow Separatists in Holland produced little more than enough to barely get by.

The inadequate income earned by the English Puritans in Holland was a significant factor in the decision to leave Holland for the New World. Another was that most of Rev. Robinson' Puritan congregation were farmers or farm laborers who were fish out of water in Holland. Moreover, after the Puritans learned skills related to processing cloth, the Dutch controlled craft guilds did not welcome the competition and thwarted career advancement by the English. Additionally, as foreigners, they were unable to fully engage in Dutch civil, political, and religious affairs.

The political and economic stability of Holland was also under threat during this time, as an armistice between Spain and Holland came to an end in 1621, renewing the threat of religious persecution by way of the Spanish Inquisition. That was not a pleasant prospect for a Protestant to be sure. Further, there was concern among the Puritans that their children were losing their English language skills and heritage which wouldn't do at all.

Migration to the English Colonies
Like most Americans, I know only bits and pieces about the history of the *Mayflower*. I had never taken the time to read about its origin. As for the other early ships carrying Pilgrims to the Plymouth Colony, I knew virtually nothing. Over the course of my research on Stephen, I learned quite a bit about the *Anne* that arrived at Plymouth in 1623 with Stephen on board. But, beyond that there was a big void. I thought it would be prudent for me to have at least a rudimentary familiarity of the story of the Puritans' departure from Leiden for Plymouth. I was to find out that they actually left Leiden with sails set to take them to the Virginia Colony.

As I understand it, because of the unfavorable economic and social conditions related above, the Leiden congregation sent two of their members, John Carver and Robert Cushman, to do business with the Virginia Company of London. The emissaries were to explore options in getting to the nascent Virginia Colony in Jamestown. The Virginia Company granted them a land patent, but, for some reason I've failed to determine, it didn't work out. Instead, the Leiden congregation opted for an association with a group of private backers and adventurers in Virginia headed by London merchant Thomas Weston. Weston, in fact, pops up often in the chronicle of establishing a colony in the New World.

In 1618 Leiden representative Carver received a patent for land from Weston in the Virginia Colony. Despite the change in companies the original destination continued to be Virginia, not New England. The Leiden congregation members chosen to make the initial voyage sold their estates and invested in common stock with Weston and the *Company of Merchant Adventurers of London*. For the merchants it was strictly a business deal aimed at making stockholders a profit. The company arranged for the ship *Speedwell* a 60-ton pinnace (type of sailing ship) to take the Pilgrims to England where both the *Speedwell* and the *Mayflower* were scheduled to set sail for Virginia.

If I've got the sequence right, on July 22, 1620 the ill-fated *Speedwell* left the harbor at Delfthaven, Holland bound for Southampton, England. On August 5, the *Speedwell* and the *Mayflower* departed from Southampton with a total of 120 passengers, arriving at Dartmouth on the River Dart in Devon County on the 23rd with the *Speedwell* having sprung a leak. Both ships continued on to the harbor town of Plymouth in Devon County on the 31st where the unseaworthy *Speedwell* was abandoned. Eighteen passengers gave up the voyage and the remainder crowded into the *Mayflower* departing on the 16th of September. The timing was most unfortunate, as a fall departure meant that the ship would arrive at its destination in the winter. But, then, maybe it was thought that the weather in December would not be so bad in the Colony of Virginia.

I've been unable to find out how the Leiden Pilgrims were chosen to make the first voyage, leaving many behind. Among those on the Delfthaven dock waving goodbye to their friends on the *Speedwell* may have been Stephen and Tryphosa Tracy. We know they were in Leiden after the *Speedwell* sailed as they are both listed in the Leiden census for October 16, 1622. Stephen would join his mates in Plymouth about 10 months later.

It is interesting to note that many *Mayflower* passengers had close connections to Stephen's home county of Norfolk, England. While the origin of numerous passengers is not well known, those who are recognized to have been from Norfolk include: Thomas Williams and John Turner and his two sons of Great Yarmouth; Edward, Ann, and Dr. Samuel Fuller of Redenhall; John Hooke and Desire Minter of Norwich;

Edmund Margesson of Swannington; and Thomas Tinker and wife and son of Neatishead. The names of several communities in New England based on towns in Norfolk lend credence to the close association between the county and the Colony. For example, Norwich, Connecticut and Yarmouth, Massachusetts are named after cities of the same names in Norfolk County, England.

Is it only me who thought that all passengers on the *Mayflower* were Puritans? Not so, I learned. Of the estimated 102 passengers and 30 crew members on the vessel, only 37 to 41 were Separatists Puritan "Saints" from Leiden. No one seems to have the exact numbers of people or the composition of men, women, and children. All non-Puritans, who were called "strangers" by the Puritans, agreed to abide by the authority of the Merchants and Governor John Carver. Carver, by the way, was the first Governor of the New Plymouth settlement, but he died in April 1621 soon after their arrival. The *Company of Merchant Adventurers of London* replaced him with William Bradford.

Mayflower and the Mayflower Compact
A word or two about the *Mayflower and the Mayflower Compact* seems appropriate at this point. If you weren't absent from high school on the days it was discussed, you are probably familiar with it. If you're like me you know it was important, but don't really know exactly why. It turns out that who actually signed it and its significance have been the topics of debate and dispute for centuries. It seems to remain unresolved among present-day historians. I'll leave it to those of you who are interested to explore the arguments at your leisure.

As every third grader knows, the *Mayflower,* landed near a big rock close to present-day Cape Cod, Massachusetts. The ship was blown off course on its way to Virginia by severe storms and it lacked the provisions to continue to its original destination. Since the ship had not reached Virginia, the "strangers" on board argued that they were no longer bound by their agreement to be subject to the governance of the Puritans. This didn't sit well with the Puritan "Saints" who, naturally, assumed that God would want them to be in charge. They hadn't come all that way to hand over authority to a bunch of unsaintly "strangers."

To head off a rebellion, the Puritans came up with a clever proposal to ensure social order and increase the prospect of living through the winter. Not incidentally, the plan led to the creation of a formal government structure which became known as the *Mayflower Compact*. The Compact was a social contract in which the settlers agreed to abide by its rules and regulations to maintain order and to survive. It also affirmed allegiance to the King. Not all signed onto the agreement, but apparently there were enough signees to ensure its enforcement. Caleb Johnson's *Mayflowerhistory.com* lists forty-one male passengers who signed the contract (*http://mayflowerhistory.com/mayflower-compact/*). I'd like to know how many of those who signed were Puritans, as well as how many men chose not to sign.

The Fortune, Anne, and Little James

About a year after the landing of the *Mayflower*, the struggling colonists were surprised one chilly November morning in 1621 to look out in the harbor and see a British ship. It was the *Fortune* sent by the *Merchant Adventurers*. It was a small vessel and carried only 35 passengers, mostly men (their wives and children came later on the *Anne* and *Little James*). Governor Bradford was not pleased to see a ship anchored in the harbor as its arrival was completely unexpected. The last thing he needed were more mouths to feed and shelter. Unless, he fervently hoped, it was filled with needed food and supplies. Alas and alack, there were none. Can you imagine the man's frustration? Why would the *Merchant Adventurers* send only passengers with no supplies for the colony? There was, however, little choice but to make the best of the situation and welcome the new colonists.

Weston Settlers and the Sparrow

Have you ever heard of the Weston Colony on Massachusetts Bay in 1622, merely one year after the Plymouth Colony began to set roots? No? How about the Weymouth Colony? Or perhaps, the Wessagusset Colony, as it was also known? Well, me neither. It came as surprise to me to find out that Thomas Weston had left the *Company of Merchant Adventurers of London* to seek his fortune with his own company and settlement in New England. To this end he embarked on founding a colony off the coast of present-day Maine.

In May, 1622 Weston's ship the *Sparrow* anchored at Damariscove (sic) Island. From there he led a group of ten men to Plymouth sailing in a shallop (a light sailboat). They arrived May 31. The group was welcomed at Plymouth while they waited for the main party of the Weston settlers to arrive from England on the *Charity* and the *Swan*. When the two ships arrived sixty more men called by Governor Bradford as "lusty men" were added to the 80-odd colonists living in the Plymouth settlement. The good Governor was not happy to have to accommodate such a large group. Their presence added enormous stress to an already very fragile situation. They stayed July and August before departing to attempt to establish a new colony about 30 miles north at present day Weymouth, Massachusetts.

Apparently, the fifty to sixty men who landed at the Weymouth site were ill-prepared for life in the wilderness and the settlement failed. The men had to be rescued by Miles Standish and some other Plymouth colonists. A few of the rescued men chose to stay in Plymouth, the remainder returned to England probably glad to have left the prospect of a life filled with unfamiliar adversities in the New World. Thomas Weston, however, was far from being finished.

Arrival of the Anne & Little James

In early 1623, a year or so after the Weymouth debacle, a large supply and passenger ship of 140 tons named the *Anne* set sail from the Port of London for the New Plymouth Colony. Soon afterwards the much smaller 40 ton *Little James* followed. The *Anne* arrived on July 10, 1623 and the *Little James* came about ten days later. Both ships were financed by our old friend Thomas Weston who had also financed the *Mayflower* and the

Fortune, as well as the ill-fated settlement in Maine. The *Anne*, captained by William Pierce, carried 60 passengers and 60 tons of badly need supplies. Combined, the *Anne* and the *Little James* carried about 90 passengers. There are no separate passenger lists as they were grouped together under the *Anne* when land distribution was made in Plymouth in 1623.

Sixty of the 90 souls on board the two ships were Puritan/Pilgrim Separatists. This included Stephen. The remaining 30 passengers were an independent group unaffiliated with the Separatist movement. Those folks had paid their own travel expenses and were, therefore, not beholden to the joint stock company of Separatists and the *Merchant Adventurers* that had been formed in Leiden in 1620. Unlike the so-called "strangers" aboard the *Mayflower*, this group was referred to as "the Particulars" having made the voyage *"on their own particulars."* This was a quaint way of saying they had paid their own way.

The leader of the autonomous group that arrived in 1623 was John Oldham. While a Puritan, Oldham was more motivated by ambitions for wealth than creating a religious refuge in New England. His group was promised separate living arrangements in Plymouth, but things didn't quite work out as planned. Oldham's different perspective on the primary purpose of the Plymouth settlement, accompanied by an ugly confrontation with the fiery, but popular, Miles Standish, led to his banishment. Oldham was out of sight, but not out of mind. He later plays a significant role in our story.

Governor William Bradford's *History of the Plimouth (sic) Plantation* is a treasure trove of detailed information on all things early Plymouth. We learn from his book that from the beginning of the arrival of the Oldham's "Particulars" Governor William Bradford was concerned that they would not feel obligated to work for the "common good." He also had good reason to be concerned about how even the Pilgrims would adjust to their new surroundings as Bradford observed that the new arrivals were *"so 'daunted and dismayed' by the ragged and emaciated appearances of the settlers that 'some wished themselves in England again; others fell a-weeping, fancying their own misery in what they now saw in others."* It didn't help that Bradford demanded strict moral and religious standards of everyone. As a result, many who came on the *Anne* and *Little James* threw in the towel and returned to England bidding a jolly good riddance to the Colony and its uptight leaders.

Even those who stayed had many complaints about living conditions, including gripes about not being able to enjoy their usual British cuisine which they sorely missed. No doubt food connoisseurs from France and Italy might have found that to be quite ironic given their opinion of English gastronomy. Hey, I love English food, but the English settlers from Leiden had no experience with, or stomach for, venison, wild turkey, or seafood. It was noted that the best food that the Pilgrims could offer the newcomers on the *Anne* and *Little James* were lobsters, clams, or striped bass fish without bread or anything else but a cup of water. And what respectable Englishmen worth his salt could live on such abysmal fare? There was, of course, the occasional wild fowl and deer. Not to mention nuts from an unnamed wild vine with nut-like tubers on its roots. This was not so palatable to people who wondered "where's the beef" or, for that matter, the lamb and pork. And where were the ubiquitous English peas to be washed down with a pottle (two quarts) of weak lager beer? Fortunately, the year 1623 produced a bumper crop of garden staples with which the English settlers were more familiar.

Despite Bradford's apprehensions regarding the new arrivals on the *Anne* and *Little James*, he writes that he was pleased to see many of his friends and colleagues from Leiden. And, of course, many of those on-board were overjoyed to be reunited with their Puritan friends and family with whom they had worked, lived, suffered, and worshiped in Leiden. This included their old friend and my favorite Pilgrim, Stephen Tracy.

All the Colonists were also glad to see that the *Anne* carried livestock, including three "Kerry breed" cattle which they nicknamed the *Great Black Cow, Lesser Black Cow,* and *Great White Backed Cow.* By 1627 these three "cows" had produced 16 head of cattle. Before you ask if there was a bull among the cows, check your Merriam online dictionary. It gives a second definition of cow as a bovine animal regardless of gender. In this case, rumor has it that there was one bull and two heifers. The livestock on the *Anne* also included 22 goats.

Chickens had been brought with the Pilgrims on the *Mayflower*. Having chickens turned out to be most fortunate as chicken soup played a significant role in sustaining the Colony. Edward Winslow gave it to a very sick Wampanoag sachem (Chief) named Massasoit. Following his recovery, Massasoit remained a lifelong friend of the Pilgrims. Do we owe the success of the colony to chicken soup? My mother probably would have thought as much given all that she said it would cure! She did prepare a delicious simmering pot from freshly dressed poultry my dad brought home live from the corner store for Sunday dinner.

I mentioned earlier that Tryphosa and her infant daughter, Sarah, may not have traveled with Stephen on the *Anne*. There is documentation to support that they were and there is documentation to support that they weren't. It isn't unusual to find conflicting possibilities such as this. When I do I tend to follow the lead of genealogists who have well established reputations among contemporary researchers. However, in this instance, I must confess that I have written elsewhere that the family came together on the *Anne* based on ship passenger lists. I've given this a lot of thought and looking at the evidence again in writing this narrative, I'm going to change my mind. I hope you aren't one of those who get upset with people who change their mind based on new evidence or on a new perspective on the evidence. I'm definitely doing a flip-flop! It is better to be correct than consistent, as long as you don't have political aspirations!

In re-reading examinations of this topic by such genealogical luminaries as Charles Robert Anderson and Robert S. Wakefield, I'm more or less convinced that Stephen's wife and daughter came on the *Jacob*, arriving at Plymouth in 1625. These two distinguished fellows persuasively argued that Tryphosa was pregnant soon after the birth of Sarah which, according to Wakefield, was in 1622. He suggested that Tryphosa did not want to risk an ocean voyage with an infant and carrying for another. Staying in Leiden, she gave birth to a daughter, Jane, in early 1623 in Leiden. Robert Charles Anderson has observed that Tryphosa was in London on May 1, 1624 when she applied for a *"license to pass from England beyond the seas"* with a daughter. Sadly, applying for travel with only one child implies that Jane died sometime between her birth and May, 1624.

One problem with this scenario is that Sarah's birthdate is recorded on a website called *Find a Grave* as January 16, 1623. This would not be possible under the Anderson and Wakefield theories. *Find a Grave* is very helpful in locating places of burial of ancestors and I've used it frequently, but the data are not necessarily based on historic records or documents and it is not all that unusual to find a mistake. The international marriage document for Sarah and her husband, George Partridge, gives her birth year as 1621 which confirms the date noted by Anderson and Wakefield.

4

STEPHEN TRACY, JR. – PLYMOUTH & DUXBURY

One of the first things I wanted to know about Stephen when he lived in Plymouth was how much land he owned. This was important to me because I figured he might have fared better than others because of his acquaintances among the Pilgrim leaders with whom he had lived in Leiden. That familiarity, I thought, would have improved his odds of acquiring good land. Keep in mind, his profession was as a say-maker or serge-maker, hardly good preparation for making a living as a farmer. So, good, fertile land for farming would have been a plus.

Before Stephen arrived all the land at Plymouth was held in common. There was no private ownership. That experiment in communality was short lived. Low production of crops was partially attributed to the lack of private incentive to work land owned by the community. To correct the situation, in 1623, the year Stephen arrived, the land was divided into privately owned acreage among the passengers of the abovementioned four ships that carried passengers to Plymouth: *Mayflower* (1620), *Fortune* (1621), *Anne* (1623), and the *Little James* (1623).

A total of ninety-five acres were granted to all who came on the *Anne* and *Little James*. Twenty passengers on these two ships were allocated a total of fifty acres southward of both sides of Wellingsley Brook. Stephen received three acres near land owned by Governor Bradford. I'm guessing that the Governor was allocated some choice property. At that time, the brook was apparently filled with trout. A restoration of the brook was undertaken in 2012 to restore it to its former glory by removing several small dams. This enabled the return of the Sea Run Brook Trout to the heart of Plymouth.

How much land constituted an acre in the 1600s? Apparently, the answer to that isn't as simple as one might think. Historically, it was the amount of land tillable by a yoke of oxen in one day. But to my limited knowledge the Pilgrims didn't have any oxen. Would a yoke of cows till as much? Putting flippancy aside, I got a definition from a land surveyor who lives in Duxbury, Massachusetts. His name is Lamont "Monty" Healy. I'll have more to relate about him later. He informed me that when the Pilgrims referred to a grant of five acres in breadth, it meant a square acre with 208.71 foot sides. As much as I appreciated the definition, it didn't clarify it much for the likes of math-challenged me. I called upon the talents of my nephew, Tracy Karnavas, a high school math teacher to give me a lesson. He explained that *"if a grant of five acres in breadth meant a square acre with 208.71 foot sides then 208.71 squared would be 43,560 square feet which is the same as today's definition of an acre."* He further explained that this would mean that five acres in breadth would equal 1 acre today in square footage. That works for me.

One other interesting feature that I learned about Plymouth Colony is how it was financed and how that defined land ownership. From its inception in 1620 until early 1627, the Plymouth colony was financed by the *Merchant Adventurers* in London. Therefore, while individuals were awarded land to live on and farm, early on there was, as noted, no individual land ownership. What was not assigned to families was given to the Colony for everyone's use, such as the "commons" area where anyone could bring their livestock to graze. It is characteristic of the "company towns" historically found in the Appalachian coal country in Eastern Kentucky and West Virginia. Hershey, Pennsylvania, home of the famous chocolate candy, had a similar approach. It sounds much more ideal than it actually was.

The arrangement with the *Merchant Adventurers* did not last long thanks to the efforts of a Plymouth Pilgrim named Isaac Allerton. He was the primary negotiator behind an agreement that was made on October 26, 1626 for the colonists to purchase all of the Plymouth stock and land from the Adventurers for £1,800 ($418,000 in 2016 currency). Stephen was one of 53 settlers to sign the agreement (his name is spelled Steeven Trasie in the document). His participation in the deal also gave him privileges in all future land purchases and grants.

The acquisition of the land was a huge boon for the privileged 53 settlers. Each man who signed was awarded twenty acres for himself and twenty acres for each member of his household. Thus, Stephen received 80 acres for his family of four. He and Tryphosa had a second daughter, Rebecca, who was born in 1625. By the end of 1624, the population of Plymouth was about 180 people dwelling in 32 houses within a fortress about one-half mile in circumference.

Each twenty acre lot allocated under this agreement was five acres wide facing the shore, and four acres deep. As I now know, if these were five acres in breadth, the total allocation was really for only four acres, not twenty and one, not five, on the shoreline. There apparently were some "inland" lots, but the inland areas primarily stayed in possession of the Colony as a whole for use as common areas, for distribution to later immigrants, or for later sales to second generation children of the early settlers or others. Accordingly, Stephen and other early Pilgrims had land closest to the ocean, with prime waterfront lots. Since private ownership was a new concept, rules were adopted for giving rights, or limitations, regarding rights of way, hunting, and so on.

The bad news is that the agreement with the *Merchant Adventurers* left the colonists with a significant debt. I hadn't known that such a familiar ominous national financial situation had started so early in American history! But there it is. Allerton, Bradford and others took on the debt by agreeing to give the London merchants a monopoly in the fur trade. Unfortunately, the area around Plymouth didn't contain enough wild game, especially desirable beaver fur, to ensure the colonists' capacity to pay off the debt. Isaac Allerton once again came to the rescue by acquiring a land grant from the King in what is now Kennebec County, Maine. The hunting expeditions and processing of fur for shipment to England was managed by everyone's friend, Plymouth resident, and Pilgrim leader, William Brewster. According to Dr. Jeremy Bangs, the debt was paid in full by 1632 with grants of land in Scituate, Massachusetts.

Once the land had been purchased from the *Merchant Adventurers*, the question arose about what to do with the cattle, goats, swine, and poultry that had also been the company's property. It was decided to distribute the livestock to all families and their members of the colony. On May 22, 1627 an agreement was reached known as the "Division of Cattle." The title is a little misleading presumably in the interest of brevity as all the livestock was divided into 12 lots of animals to be shared by 13 people. The four members of Stephen's family shared in the 10th lot which consisted of a *"heifer of the last year called the white bellied heifer and two she goats."* Another person who shared in lot #10 was Thomas Prence whose daughter, Mary Jane, later married Stephen's son, John. The original document of the *Division of Cattle* has been preserved and is a very valuable source because it lists every individual living in Plymouth in 1627.

Stephen in Duxbury, Massachusetts

I assume that Stephen did well economically and socially in the years he spent in Plymouth settlement, although I don't have primary evidence to back that up. Secondary evidence does support the assumption that he was economically well off. He was clearly highly thought of in the community. For starters he had become one of the freemen. That made it possible for Stephen to be closely associated with the primary "movers and shakers" of the Colony. Indeed, in more than one historical book Stephen is referred to as *"a leading man in the founding of the Plymouth Colony."* I don't have any details on what made him a leading man in Plymouth village itself.

Fortunately, there are multiple descriptions of his success and high status in the settlement of Duxbury of which he was an original founder. He moved to Duxbury from Plymouth in 1633, ten years after his arrival at Plymouth. Duxbury was located across the bay from Plymouth about 10 miles north by land. The settlement was on property originally occupied by the Pawtuxet Indians of the Wampanoag tribe. The tribe was wiped out by the plague, except for one person. The lone survivor was Tisquantum, better known as Squanto. Squanto played a critical role in helping the Pilgrims get through the early years. He died in 1622, one year before Stephen arrived at Plymouth.

At some point the land in Duxbury was obtained by Captain Miles Standish. He named the area after his family ancestral property, Duxbury Hall, in Lancashire County, England. Stephen and others apparently moved from Plymouth because it had become too small to accommodate the needs of farmers who depended on more land for grazing and raising crops. William Brewster, Thomas Prence and others had been using the land at Duxbury for a couple of years before 1633 in summers, returning to winter in Plymouth. The movement outward from Plymouth was another big headache for Governor Bradford because he felt that the dispersal of the community would undermine its religious mission. He was ultimately proven right!

Three years before he helped found Duxbury, Stephen and Tryphosa had been blessed with another daughter, Mary. Stephen must have seen the Duxbury settlement as an opportunity for him to improve his livelihood with his growing family and livestock. Governor Bradford obviously concurred as he granted Stephen 60 to 80 acres with a meadow in Duxbury in 1634. In that same year, Stephen and Tryphosa had their fourth and final child and only son, John, who was born in Duxbury. The next year, on October 1, the Colony Court appointed Captain Standish, William Collier, Jonathan Brewster, William Palmer, and Stephen Tracy to lay out highways in Duxbury before November 15 of the same year.

William Palmer must have been a good friend of Stephen. This seems evident from Palmer's will in which Stephen was left a bequest. What the bequest specifically entailed is unknown. Palmer died on November 7, 1637. He had been a passenger on the *Fortune* that arrived at Plymouth in 1621. His wife came later in 1623 on the *Anne*, the same ship on which Stephen was a passenger. Palmer was one of the original proprietors of Duxbury and later settled in nearby Yarmouth, Massachusetts.

By 1637, nine of the 27 heads of families who had arrived on the *Fortune* had resettled in Duxbury. On March, 21 1637, Stephen was one of five men from Duxbury appointed by the General Court to explore the possibility of moving Plymouth a little to the north and Duxbury a little to the southwest. The idea was to create a new settlement either near the Jones River or Morton's Hole (a deep hole on the flats west of Captain's Hill). The projected "Jones River" settlement was to be located about half way between Plymouth and Duxbury. The men appointed from Duxbury were joined by five men from Plymouth, including Captain Miles Standish. Nine of the ten men showed up at the meeting to decide on which place to recommend. Seven men on the committee suggested the Jones River settlement and two favored Morton's Hole. I don't know which location was preferred by Stephen. However, it is a moot point as the idea seems to have gone over like a lead balloon and was dropped. Incidentally, the property referred to as Jones River is now part of Kingston, Massachusetts. The river was named for the Captain of the Mayflower, Christopher Jones.

As for the precise location of Stephen's land in Duxbury, at first all I could find were indirect references to his property. For example, one record of his land made in 1636 states that "...*whereas there is reported to be certaine wast land between the lott of Stephen Tracy & that of Liuetent Will Holmes at the request of Mr. Will Bradford, such land was granted to him ....*" This wasn't much help. Nor was a later reference that gave the directions to the Governor's house "*through a valley to Abraham Pierce's, turned northerly to the house of Stephen Tracy, leaving Gov. Bradford's house on the west.*"

Another elusive clue I found was that *"The house of Stephen Tracy stood near the site of John H. Parks, and the easterly line of Gov. Bradford's land ...."* These citations are taken from a book by Thomas Bradford Drew written in 1897. Drew did place Stephen's property at Jones River in the vicinity of Governor William Bradford's land: *"Among those who had secured lands and more or less permanent settlements at Jones River, prior to 1636, were Gov. Bradford, John Howland, Stephen Tracy and Abraham Pierce."* A book about Governor William Bradford notes he also acquired 300 acres of land near the Jones River by 1636 for certain and possibly as early as the second division in 1627.

I suspected (hoped!) that more detail might be available somewhere that would give a better read on the location of Stephen's Duxbury property. To investigate I sent an email on April 27, 2016 to the *Duxbury Rural and Historical Society* which for some reason I had only just discovered. Not having written to the Society before, I thought it would be worth an inquiry to see what treasures they might have relating to Stephen. Lo and behold not 15 minutes after sending my email I received a response from the aforementioned Society's archivist and historian, Carolyn Ravenscroft. She provided me with the only reference she could quickly put her hands on. I was a bit taken aback that given Stephen was a founding father of Duxbury the Society had so little material on him. The document at hand was a brief article published in the *Duxbury Clipper* on October 1, 2014 entitled *"Stephen Tracey (sic) and the Loring Family."* Fortunately, it proved to be a very helpful article in that it described in detail the location of the land granted to Stephen in 1627.

Ms. Ravenscroft was also kind enough to forward my email to the author of the *Duxbury Clipper* article, Lamont R. Healy. Soon afterwards I received a reply from him. Monty, as he prefers to be called, proved to be a treasure trove. For starters, he is a professional land surveyor with an intense interest in who owned what and where in Duxbury at its beginning. And, while he has only a passing interest in Stephen, he was more than willing to share what he had. What luck, say I. Monty sent me two packages by snail mail with very detailed worksheets (maps) of early Duxbury and a related article from the *Duxbury Clipper* on *"The Kingston Nook – No Man's Land."*

Monty pointed out that it was not 80 acres that were granted to Stephen, as recorded elsewhere, but *"more like 60."* The October, 2016 article shows a map of Stephen's land running west to east from Tussock Brook to Kingston Bay, just north of the Jones River. Tussock Brook is currently the boundary between Kingston and Duxbury. Stephen's property bordered the settlement of Kingston to the South. Kingston did not become a town until 1726. Monty explained that in 1857 the Duxbury town line was diagonal across Stephen's land when Kingston, after a lengthy legal battle with Duxbury, annexed "The Kingston Nook."

Monty said that Stephen's land grant was just south of the property of Joseph Rogers. They shared a meadow. This location is also acknowledged by a copy of a paper written in 1814 or 1884 by a Mr. Bradford. At some point it had been copied and revised by Henry A. Fish. The copy is now held in the Vertical Files of the Local History Room in the Kingston, Massachusetts Public Library. The library obtained it from Emily Fuller Drew, a Kingston historian. The Kingston Library's Archivist, Susan Aprill, was nice enough to send me a PDF copy of the paper. As for Joseph Rogers, he was one of the original members of the Puritan Leiden congregation, so he would certainly have known Stephen from Leiden. Rogers came to Plymouth with his father, Thomas, on the *Mayflower*. Stephen's son, John, lived on the Tracy property in Duxbury for nearly 50 years.

According to Monty, Lt. Thomas Loring, a boat builder from Boston, purchased the land from John Tracy on December 3, 1702. The Loring family owned the property into the 1900s. The tract became known as *The Bay Farm*. I'm very happy to report that the farm is now an expanded "Bay Farm Conservation Area." It is held under the protection of the Duxbury Board of Selectmen and managed by the Duxbury Conservation Commission. According to an online brochure *"It has become a popular area for dog walkers, cross-country skiers, hikers, joggers, and birders who enjoy the large open, grassy field."* It has a 1.7 mile looped trail. There is a nice photo of *The Bay Farm* online at http://www.wickedlocal.com/article/20101108/ NEWS/311089404.

Continuing to look for references to Stephen's land one source I found gave a 1637 reference to the road to Duxbury. According to the source, the road from Plymouth to Duxbury began *"at the ferry at Jones River passing by Stephen Tracy's property to the bridge at John Rogers' property, continuing past Jonathon Brewster's cow yard, through a valley near the house of Thomas Prence and Christopher Wadsworth's property."* Another description is provided by historian Hamilton Hurd who wrote in 1884 that *".... there were three routes from Plymouth over Jones River to the common point at Stephen Tracy's house, which probably stood on the present estate of Mr. Samuel Loring of Duxbury."* Hurd also mentioned the location of Stephen's house next to the property of William Bradford.

In 1640 a document recorded that the bounds between Duxbury and Plymouth were *"from a little brooke (sic), running from Stephen Tracy's, to another little brooke, falling into Blackwater from the commons left to Duxburrow (sic) and the neighborhood thereabouts."* The little brook may have been Island Creek or Wellingsley Brook that abutted Stephen's property. Blackwater Pond is actually a small lake that still exists as a popular fishing spot. It is about five miles southwest of Duxbury near the town of Kingston. Stephen's property seems to have been about equal distance from the villages of Duxbury and Plymouth. Stephen is also known to have a received a grant of land at Namassakeeset which was annexed by Duxbury in 1658.

You would be justified in asking the obvious question: why so much detail on the location of Stephen's Duxbury land? Well, first of all it has taken me years to find an accurate description and I'm not about to leave any of it out. Secondly, and more importantly, the location plays a critical role in supporting my theory that Stephen and Thomas might well have known each other. The fact that the families of Stephen and Governor Bradford were neighbors lends itself to this audacious idea. I'll explore this is great detail in a later chapter.

Given the apparent paucity of information on Stephen in the Society's holdings, I immediately emailed an attachment of what I like to think is a well-documented write-up that I had prepared in 2014 entitled: *Stephen Tracy (1596-1654) of Plymouth & Duxbury, MA*. I try to get in my digs whenever I can! And this was a great opportunity to increase the Society's holdings on Stephen. I also sent a copy to the Kingston Public Library. It was gratefully received by both institutions.

Continuing my investigation of who got what land, I found a reference to a relevant land distribution decree by Governor Bradford. On March 2, 1640, the Governor announced that he would surrender the land patent of Plymouth Colony which was in his name to the Plymouth freemen, reserving three tracts of land for the "old comers." Passengers on all of the first four ships qualified as "old comers." They were later designated as "Forefathers." Stephen was included in these groups because he arrived on the *Anne* and also because he had been a freemen since at least 1633. Stephen benefited from being included in this elite group by receiving an additional 40 acres in Duxbury.

Stephen's son-in-law George Partridge (1617-1695), husband of his daughter Sarah (1621-1708) was also awarded 40 acres in Duxbury. The property was north of Stephen's near the present-day intersection of Tremont Street (State Route 3A) and Parks Street. Stephen acquired more land on November 2, 1640 when the General Court awarded several men property. Stephen received "fourscore" acres with some meadow at the North River. The North River, I'm pleased to say, is alive and well after all these years. It is popular with kayakers and a habitat for striped bass and bluefish. The North River Wildlife Sanctuary near Marshfield looks like a wonderful, restful place to visit.

By your leave, let's pause here a moment in Stephen's progression to examine what I discovered about how one became a freemen and what it meant. All of the original stockholders in the joint-stock Company of Merchant Adventures were freemen, but not all freemen were stockholders. I don't know if Stephen was an original stockholder. Possibly not, since he was not in the first group to leave Leiden on the *Speedwell* and *Mayflower*. However, I do know that he is listed as "*one of the Freemen of the Incorporation of Plymouth, 1633.*" Moreover, he is included in the 1639 list of Duxbury freemen and is also listed as a freeman of Duxbury in 1643 and in 1646. In that document his name is shown as *Steephen Tracye* (sic).

Actually, it was very helpful to find the spelling of his name as *Tracye*, as I used that spelling to search and locate several references to him that did not show up when searching *Tracy* or *Tracey*. Other spellings of Tracy that made searches more challenging include *Trasey, Traccy, Trassey, Trassie, Trass, Tress, Traice, Tracies, and Trace* to name a few of the variations. In fact, there are 30 different ways of spelling it. As the late Australian Steve Irwin would put it, "*crikey mate*", how many ways are there to spell a five-letter name?! Can you imagine what family genealogists are confronted with if the surname being researched is more than five letters? In addition to the multiple ways I ran across the spelling of Tracy, I also saw Stephen spelled *Steeven, Steeuen*, and *Steph*. You have to give them credit; the scribes of the times came up with really creative ways of spelling names!

In order to become a freemen in the Plymouth Colony, other than those who were freemen by virtue of being a stockholder in the company, a man (and rest assured it was only a man) first had to be approved by of all of the freemen of the town where the person lived. Then he (only men) was recommended to the *General Court of Freemen* for final approval. Land ownership was not a requirement, but one had to give an oath of allegiance to the Colony. Freemen were required to attend town meetings and the General Court sessions on a regular basis. Heavy fines were imposed on those who did not fulfill their civic obligations.

There were many advantages to being one of the freemen in the Plymouth Colony. Only freemen could vote for the Governor. Only free-men could vote for town representatives to the General Court, known as "deputies." And only freemen could be deputies. Another nice perk was that only freemen had a right to be tried by a jury of twelve men and could even challenge who served on the jury. This must have come in very handy and swung the scales of justice toward their side when being taken to court by non-freemen.

For some unknown reason Stephen's name isn't included in a list compiled in 1643 of the men in Duxbury who had a right to bear arms. Yes, gun control was strictly enforced and typically limited to freemen. His absence on this list may have caused later researchers to assume that he had already returned to England. As I'll explain shortly, while it has been proven he didn't return until about 1654, a number of authors apparently didn't get that memo and give an earlier date for his departure back to England as being most probable.

Stephen's Civic Roles in Duxbury
As we've seen, Stephen owned a great deal of land in Duxbury. Having land is good, but I wanted to know how he used his land ownership and apparent wealth for the public good through civic activities. The absence of histories about such activities in Plymouth gave me pause. It was most welcome, then, when I found plenty of sources giving evidence regarding his civic engagement in Duxbury. Much of this was recorded by Nathanial B. Shurtleff in the compilation of the eight volume *Records of the Colony of New Plymouth*. Shurtleff was very active in the American Antiquarian Society.

The *Records* reveal that Stephen was deeply involved in the establishment of Duxbury from the very beginning. For example, he was one of a five-member committee to select a site for the meeting house in Duxbury. After the community was created, there is a long string of his civic activities. He was appointed tax assessor in 1634, selected for the coroner's jury in 1635, appointed a member of the first General Court of the Colony in 1635, and served on the grand jury in 1636. In the same year he was appointed to a Duxbury committee to meet with a committee from Plymouth to work out exactly where one community began and the other ended.

The list of activities continued to grow as I did more research. On March 20, 1636, several men were appointed to *"view all the hey (sic) grounds"* that had been assigned to the inhabitants of Plymouth, Eele River, and Duxbury. Stephen and Jonathan Brewster were specifically assigned to view the hay grounds from Island Creek to the River beyond Phillp Delanoy's property. The purpose of the survey seems to have been to determine which grounds were to be used as grazing pastures.

On December 30, 1637 Stephen worked once again with Jonathan Brewster, along with Christopher Wadesworth, to lay out an access road to Ralph Partrich's land. In 1638 and 1639 he is recorded as having been appointed constable for Duxbury. In 1638 and 1642 he was designated as an arbitrator by Governor Bradford. From 1639 through 1642, he served as a grand juror. On June 2, 1640 he was appointed a member of "The Grand Inquest" which sounds rather more ominous than it really was since it just refers to the Grand Jury and not an inquisition of the Spanish kind! Although I'm sure there were those at the time who would argue with that distinction.

It appears to have been the norm to have quarrels, squabbles, and disputes, even minor ones, given to juries for resolution. The juries would decide whether or not the alleged crime or affront was of significant import to send to the General Court. If the dispute was not forwarded to the General Court, the local jury would determine what punishment, if any, should be given. I don't know what was behind this legal process other than to speculate that it beat resolving issues by fisticuffs or more violent means, although that certainly happened. It does show that a legal process was firmly in place. Part of the process was for the Governor and Assistants to appoint jurors. Stephen's respected reputation in the Plymouth Colony is evident from the numerous times he served on Grand Juries as documented in March, 1636, January, 1637, August, 1638, September, 1640, June, 1641, and December, 1641.

On one occasion that took place September 7, 1642 Stephen participated as a character witness on behalf of Abraham Pierce. The case involved a suit brought against Mr. Pierce by William Hanbury concerning some swine that had been killed. In fact, swine (the four-legged kind) seem to have been at the root of many disputes between neighbors. Apparently hogs roamed freely resulting in considerable damage to neighbor's crops.

Despite the significant role that Stephen played in the development of Duxbury, the history of his branch of the Tracy family hasn't received a great deal of attention. When I checked with the *Duxbury Rural & Historical Society* I was told that the only material on the Tracy family in its archives was a book written by Dorothy Wentworth in 1972. It provides only a very brief sketch of Stephen. Similarly, the *Kingston Public Library* only had the article written by Lamont Healy. This isn't much material for a Leiden Pilgrim, "Forefather", founding father of Plymouth and Duxbury and friend and neighbor of Governor Bradford. Happily, both the Society and the library are very receptive to any material I can give them. As noted, I've already sent them what I have and will send them an update that I'm preparing.

It isn't only Stephen who has not received much historical attention. The Plymouth Colony and off spring communities like Duxbury weren't a favorite focus of historians in the 17th and 18th centuries. I discovered that one reason for this is the relative obscurity of Plymouth following the Great Migration and expansion of the Massachusetts Bay Colony from 1630 to 1640. The Pilgrim community of Plymouth was not greatly researched or written about for a long period of time. It was simply overshadowed by the mass immigration in the Boston Bay area and the subsequent settlement into the Connecticut Valley. Consequently, Plymouth and Duxbury were pretty much relegated as "backwater" locations in the face of the growth of

Boston and the Bay area. Only the most well-known of the "Forefathers" like Governor William Bradford or the swash-buckling Miles Standish receive much historical attention. But don't take my word for it. Check out this analysis in the works of contemporary early American Harvard historian, Professor Bernard Bailyn, in particular *The Barbarous Years: The Peopling of British North America: The Conflict of Civilizations, 1600-1675.* It is an informative and enlightening read.

Date Stephen Left Duxbury for a Trip to England
One of the so called genealogical "brick walls" that I've encountered in researching Stephen is the date that he left Duxbury for a trip to England. Until very recently, the predominating view was that this had occurred as early as 1643. That date was given some credence in *The Great Migration Directory: Immigrants to New England, 1620-1640, Volume I-III, P-W* written in 1995 by every genealogist's favorite guru, Robert Charles Anderson. In that edition Anderson had this entry on Stephen Tracy: "*Returned to England permanently, perhaps as early as 1643, and certainly by 1654.*"

Because there wasn't any real evidence to support either date, I've spent an extensive amount of time trying to find which was more likely. I mentioned earlier that searching sources for Tracy spelled *Tracye* led to several new references regarding Stephen. Well, that was the key to unlock this particular mystery box. More specifically, I found a reference to the deeds recorded in the *Records of the Plymouth Colony* that showed *Steven Tracye* as having been one of several Plymouth Colonists who purchased land in 1652. This, in turn, helped me locate a 1981 publication by Leon Clark Hills which noted that: "*In March, 1652, Stephen Tracy, Francis Cooke and others acquired a large tract of land to the west* [of Plymouth], *later called Dartmouth. These two men had one share each in the venture. For some reason about this time Stephen decided to leave the country.*"

The Dartmouth, Massachusetts property mentioned by Hills was purchased by William Bradford, Miles Standish, Thomas Southworth, John

Winslow, John Cooke, and 31 other "associates". Most importantly for me, the list of purchasers included Stephen. The acquisition involved several thousand acres of land 35 miles to the southwest of Plymouth on the coast. The land was bought from Wampanoag sachems Massasoit and Wamsutta. To be precise the price was thirty yards of cloth, eight moose skins, fifteen axes, fifteen hoes, fifteen pairs of shoes, one iron pot, and ten shillings' worth of assorted goods. There were 34 shares owned by 36 people. Stephen received one whole share of 3,200 acres. The original list of the sale of the land was lost for several years, along with the list of shareholders. Both were reconstructed from memory until the original deed was found.

After I had discovered that Stephen was, indeed, still in the Colony in 1652, I informed the Massachusetts Society of Genealogists (I'm a long-time member). I never received an acknowledgement, but I couldn't help but notice that in the 2015 publication of Anderson's *The Great Migration Directory: Immigrants to New England, 1620-1640 A Concise Compendium* the entry for Stephen had been revised to "*returned to England permanently by 1654.*" The reference to 1643 had been dropped. You may correctly assume that I was pleased no end.

Dartmouth was named after a town of the same name in Devon County in southeast England. It was the originally planned point of departure for the Puritans in 1620. The land bought by the Plymouth Pilgrims was later sold to the Religious Society of Friends or Quakers, who wished to live outside the stringent religious laws of the Puritans. It also attracted Baptists and even 10 of the 36 men from Plymouth who purchased the land. Unlike other Plymouth communities, it had neither church nor town center. I have been unable to find out how much the original purchasers received in payment for the land or if it was sold separately by each owner. Regardless, I would speculate that Stephen's sale of his 3,200 acres would have netted him a handsome sum of wampum! It would be more than enough to finance a trip home and back. If only I knew the purpose of that trip.

Stephen's Return to England

Although I now had a more accurate idea as to when he took a trip to England, I was none the wiser as to why Stephen would engage in such a journey. I can't help but wonder if his financial windfall from his full share of the Dartmouth property was a factor. He may have gone for business or family reasons. Stephen may have also been anxious to return to an England that was much more receptive to the Puritan cause under the rule of Protector Oliver Cromwell. There may also have been some connection between his trip and the apparent death of his wife, Tryphosa, before his departure. Her exact date of death is not known, but it appears to have been before he went to England.

Travel to England was risky on many fronts. One was confronted by the real possibilities of shipwreck, accident, illness, and disease. It was farsighted for anyone venturing across the big pond to leave instructions on how they wanted to leave their worldly goods should they not return. Stephen had this covered by giving power of attorney to his *"loving friend"* John Winslow before he left for the motherland. The power of attorney was equivalent to a will. John Winslow was a brother of *Mayflower* passenger Edward Winslow. John had been one of the many Puritans who remained in Leiden in 1620, along with Stephen. He came to Plymouth aboard the *Fortune* in 1621 one year later and two years before Stephen arrived.

In his power of attorney Stephen asked Winslow to divide his lands and chattels at Duxbury between Stephen's son John and his daughter Ruth. He also specified that *"...what Cattle I have more (maryes two cows being cast in amongst them) to be equally Divided among my five children lieving (sic) in New England...."* He was in Great Yarmouth, possibly London, on March 20, 1655 when he became ill and died soon after. His son John apparently ended up as sole owner of the Duxbury property because it was still in his procession when he sold it to Thomas Loring on December 30, 1702.

Children of Stephen & Tryphosa

To save you the trouble of going back several pages to refresh your memory as to the family makeup, I'll remind you that Stephen and Tryphosa had six children: Sarah, Jane, Rebecca, Ruth, Mary, and John. Jane died in infancy. At the time of Stephen's departure for England and death, two of his four daughters, Sarah and Rebecca, are documented as being married. His daughter Mary was also most likely married because, like his other married daughters, he did not include them in the division of land. A bequest was made for his only unmarried daughter, Ruth. Regrettably, I cannot find what became of her. John was unmarried at the time but at age 22 had reached maturity when he became eligible to receive the inheritance.

With the exception of Ruth, I've been able to find out some details of the lives of Stephen's children. I'll start with Sarah whom, you'll recall, was born in Leiden in 1623. She married George Partridge on November 28, 1638 in Duxbury. She was only fifteen but marriage at that age for a girl was not all that unusual at the time. Her 21-year old husband, George, came from England to Duxbury in 1636. He was a tailor and the son and the grandson of ministers in Kent County, England. I occasionally run across online postings of the numerous descendants of Sarah and George.

Stephen and Tryphosa's second child and daughter, Rebecca, was born in 1625 in Plymouth. She married Ensign William Merrick (or Myrick) in 1644 in Eastham, Massachusetts. Eastham was a new community, reflective of the efforts of Plymouth Colonists to establish new towns on the peninsula. Eastham is a little over 60 miles from Duxbury in Barnstable County next to Cape Cod County. William Merrick, born in Wales in 1603, was 22 years Rebecca's senior. Such an age differential was also not unusual for the time. William had come to the Colony as an indentured servant but had acquired his release before 1636. He was granted land in Duxbury and in Green's Harbor. He was elected freemen in 1658. William and Rebecca had ten children and a host of descendants. If I may make a side comment, it is interesting to note that Barnstable County is named for Barnstaple, Devon, England. Recall that the Turgis de Traci (sic) was the Baron of Barnstaple. He laid the foundation for the Tracy family of Gloucestershire, as well as Devon.

Stephen and Tryphosa's only son John was born in Duxbury in 1633. He made quite a prominent record for himself in Duxbury, serving on numerous jury sessions involving civil cases. He was a Selectman (elected town official) eleven times. He was also elected Deputy to the General Court three times and, like his dad, was a town Constable. John is the subject of numerous discussions in the literature. He married Mary Jane Prince in 1660 at age 27. Mary Jane was born in Duxbury in 1635 and 25 years old at the time of the marriage. Both were above the average marrying age. She was the daughter of Massachusetts Governor Thomas Prence. Prence was a founder of Eastham and served as Governor of Massachusetts three times (1634, 1638, and 1657-72). John and Mary had five children and countless descendants.

The Mysterious Case of Mary, Daughter of Stephen
With some trepidation I go once more into the breech when I venture to discuss Stephen and Tryphosa's fifth and final daughter, Mary. To say that she is somewhat of an enigma is a gross understatement. Her birth is not in question, as there is solid evidence that she was born in 1630 at Plymouth. It is also probable that Mary was alive when her father died in England because he mentioned her in his power of attorney. Although Mary was mentioned in the document, it was only done parenthetically. She was not named in his bequest. It bears repeating that the incidental reference to her may have been because she was already married and, therefore, did not receive an inheritance. Besides this circumstantial evidence, knowledge about her is a bit dicey. Well, more than a bit, it is extremely fickle.

The questions are: did Mary marry? No record. If she did marry, whom did she marry? No record. Did she die before marriage? No record. When did she die? No record. This is sounding like a broken record! Of course, it could be that there are no records of her after age 25 because she was married and, like so many other wives and mothers of the time; she simply slipped into marital anonymity. Am I employing the fallacy of circular reasoning? Murray State beloved philosophy, ethics, and logic professor Dr. Robert Perkins where are you when I need you?!

I've been drawn to know more about Mary, because she may have been the wife of Francis Griswold. This is important to me because Francis Griswold's daughter, Mary (1656-1711) married Jonathan Tracy the third son of Thomas Tracy. Therefore, she and Jonathan are my 6th Great Grandparents. But was Mary the mother of Jonathan, Mary the daughter of Stephen Tracy?

There is a widespread myth that the wife of Francis Griswold was a daughter of Thomas Tracy. This idea seems to have its roots in a book written in 1902 by a well-meaning, but misinformed historian named Elizabeth Todd Nash. In her book entitled *Fifty Puritan Ancestors 1628-1660* she writes: "*Francis Griswold, son of Edward and Margaret Griswold, born 1629; married Mary Tracy, daughter of Thomas; settled in Saybrook 1655-6, was 'one of the first proprietors of Norwich 1660...*" This is a classic example of how the moral of following lemmings into the abyss manifests itself in genealogical books and articles. Despite the fact that Thomas Tracy did not have a daughter named Mary, for years Nash's statement went mostly unchallenged by a host of people who should have known better. Nash gave no source for the claim and many did not bother to verify. As a result, there are plenty, and I do mean plenty, of publications and postings on websites that show the wife of Francis Griswold as Mary Tracy, nonexistent daughter of Thomas.

I suspect, and this is not original with me, that Nash assumed that Francis' wife was the daughter of Thomas because of Thomas' friendship with father and son, Edward and Francis Griswold. Plus, Francis and Mary were about the same age, 23 and 22, respectively when Francis married. The monumental and insurmountable problem with this theory remains that Thomas did not have a daughter named Mary. He had a daughter named Merriam, but she married Thomas Waterman.

Faced with the overwhelming evidence that Thomas Tracy's daughter did not marry Francis, numerous genealogists have come round to the idea that the wife of Francis Griswold was not a Tracy at all. Not so fast, say I. Having been bandied about for several centuries, there are more than a few other theories as to the identity of the wife of Francis Griswold. I must say that it is fascinating that her identify has generated so much interest!

My personal favorite theory is the one noted above that suggests that his wife and widow was Mary Tracy, daughter of Stephen and Tryphosa Lee Tracy. I was first made aware of this possibility a few years ago in an exchange of emails with Coralee Griswold, a Griswold family genealogist. In April, 2008 she sent me an email with the following quote from a 1999 publication held in the *Family History Library* in Salt Lake City, Utah: "*In 1990, Robert French stated the following for his research in The Greswold (sic) Family: 12 Generations in England: 'No authority can be found that gives Thomas TRACY as having a daughter 'Mary'....... 'Secondary sources state she was the daughter of Thomas Tracy but there is no record of him having a daughter, Mary. She may have been the daughter of Stephen and Tryposa (sic) (Lee) Tracy (Boston Transcript 7210).*" It is the last sentence that sent my heart a flutter. But, before it could fly, I needed verification.

Upon further research I found that "*The US and International Marriage Records Prior to 1700*" lists the marriage of Francis Griswold to Mary Tracy of Massachusetts. No date of the marriage is recorded. The location of the marriage is listed only as "New England." The fact that the bride is listed as being from Massachusetts leads one to assume it is a reference to the daughter of a Tracy from the Bay State. At the time, there was only one Tracy family in Massachusetts. That would be the family of Stephen Tracy of Plymouth and Duxbury. Marriage records in this data base are based on information from over 500 years of marriages extracted from family group sheets, electronic databases, biographies, wills, and other sources. It is way above my pay grade to ferret out the source of the marriage record that shows a Mary Tracy of Massachusetts, not Connecticut, as Francis' wife.

A serious fly in this buttermilk is that the well-respected genealogist Donald Lines Jacobus tells us in his book on the Waterman family from which I've drawn a lot of material that *"no Mary Tracy has been found who could have been his* [Francis Griswold] *wife."* As a young person might say using today's lexicon, *"when I read this I was, like, I mean, you know, I mean, really bummed out."* Further, this would be said as though it was an interrogative sentence. It reminds me that language evolves, like it or not.

The more research I do on the identity of Mary Tracy, the more I am intrigued by Jacobus' observation because he knew that Stephen had a daughter by that name and he knew that there was interaction between the Plymouth and Connecticut Colonies. Moreover, it was Jacobus who wrote in 1939 that *"The probability is that our Thomas Tracy sprang from the Tracys of Norfolk County, England, and was related to Stephen Tracy of Plymouth."* I assume he drew his curious conclusion that *"no Mary has been found who could have been [Francis'] wife,"* because there isn't any evidence showing what ever happened to Mary Tracy.

The level of complication in the tale of the wife of Francis Griswold increased with his death in 1671. This is because "she-who-has-no-identity" didn't stay a widow long. A couple of years later, in about 1673 she became the second wife of William Bradford IV, son of Plymouth Colony Governor William Bradford, III. Despite the high status of the Bradford family and a zillion descendants from this *Mayflower* family, to my knowledge no one has been able to track down the surname of the William Bradford IVth's second wife. This is so even though they had a son together, Joseph Bradford, in 1675. She-whose-name-remains-unknown died a year later.

I must confess that having looked long and hard at all of the evidence as to the identity of the wife of Francis Griswold and the second wife of William Bradford IV, I've come to the cautious conclusion that she was, indeed, Mary Tracy daughter of Stephen. This is really an educated guess, but then so are all the other suppositions I've found in the literature. I've included Mary as the wife and widow in question on my Ancestry.com posting. I've done this because I can document that Francis is my 7th Great Grandfather through his and his wife's daughter, Mary Griswold. Since Mary Griswold married Jonathan Tracy, son of Thomas, they are my 6th Great Grandparents.

Posting Mary Tracy as Francis Griswold's wife may be irresponsible of me, but I do think the preponderance of evidence makes it a reasonable claim. To obtain a more definitive answer would require a DNA test of a known descendant of a Griswold. If there was a close match with me, a known descendant of Jonathan, we might be onto something.

Well, enough idle chit chat of what might have been or might be. Let's delve into something that is provable. I'm speaking of my verified direct English ancestor, Thomas Tracy, my 7th Great Grandfather who came to the Colonies in 1636. However, before discussing the life and times of Thomas, I need to share a bit about *The Great Migration* of 1630 to 1640. This momentous event is not to be confused with the identically named *The Great Migration* related to the movement of six million African-Americans from rural southern United States to the urban north from 1910 to 1970. That's a whole different story of migration due to social and economic persecution and the desire to be free.

The Great Migration

The Great Migration period I'm referring to took place from 1630-1640, give or take a year or two. It is frequently cited only as *TGM* by us genealogy nerds. Only the initials are typically used because it was such a defining moment in the development of New England. TGM quickly overshadowed the backwaters of the Plymouth Colony. I soon discovered that it all started when the *Massachusetts Bay Company*, a joint stock trading company, received a charter from King Charles I in 1629.

The charter was initially a commercial venture aimed at colonizing a vast area of New England extending three miles north of the Merrimack

River to three miles south of the Charles River. Ominously, the company was quickly taken over by a group of non-Separatist Puritans led by John Winthrop. In order to acquire the company, Winthrop, who was quite wealthy, promised to sell his English estate in Groton, Suffolk County, England and put the money into the company and take his family to the colonies. The *quid pro quo* in the deal was that the company government and charter were to be placed under his exclusive control. The company agreed and appointed him Governor.

I'm fascinated with the revelation that a major incentive behind the founding of both the Plymouth Plantation and the Massachusetts Bay settlements was economic. I don't know why I didn't see that coming. Neither would have gotten off the ground without English investors whose primary motivation was profit. I'm sure that this is common knowledge, but don't most of us share the illusion that it was all more about religious freedom than the accumulation of wealth. That may have been true for many of those who came to New England, but it was not the primary purpose of the investors. Why am I not all that surprised?

Oh well, for whatever its underlying reasons for existing were, TGM had a profound impact on the establishment and expansion of the colonies. Fortunately, the history of TGM is well detailed and easy to access. The so called Winthrop Fleet consisted of a group of 11 ships that carried about 1,000 Puritans plus livestock to Massachusetts in the spring and summer of 1630. The first four ships departed from Yarmouth, England on April 8. When I first saw a reference to the point of departure I thought it makes sense these Puritans would depart from Great Yarmouth, Norfolk. Alas, once again I was misled by logic. The actual port really was Yarmouth, but it was Yarmouth, Isle of Wright, some 245 miles southwest of the city of Great Yarmouth.

The first company charter ship arrived in Boston, Massachusetts Bay Colony in 1630. By the time TGM ended in 1639/1640 some 30,000 folks had stormed ashore putting into motion our embryonic nation of immigrants. More ships were licensed to take passengers to New England in 1640, but with the dissolution of Parliament by Charles I potential immigrants returned or stayed at home *"in expectation of a new world."* The English Civil War (1642-1651) that followed effectively ended, for the time being, the TGM and the tide of immigrants.

Oddly, although the fleet departed from the Isle of Wright rather than the harbor at Great Yarmouth in Norfolk, most of the Puritans on the ships were from East Anglia. Indeed, Winthrop himself was from the East Anglian County of Suffolk. He led Puritans out of East Anglia who felt threatened by King Charles I and his influential wife, Henrietta Maria, a French princess who was a devout Catholic. I gather that Charles I granted the Charter to the *Massachusetts Bay Company*, in part, to get rid of Puritan troublemakers.

Winthrop and associates had their own agenda and soon bent the charter to achieve it. Winthrop's goal was to use the *Massachusetts Bay Company* to create a religious commonwealth indicative of a *"shining city on a hill."* If you haven't heard a contemporary politician or minister sing that song, you've been living under a rock or, understandingly, have little taste for politics. The *shining city* reflected Winthrop's vison of an ideal Christian community. Crucially, a Christian community did not equate with a democratic one. In point of fact, Winslow established a virtual theocracy that did not look kindly on dissension and opposing views. Just ask Anne Hutchinson and her sort. Look it up. It is no wonder, then, that Baptists, Quakers, Jews, and audacious women were not welcomed in Winthrop land and were banished or worse, much worse. Many of the outcasts were able to find refuge in Roger William's the community of the more tolerant and religiously diverse Rhode Island.

Winthrop was Governor 1629-1634, 1637-1640, and 1646 to1649, the year he died. After his death, things got really messy. I'll keep it simple by just noting that much of his vision of a *shining city* was pretty much assigned to the dust bin of history when King Charles II, an anti-Puritan and strong supporter of the Church of England, revoked the *Massachusetts Bay Company Charter* in 1684. The Bay Company's influence over social, religious, and economic policies, however, had greatly diminished long before then. The cancellation was just the last nail in the proverbial coffin.

There is one more lesson that I learned about the *Massachusetts Bay Company* that I'll share before moving on. In constructing his "*shining cities*" Winthrop took a cue from the difficulties experienced by English colonists in Jamestown, Virginia. While the theocracy thing didn't work out, the man was a genius in designing sustainable, viable communities. Avoiding the bedlam of the English settlements in Virginia that were left to their own devices, Winthrop adopted a carefully crafted approach to developing his ideal community.

He began by platting seven towns for immigrants and recruiting whole non-Separatist English Villages. He wanted likeminded groups and extended families to be the glue to holding settlements together. His brand of Puritans spoke of the family as a "*little commonwealth*" which became the foundation for the larger society. Hence, whole families and even entire non-Separatist Puritan congregations in England were encouraged by Winthrop to come to the Massachusetts Bay Colony.

Winthrop also sought "planters" who were men with a wide variety of skills and a strong sense of community. Planters, it should be noted, were not necessarily people who planted seeds in the ground. They were people who were "planted" abroad for colonization purposes. It was the underpinnings of the Commonwealth of Massachusetts and way beyond. Pennsylvania, Virginia, and Kentucky are the other three Commonwealths.

The *Massachusetts Bay Company's* chances for success were improved by helping immigrants to be much better prepared to survive based on the experiences of those who had come before. Reverend Francis Higginson of Salem, Massachusetts played an important role in informing immigrants of what was needed for survival and comfort. His catalogue of needful things included a year's provision of food consisting of meal, peas, oat-meal, vinegar, oil, and butter. He also gave explicit instructions on tools that would be required to make a go of it. The Massachusetts Bay Colony eventually published lists of necessities to survive what might be titled today as an *"Idiots Guide to Living in the Colonies."* Similar lists were posted on advertisements for prospective planters and their families in England.

Each settlement in the Bay Colony followed Winthrop's brilliant village hub-and-spoke design. Houses were constructed close together around a central village green with a church and fortified meeting house (the hub). The homes of planters were required to be located within walking distance of both their farms and the village green in a spoke like fashion. This worked for short period until towns got too crowded, which they quickly did. Because of the need for expansion Governor Winthrop established a policy that required three to five prominent men to request a charter to establish a new plantation. Such requests had to clearly demonstrate to the Governor that there were families with neces-sary skills to establish a maintainable community. The petitioners also had to have a minister in place who agreed to tend to a congregation in a new plantation.

Petitioners were typically given three years to create a sustainable com-munity or lose their charter. By 1640 twenty towns had been established in this manner in the Massachusetts Bay Colony. It was a very clever way of constantly increasing the growth of the colony through a built in mecha-nism that created a situation whereby people were self-motivated to create new communities. Winthrop was a very crafty fellow who knew how to grow his territory.

Once a charter was approved, the petitioners were required to establish a governmental structure that met Winthrop's standards. This included a pre-arranged method of land distribution, a church, criterion for citizen-ship, and an elected leadership. As noted, it was totally different from the helter-skelter approach that took place in the Virginia colony at the same time. I bring this up, because this is the precise manner how three of the five settlements where Thomas lived were established. Speaking of Thomas, finally as promised, let's explore what I learned that makes him not only an intriguing ancestor, but a man of character who overcame great odds to make something of himself of which his descendants can be justly proud.

5

WAS STANWAY THE BIRTHPLACE OF LT. THOMAS TRACY?

I have been doing research on Thomas off and on for over 20 years. His place of birth has long been in question. As Winston Churchill might have said *"it is a riddle wrapped in a mystery inside an enigma."* In fact, he did say that in October 1939, but he was talking about Russia not Thomas Tracy. Until very recently I bought into the opinion of the overwhelming majority of Tracy family genealogists that Thomas was of English aristocracy. I had been lured into accepting the idea that he was a child of the Tracys of Stanway, Gloucestershire by the prodigious number of books, articles, and online postings that support that theory. In the process of preparing this current account of Thomas my admiration has grown for him multifold precisely because I now suspect that in all probability he was not a Stanway Tracy. I lean toward the theory that he was a carpenter of meager means from Norfolk County, England who sought and achieved personal advancement in the New World.

Have multitudes of Tracy descendants of Thomas been taken down that well-known garden path with regards to his alleged pedigree? I'm inclined to think so. But I'm obliged to vacillate and resist making an unequivocal statement because I have neither proof that he was nor any proof that he wasn't a son of the aristocratic Tracy family of Stanway Manor. It isn't just me who is caught in this quandary. Three hundred and thirty-two years after his death in 1685, no one has verified his pedigree one way or the other. Throughout this text I'm going to employ the dubious device of indirect evidence and try and convince you to join me in doubting popular belief or, at the very least, questioning it. Although I'll attempt to challenge conventional wisdom, at the end of this account my hope is that your grasp of who he was as a pioneer will transcend the relevance of where he came from.

Aristocratic Blue-Blood Family Line: Fact or Fantasy?

Before proceeding about the life and times of Thomas in the New England Colonies, let me spend a few moments examining the elephant in the room whenever there is an actual or virtual gathering of Tracy family genealogists. We all agree that he was born in England about 1610. Ah, but the question is where in the "Land of Hope and Glory" that is the England we all know and love might this have been? It is a very dodgy issue, indeed. The majority of my cherished Tracy kin of all stripes believe that he was born in Stanway. A few, conversely, believe it is more likely that Thomas was from Norfolk County, England. Given the disparity, I wanted to find the sources of both theories. In this chapter I'll explore the *"Thomas-from-Stanway theory"* (remember I'm using Stanway as a catchall term for Tewkesbury, Toddington, and Gloucestershire County). I'll examine the Norfolk Theory in Chapter 7.

Reuben H. Walworth

Ever since I got started on my path of inquiry, I've been curious about the origin of the idea that Thomas was from Stanway. Where did it first appear in print? The earliest readily available reference I could find is in a book written in 1864 by Reuben H. Walworth, LL.D. He was a New York attorney, judge, and Democrat U.S. Congressman. Walworth was born in 1788 and died in 1867. He is best remembered as the Chancellor of New York which was the highest judicial position in the state. As it turns out he was the last Chancellor since the position was abolished upon his retirement.

He was known as a great equity jurist and an early friend of the temperance movement.

Walworth County, Wisconsin is named after Reuben. To illustrate the weird and serendipitous connections one often makes in the pursuit of genealogy, I found out the source of the Wisconsin county name in a very circuitous way. I'm working on improving the strategic planning process of our local United Way. To keep from reinventing the wheel, a few weeks ago I was examining a promising United Way model adopted in Walworth County, Wisconsin. Walworth County is comparable in size and demographics to Calloway County, Kentucky where I live. In the process of learning more about Walworth County, I wondered if the county name might be connected to Reuben Walworth. Walworth, after all, is not all that common a name. Sure enough, the founders of the county apparently were great admirers of the Chancellor and honored him by taking his name. You never know what you'll find under a rock. One thing for sure is that you've got to turn it over to see what's there.

Walworth's connection to the Tracy family was through his paternal grandmother, Jerusha Tracy (1723-1764) who married Jedediah Hyde (1712-1761). The judge claimed that he was a descendant of Thomas Tracy of Connecticut son of Nathaniel Tracy of Stanway, born about 1551. Further, Walworth asserted that he, through that family line, was directly related to King Egbert of Wessex, the first Saxon King who died in 839. Walworth certainly had the credentials to conduct research as he held degrees from Princeton, Yale, and Harvard. The short title of his two-volume opus is *The Hyde Genealogy*. While the primary focus was on his Hyde family ancestry, he included considerable information on his Tracy lineage. Both volumes of the treatise are accessible online at *Hathitrust.org*.

Initially, the cynic in me couldn't help but wonder if being a descendant of a King and Baron of the English realm would have been beneficial to his political, social, and judicial status, as well as his ego. No doubt he had blue-blood friends who liked to tout their own English aristocracy.

Chancellor Walworth wouldn't have let them lord it over him, now would he? I'm just saying! In retrospect, however, I believe that I misjudged the judge as discussed below.

So where did Walworth get the idea that Lt. Thomas Tracy was related to King Egbert and the Tracys of Stanway? In Volume I of the *Hyde Genealogy* Walworth cited two primary sources. One source was the 1856 edition of *Burke's Peerage*. The other was unpublished research conducted in England in 1846 by F. P. Tracy of San Francisco. My initial step was to examine his reference to *Burke's Peerage* which was first published in 1826. It can be found online under the title *A Genealogical and Heraldic Dictionary of the Peerage and Baronetage of the British Empire*. There are 106 editions of the work, the last in 1999. The 1856 edition cited by Walworth was the 18th. All editions are highly regarded as reliable and accurate accounts of English peerage.

Okay, at first blush that looked good for Walworth's claim. He referred the reader to Appendix B in Volume II of *Hyde Genealogy*. Appendix B contains an outline of the lineage of the Tracy family of Stanway wherein Walworth showed Lt. Thomas Tracy as a member of the 29th generation of the family line, son of Nathaniel Tracy. Based on *Burkes' Peerage* the chart is an accurate sketch of the various ancestors of the Tracys of Stanway up to Nathaniel Tracy. But *Burkes' Peerage* doesn't include a Thomas Tracy, son of Nathaniel. No edition of *Burkes' Peerage* written before 1864 mentions a Thomas Tracy, son of Nathaniel. For that matter, I can't find such a reference in any other genealogical and heraldic work before 1864. I must confess to not being able to access the 1856 edition, but I did access the 1852 and 1866 editions of *Burkes' Peerage* and found no reference to Thomas born in or near 1610, son of Nathaniel or any other member of the Stanway household. If it had been in the 1856 edition as implied by Walworth one would expect to find it in the 1866 edition.

According to Burke and numerous other experts in English peerage, the Stanway Tracy line actually began when Richard Tracy (1501-1569) was given Stanway Manor by his father Sir William Tracy of Toddington about 1533. Stanway is a little over two miles from Toddington. Richard Tracy is a fascinating character worthy of a brief sidebar. He was a 1515 graduate of Oxford University and a descendant of William de Tracy of Devon (d. 1189), one of the four knights who assassinated Thomas Beckett in 1170. William de Tracy was the grandson of William de Tracy, illegitimate son of King Henry I discussed on page 4.

Richard was also a close friend of King Henry VIII. Henry issued his famous (infamous?) directive *"Dissolution of the Monasteries"* between 1536 and 1541. This decree closed hundreds of small Abbeys, including Hailes Abbey which had been a Catholic Monastery since 1245. The Abbey is only three miles from Stanway. The King gifted the property to Richard Tracy in 1553. Presumably the gift was in appreciation for the Lutheran Richard's role in Protestant reform. Richard was the father of Paul and Nathaniel, among other sons, who play a potential central role in our story. If you are interested in learning more about Richard, I recommend a book chapter on him by Catharine Davies in *Broken Idols of the English Reformation* edited by Margaret Aston.

Since I could find nothing in any edition of *Burkes' Peerage* to backup Walworth's claim, I assumed that he had found support for his theory in another peerage publication. I dug a little deeper and found several other potential sources, including an 1840 publication by John Britton entitled *Graphic Illustrations with Historical and Descriptive Accounts of Toddington, Gloucestershire, the Seat of Lord Sudeley*, as well as an 1841 publication by John Burke and Sir John Bernard Burke entitled *A Genealogical and Heraldic History of the Extinct and Dorman Baronetcies of England, Ireland, and Scotland*.

I also examined *The Peerage of Ireland: A Genealogical and Historical Account* (1768), *The History of Tewkesbury* (1830), *The Visitation of the County of Gloucester, Taken in the Year 1623* (1885), *The Hanbury Family* (1916), and the *Family Tree of the Tracys of Stanway and the Charterises of Amisfield, Earls of*

Wemyss. The latter is a chart I obtained from the Gloucestershire Record Office several years ago. Conspicuous by its absence, none of these works mention a Thomas Tracy of Stanway born around 1610. I surmised from this that Walworth's inclusion of Thomas in the Stanway Tracy lineage came from a source other than genealogical and heraldic works published before 1864.

I recognize that only the more prominent of the many sons and daughters are noted in Burkes' and other English peerage books leaving room for speculation that Thomas could have been one of many children, and there were many, whose professions or social status didn't warrant inclusion in the Sudeley-Hanbury-Tracy family pedigree charts. Plus, there is always the argument that if Thomas had left the family to go out on his own far away from England, he might not be mentioned. Be that as it may, there was no reference to a Thomas Tracy that substantiated Walworth's claim.

Giving Walworth the benefit of the doubt, I turned to the second source he highlighted in the preface to Volume I of the *Hyde Genealogy.* This was his reference to F. P. Tracy. Walworth noted that he (Walworth) *"availed himself of much useful information furnished by the late Judge F. P. Tracy of San Francisco, as to the Tracys who are descendants of the first William Hyde, and also to their English and French ancestry."* Walworth had some assistance in spreading the theory. The media, such as it was in the 1860s, picked up on the theme. An article with the heading *"Tracy Pedigree"* was published in the *Willimantic Journal* on December 7, 1865 based on the Walworth's *Hyde Genealogy.* The article noted that *"The facts embodied in this pedigree, were gleaned from archives and records in England, by the late Judge Frederick P. Tracy, of California, a native of Windham (Scotland)* [Massachusetts], *who was most indefatigable and thorough in his investigation."* Aha, I thought, this F. P. Tracy constitutes a clue that needs pursuing. Who was this F. P. Tracy upon whom Walworth relied so much? What did F. P. Tracy know, when did he know it, and who did he tell?

The Mysterious Research of Frederick Palmer (F. P.) Tracy
The influential F. P. Tracy turns out to be Frederick Palmer Tracy. He played quite a significant in the development of the prevalent *"Thomas-from-Stanway theory"*. He was born in Windham County, Connecticut in 1815, the son of a machine shop owner. Young Frederick went into the ministry at age 18, being ordained in 1835. His first church was in Hebron, Connecticut, followed by a stint in Salem, Massachusetts. He was a minister in several towns in Massachusetts, including the Methodist Church in Williamsburg, Massachusetts in 1844. He also ministered at the South-Street Methodist Episcopal Church in Lynn, Massachusetts. In 1846, due to exhaustion from work he and his wife embarked on a two-year trek to Europe. The trip was paid for by one of his parishioners at his church in Williamsburg. His first stop was apparently at Gloucestershire County, England where he conducted research on the Tracy family of that area.

It hadn't dawned on me until recently when I was reading *Tudors: The History of England from Henry VIII to Elizabeth I* by Peter Ackroyd that the date F. P. departed for England was in the middle of *The Great Hunger*, known outside Ireland as the *Irish Potato Famine*. This terrible tragedy lasted from 1845-1852 resulting in the emigration of over a million Irish, 20 to 25% of its population. Not to mention the million who died of starvation. I wonder if F. P. was aware of the calamity occurring across England's northern border. Of course, New England, especially Boston and New York, were forever impacted by the arrival of the poverty stricken Irish.

Genealogist Matilda O. Abbey wrote in 1888 that *"Frederick Palmer Tracy made a careful examination of the records of Gloucestershire, when in England, which proved the royal descent of Thomas Tracy, of Norwich, Conn."* Dentist and genealogist Dwight Tracy, M. D., D.D.S. observed in an article he wrote in the *Connecticut Magazine* in 1907 that when F. P. Tracy was in England *"he visited Toddington and was received with all the courtesies due kinship by Lord Sudeley, the Right Honorable Charles Hanbury Tracy, Lord of Toddington Manor. In his searches there he did find a Thomas Tracy, a younger son of the same general family of Tracys."*

Dr. Tracy went on to say that *"Judge Tracy communicated the result of his researches to Chancellor Walworth, who was then compiling his notable 'Genealogy of the Hyde Family' and he was so impressed with its importance that he presented the matter in full in his Ethelred* (lineage)" To refresh your knowledge of English history Ethelred "The Unready" was King of the English 978-1041. Since Thomas does not appear in any peerage book, I draw from Dr. Tracy's statement that once Walworth thought he had confirmation that Thomas was from Stanway that he simply took it upon himself to add Thomas to the lineage of the Stanway Tracy line.

Armed with this new perspective on how Walworth came by his theory, the question that came to mind was who was the Thomas Tracy that Dr. Dwight Tracy thought Reuben Walworth had discovered from the research of F. P. Tracy? To try and get to the bottom of this question, I re-read the *Connecticut Magazine* article by Dr. Dwight Tracy and another article on the same topic he wrote in 1908 entitled "*Recently Discovered English Ancestry of Governor William Tracy of Virginia, 1620, and of His Only Son, Lieutenant Thomas Tracy of Salem, Massachusetts and Norwich, Connecticut.*"

Dr. Dwight Tracy claimed that the Thomas he thought to be Lt. Thomas Tracy was the son of a William Tracy. The William Tracy in question was born in the Tracy Manor of Toddington about 1580. William took his family, including his young son, Thomas with him to the Berkeley Colony in Virginia in 1620. William was killed by Indians on April 8, 1621. His family returned to England. Despite the efforts and contentions of the good Doctor, our Thomas is unequivocally NOT the son of the William Tracy of Toddington Manor who went to the Virginia Colony. Jacobus examined the theory in 1939 and said that he found it to be a "*specious*" one. It was further refuted by John G. Hunt in 1965. Other imminent genealogists such as Dr. David L. Green and Paul C. Reed also rejected the son-of-William theory out of hand. Later, I'll have more to say about their deductions.

Something else is seriously questionable with Dr. Dwight Tracy's theory. Dr. Tracy clearly stated that he based his theory that Thomas was the son of William of Toddington on the research of F. P. Tracy. He also made it crystal clear that he referred to the same research upon which Walworth based his theory. But, hold on here. Walworth said that he concluded Thomas was the son of Nathaniel Tracy of Stanway based on the research of F. P. Tracy. If they used the same research as a source, what is the explanation for using the names of proposed different fathers of Thomas? I'm at a loss to explain the discrepancy.

I thought wouldn't it be great if F. P. Tracy's research was available for examination? If it were, perhaps one could ascertain who F. P. claimed to be the father of Thomas and the reasoning behind the claim. So what happened to F. P.'s research report? I went online to see if I could find a reference to any reports by F. P. Tracy that had somehow been protected from destruction or loss. Presto, I found an online reference to Frederick Palmer Tracy in a collection of papers housed at the Bancroft Library at the University of California at Berkeley.

Thanks to the assistance of Lorna K. Kirwan, Bancroft Library Collections Manager I learned that the entire collection is entitled: *"Tracy Family Papers, circa 1800-1888. BANC MSS Z-Z 107 v.1; BANC MSS Z-Z 107 v.2:1; BANC MSS Z-Z 107 v.2:2; BANC MSS Z-Z 107 v.3."* Volumes 2:1 and 2:2 are said to contain a family genealogy that was *"probably compiled around 1848."* That fits the 1846 date when F. P. conducted his research in England, returning to New England in 1848. I also discovered a reference to the research by F. P. Tracy's son-in-law, John Swett who wrote the following about Judge Tracy's genealogical work: *"For ten years his leisure evenings were devoted to the work, and the manuscript of a thousand pages in his now clear handwriting remains in the hands of his family."* John Swett was the California State Superintendent of Public Instruction in the 1860s.

I'm fortunate to have two close cousins who are graduates of UC Berkeley and who live in the lovely San Francisco Bay area. They are

Thomas Tracy Allen, Ph.D. and Teri L. Piccolo. They own and operate an innovative and creative weather tracking business, *Eme Systems, LLC* also known as *Electronically Monitored Ecosystems.* Learn more about it at www. emesystems.com. I asked them if they might go to the Bancroft Library and see if they could find the document and make a copy of material related to the birth place of Lt. Thomas Tracy. Their first step was to register with the library. Following their registration, on October 25, 2016, they were informed that volumes 2:1 and 2:2 *"are not on the shelf."* The staff said they would continue to look for them. Bummer!

Undaunted, cousin Tracy Allen inquired at the library if volumes 1 and 3 were available. They were and he went to take a look see. He sent me an email on November 24, 2016 with a list of what he found in volume 3. It is a potpourri of documents including an article about grape growing and letters from family members. One letter date 1846 mentions that F. P. had arrived in Britain by sea at Portsmouth and that he spent ten days in Britain before departing for Paris. Another letter is from a Gardner Tracy of South Hero, Vermont dated July 4, 1846 written to F. P. Tracy. Gardner Tracy was responding a request from F. P. regarding family records that had been kept in a family bible which seems to have been misplaced.

My cousin also examined volume 1 in which he found a journal by Cyrus Tracy. Cousin Tracy noted that *"There is a lot of the navigation math mentioned in the library description, sort of a tutorial with beautiful drawings and calligraphy. But there is much more, wide ranging: doodles, a great diagram of the solar system, 'Summary of the Doctrines of the Heathen Philosophers', 'Of God', poetry, hymns, bills of sale, formulas for metal polish and gunnery fuses.* The author appears to be Cyrus Mason Tracy (1784-1860), the father of Frederick Palmer Tracy. Cousin Tracy photographed the most relevant documents and put them on a cloud for me to access.

As an aside, it is interesting to note that Frederick Palmer's Tracy's brother, Cyrus Mason Tracy, Jr. (1824-1891), was a botanist and poet in

Lynn, Connecticut. He was the author of *Studies of the Essex Flora: A Complete Enumeration of All Plants Found Growing Naturally Within the Limits of Lynn, Mass., and the Adjoining, Arranged According to the Natural System, with Copious Notes as to Localities and Habits.* You can find out more about him online at: https://myweb.northshore.edu/users/ccarlsen/poetry/lynn/tracy_mtgilead.html.

As interesting as the information in volume 1 was, I was deeply disappointed that the volume with the family genealogy had not been located within the extensive bowels of Bancroft. Without access to their content, there was no way of knowing if one of the documents in volume 2 was the research report that F. P. began but did not finish. It was all the more the pity because I still didn't know what was found that led Reuben Walworth to believe that Thomas was from Stanway. I thought that the volume may never turn up so I decided to proceed with publishing this narrative without waiting further. At my advanced age, it is better to move forward at a hastened pace to successfully see a project to fruition!

Fortunately, I put off going ahead with the publication because on December 7, 2016 Lorna K. Kirwan sent me an email informing me that the missing volumes had been located and were ready to be examined. That was music to my protruding ears! I immediately emailed Cousin Tracy with the good news. He went to Bancroft Library on December 9 where, after a brief moment of misunderstanding, he was given access to volume 2. He sent me a report on the 10th. It appeared that volumes 2:1 and 2:2 had been in the process of being sent out for scanning when we made our request. Fortunately, Lorna pulled them back in time to allow them to be examined. After we are finished with them, it will be great if they are indeed scanned so that future generations of family genealogists will have much easier access to the material in the collection.

The key question I posed to Cousin Tracy was: does the collection in both sections of volume 2 appear to be F. P.'s unpublished Tracy family research report? His preliminary inspection suggests that it does. For starters the file is about 1,000 pages. This is consistent with the approximate length of F. P. Tracy's family research as reported by his son-in-law John Swett. The volume contains 1082 sections related to the life of Tracy related persons that go back to 1066. Unfortunately, Cousin Tracy noted that there is "*no introduction, forward, or explanation, and no bibliography, nor list of resources.*" Needless to say, there is also no index. This made the task of deciphering the material much more difficult.

The text is handwritten. However, it is fairly easy to read. We've been able to read enough fragments of the document to draw the tentative conclusion that F. P. really got caught up with the enchantment of the legacy of the aristocratic branch of the Tracy family. This is reflected in the inclusion of a chart of the Tracy lineage ending with Richard Tracy who is discussed on page 45 above. As for finding any specific reference to Lt. Thomas Tracy, there is none that is apparent. Remember that Reuben Walworth, Dr. Dwight Tracy, and others claim that Thomas was a grandson of Richard. Not seeing a reference to a Thomas who could be the Thomas of New England is troubling in that I'm no closer to understanding why early genealogists believed that F. P. had not only identified, but had documented, that Thomas as a member of the Stanway Tracys.

How did F. P.'s papers end up at UC Berkeley you might ask? Well, when F. P. returned from his European sojourn, he left the ministry to begin a career in law. He chose to begin his new vocation in bourgeoning San Francisco, the Golden City by the Bay. He sailed there in August, 1849. He was an agent for the *Massachusetts and California Company,* a private company that minted gold coins in gold happy California. He apparently left that position to pursue his law career. F. P. was admitted to the California Bar in 1851. In 1854 he returned to Connecticut and brought his family back to San Francisco with him.

At the time, the most popular way to get from the East coast to the West coast was by ship. People could choose to either go around Cape Horn or go to Panama where they would trek through the jungle to the Pacific to pick up a ship to California. Travel could take up to three months. Later, he became the city and county attorney for civil business. I have no way of knowing of how his and his brother's papers ended up at the Bancroft Library, but I would surmise that a family member or close associate donated their papers to the Library.

F. P.'s ongoing family research was seemingly well known among other Tracy family genealogists of the time. His interest in family ancestry is documented as early as 1844. In that year he sent out a survey to relatives doubtless to flush out family stories and documents. He may have wanted the information before he left for England to conduct family research. He had strong credentials as a genealogist. He was a member of *The New England Historical and Genealogical Society* in 1846. He is listed as a corresponding member in 1858 after he moved to California. In 1857, nine years after he returned from Europe, he conducted another family genealogical survey. I can only guess that he included his findings from both surveys into the family genealogical document that he was still working on at his death in October, 1860.

There is an excellent biography of Frederick Palmer Tracy written by Ralph W. Allen in 1885. It is published in a chapter of a book entitled *Memorial Biographies of the New England Historic Genealogical Society*. Rev. Allen was the Corresponding Secretary of the New England Methodist Historical Society. Allen noted that F. P. was an avid reader and that *"his power of argumentation was early developed, and he became an active leader in the village debating society."* Well, that was no big revelation as it seems to run in the family. I was a high school and college debater. My son debated in high school and my wife debated in college. We're still debating!

My father, James Albert Tracy, Jr., was a university debate coach. Under my dad's photo in the senior high school yearbook of 1920-21 at Fort Morgan, Colorado is the following inscription: *"You suggest the subject and I'll argue till the smokestack falls."* All his life he didn't just talk the talk, he walked the walk. It was sometimes hard to tell just what side he was on, but I learned from him that everyone has a right to interpret information differently. Debate is a great way to learn empathy for, and understanding of, all sides of an argument and there is always more than one side! By the way, the musician and conductor Glenn Miller was a classmate of my father's at Fort Morgan High. My dad was always "In the Mood" for a good discussion.

Incidentally, under Glenn Miller's photo in the 1920-21 yearbook is *"I'm a stranger here. Heaven is my home."* He may have taken the words from a Lutheran Hymn written in 1836 by Thomas R. Taylor which are *"I am but a stranger here, Heaven is my home."*

By now you can tell that I find F. P. to be a most intriguing figure. He knew Greek, Italian, and French. His lectures and sermons were published. He had a strong reputation as an orator. His promotion of the abolition of slavery included supporting the anti-slavery candidate John C. Frémont in the Presidential election of 1856. In May, 1860 he was the chairman of the Republican delegation from California that nominated Abraham Lincoln. He married Emily Stone in 1837. They were the parents of five children. His youngest son, Thomas Garnier Tracy, born in 1845, was a cadet in the United State Military Academy at West Point in 1862 who volunteered to fight with the Union in the Civil War. He survived and was living in San Francisco in 1885. F. P.'s daughter, Mary Louise, was the wife of John Swett who as State Superintendent of Public Instruction in California made public schools free to all students in 1867. Swett was also a close friend of John Muir, founder of the Sierra Club.

As an unabashed tree hugger and proud card-carrying member of the Great Rivers Group of the Cumberland ·Chapter of the Sierra Club passionate about land and water conservancy, I couldn't have been happier to learn of this family connection to John Muir. It's hard for me to stop digging into his life and writing about it, but I suppose I should try to contain myself so that I can cover some other aspects of the origin of the *Thomas-from-Stanway Theory*. Did I mention that F. P. is described on a passport application in 1849 as being 5' 10" with a prominent nose? That fits yours truly to a tee! At least it did until gravity and aging took its toll.

Other possible Sources Available to Walworth and F. P. Tracy
An additional possible genealogical source for Walworth and F. P. is a mysterious document entitled *"Pedigree of the Tracy Family"* which was allegedly written in 1843 by a person identified only as a *"descendant of Thomas."* As a matter of fact, I've seen references to the document in several genealogies written in the late 1800s. A google search came up with a book written in 1856 listed in the catalogue of the National Library of Ireland with the short title of *"Pedigree of the Tracy Family."* Here's the weird part. The author is Martin Tracy!! That is Martin Tracy, Esq. to be precise. That's not me! I'm old but I'm not that old. Besides that Martin Tracy lived in Streamstown, County Westmeath. There is a copy in the National Library of Ireland in Dublin. I've seen a summary and the family lines which seem to have a peripheral connection to the family at Stanway. On the other hand, any excuse to go to Dublin is worth considering. It is an enchanting place. I was there in 2000 at an international research conference on the third-sector. Too bad, I was unaware of the *Pedigree* at the time.

One other document written before 1864 that could have influenced both Walworth and F. P. Tracy was a journal written by Helon Henry Tracy. A few years ago I was looking for historic material on some 2nd cousins who left Jefferson, New York in the mid-1850s for Utah and Oregon. There were five Tracy brothers who made the trek across the country at different times. Three of them were Mormon. One of the Mormon brothers who went to Utah was Helon Henry Tracy. He kept a journal that included family lore that said that Thomas Tracy was the son of Nathaniel Tracy of Tewkesbury. A copy of the handwritten journal is available from the *L. Tom Perry Special Collections* in the *Harry B. Lee Library* at *Brigham Young University*. I should note that Walworth made no mention of the journal.

The investigations into the birthright of Thomas Tracy by both F. P. Tracy and Chancellor Reuben Walworth were recognized by the

Connecticut historian John W. Stedman. In his book *The Norwich Jubilee. A Report of the Celebration at Norwich, Connecticut, on the Two Hundredth Anniversary of the Settlement of the Town, September 7th and 8th, 1859* he noted that F. P. had proposed that a meeting of the Tracy family should be held in Norwich in 1858. It doesn't seem to have happened. The Jubilee did occur. It was held on September 7, 1858. F. P. was not in attendance. Reuben Walworth was there and was very much involved in Jubilee activities. Walworth gave a talk on the Hyde family in which he mentioned Thomas Tracy and gave details about the family and descendants of Thomas's daughter Miriam who married Thomas Waterman. Walworth made no reference to Thomas's ancestry in England.

6

TRACY-FROM-STANWAY THEORIES
GONE VIRAL

I suppose it would have been reasonable for Walworth to make the leap of faith that his ancestor Thomas of Connecticut was from upper crust Tracy progenies of England. Such wishful thinking is quite understandable given he clearly believed he had the assurance of F. P. Tracy and possibly others that it was so. He may not have given the claim the serious attention it deserved because, after all, he was related to Thomas through the marriage of his paternal grandfather, Jedediah Hyde, to a descendant of Thomas Tracy. I know that I'm guilty of spending more time and effort on documenting the lives of direct Tracy relatives as opposed to their spouses. So, even though Walworth lacked primary evidence, he cited F. P. Tracy to support his claims apropos Thomas' ancestry. He ran with the idea without any apparent reservation.

The problem, for me, is that ever since his claim was put into print in 1864, it and variations of it, have propagated the *Thomas-from-Stanway theory*. Before you could say "Bob's your uncle" or the slightly elongated version of "Robert's your auntie's husband", it caught on like wildfire. The thing is that it went unchallenged until the late 1930s and continues to hold sway among the vast majority of the descendants of Thomas Tracy. In today's vernacular the spread of the idea might be described as having "gone viral." As, indeed, even a cursory review of the Lt. Thomas Tracy family lines on *Ancestry.com*, *FamilySearch.org*, and *LegacyFamilyTree.com*, etc., testify.

Impact of Walworth and F. P. on Thomas-from-Stanway Theory
Both Reuben Walworth and F. P. Tracy's shared theory on the birthplace of Thomas persuaded historian Frances Manwaring Caulkins that Thomas was from Gloucestershire County (she doesn't mention Stanway specifically, but Stanway is in Gloucestershire). In the first edition of her renowned and widely-cited work the *History of Norwich* published in 1845, she included ample material on Thomas Tracy. Notably, in that first edition she made no reference to his place of birth. However, in the 1866 edition she revised the section on Thomas Tracy writing that Thomas came from Tewksbury in Gloucestershire and was the son of Nathaniel. In a footnote on pages 201-202, she gave credit for this new information on Thomas to F. P. Tracy who *"had collected materials for a thorough historical registry of the descendants of the Lieutenant; but he died while on political tour in 1860, and the work for which he had made ample preparation has not been published."*

Caulkins also included a footnote on the importance of Walworth's *Hyde Genealogy* to her research. Such an endorsement by Caulkins was bound to have a huge influence on genealogists writing in the late 1800s and early 1900s on the Tracy ancestry. And it did! The die was cast.

In addition to Caulkins helping to spread the theory, in 1882 the renowned New England historian Hamilton D. Hurd reiterated the idea that Thomas was from Tewkesbury, Gloucestershire in his still widely cited *History of New London County, Connecticut*. The claim was further legitimized the next year in 1883 in *Americans of Royal Descent* by Charles H. Browning. In keeping with *Burkes' Peerage* and similar heraldic publications, Browning traced the pedigree of the Tracys back to the early Saxon Kings. Like Walworth, Browning showed Thomas as the son of Nathaniel Tracy. Did Browning know something earlier heraldic historians did not? He gave no sources. Therefore, reading Browning brought me no closer to knowing where the idea to insert Thomas in the family tree came from. He could, of course, have gotten it from F. P. Tracy, Walworth, or Caulkins.

In 1885 a memorial biography on F. P. Tracy by Deacon Ralph W. Allen published in volume IV of the *Memorial Biographies of The New England Historic Genealogical Society* repeated the theory, giving it even greater credence. It was further reinforced as an accepted theory when the second edition of *Americans of Royal Descent* by Browning was published in 1893 with the same information. Significantly, Browning renounced the theory in a publication in a newspaper in 1904 as revealed by Donald Lines Jacobus and discussed below. But, like retractions of the all too frequent instances of "fake news", it was too late to close the barn door after the horses had bolted.

The Impact of Charles Stedman Ripley
Before Browning backtracked on his claim in his 1889 and 1893 books, his declaration that Thomas was from Gloucestershire added integrity to the claim. Another author to pick up on the theory was U. S. Navy Lieutenant and historian Charles Stedman Ripley. Ripley's 1895 book *The Ancestors of Lieutenant Thomas Tracy* really popularized the idea that Thomas was from the Tracys of Gloucestershire and Stanway. In post-1900 genealogical books on the ancestry of Lt. Thomas Tracy, Ripley is the most cited source used to "document" Thomas' connection with aristocracy. Note, however, according to Ripley (believe it or not), Thomas was the son of Paul Tracy and grandson of Richard Tracy of Stanway. This contrasted with Walworth's and other's claim that Thomas was the son of Nathaniel, Paul's brother. Ripley argued that Walworth and Browning were in error and that Thomas was one of the youngest of Sir Paul's 21 children. Unfortunately, Ripley doesn't specify which of the illustrious works that he consulted documents that his conclusion. Nevertheless, Ripley quickly became the go-to reference to support the *Thomas-from-Stanway Theory* origin.

Indeed, Ripley's book opened Pandora's Box, leading to numerous contentions linking Thomas to Stanway. A short list of works familiar to genealogists who take an interest in the subject includes publications by Matilda O. Abbey (1888), Puella F. Hull Mason (1895), Drs. Albert & Charles Wesley Leffingwell (1897), Dr. Evert E. Tracy (1898), N. B. Tracy (1900), Mattie Liston-Griswold (1900), Judge Sherman W. Adams & Henry R. Stiles (1904), Wharton Dickinson (1904), Dr. Dwight Tracy (1907), George Norbury Mackenzie & Nelson Osgood Rhoades (1912), Sherman Weld Tracy (1936), John Matthews (1965), and Charles Edward Banks (1976). Ripley is cited by several of these authors as their major source. And several make specific references to Reuben Walworth and F. P. Tracy as resources. The theory continued to grow like a wild, irrepressible weed. Even a 1922 issue of *Americana* by the American Historical Society repeated the claim.

Francis Louis Tracy Morgan
Walworth wasn't the only person of wealth and stature who wanted to claim a connection to the aristocratic Tracy family of Stanway. You're familiar with the American financier and banker John Pierpont Morgan, aka J. P. Morgan. Well, did you know that his second wife and mother of J. P. Morgan Jr. was Francis Louise Tracy? Francis, who was born in 1842 and died in 1924, is a direct descendant of Thomas through his son John. I bring this up because once I discovered her connection to J. P. I thought that surely the Morgan family would have had a professional genealogist map out the lineage of J. P.'s wife. If so, I wondered what they found when they researched Francis's ancestry? Had they concluded that there was a connection to Stanway and aristocracy? Or had they found that she was of much more modest stock? Hmmm, weighing family aristocracy on the one hand or mediocrity on the other? Want to make a wild guess as to the connection they claim to have found?

You are so right, my friend; the correct answer derived by the chroniclers of J. P. Morgan was landed gentry! The late 19th and early 20th century genealogist who conducted the research for the Morgan family, one Wharton Dickinson, traced Francis Louise Tracy Morgan to the aristocratic Tracy family of the house of Stanway. The title of his 17- page report is a dead giveaway: *Pedigree of Tracy of Toddington Co., Gloucester and Norwich, Connecticut: autograph manuscript and typescripts, 1904 Dec. 10/compiled by Wharton Dickinson.* Methinks that there was possibly some bias afoot to keep the good name of Morgan from being dragged down to mingle with the common folk and their ilk, much as may have been the case with Walworth. According to an email I received from Carolyn Vega, Assistant Curator, Library and Historical Manuscripts, The Morgan Library & Museum in August, 2013, Francis Tracy Morgan's pedigree was traced back to Tassilo the Roman, circa 550.

I assumed that being related to Tassilo the Roman was a good thing, but I had no idea who he was. It was waving a red flag in front of a bull. I couldn't resist checking him out. A few clicks of my wireless mouse revealed that he was actually Tassilo I, King of Bavaria. He lived circa 560-609 during the rule of the Eastern Roman Empire. It would be hard to argue with Dickinson's claim that the Tracys descended from Tassilo I since it is estimated that 1,083,099 family trees are traced back to him!

Dickinson's report is available from the *Morgan Library and Museum – Pierpont Morgan Library in New York City.* I wrote to the library in September 2013 asking if I could obtain a copy. I was told that I could and they would be glad to send it to me for a fee. The estimated invoice I received was for $125 per page. Thus the 17 page document would have set me back $2,125. Even they winced at asking that outrageous amount as they offered me an 80 percent discount. But even then it would have cost me $425. As gracious as this offer was, I declined. I think the title told me everything I wanted to know. Though, I must admit that if the title had been *Pedigree of Tracy of Norfolk Co.*, I would have spared no expense! Well, I would have paid the $425. If any of you dear readers feel compelled to purchase the Dickinson document to see the progression of your Tracy pedigree since 560 AD, please do let me know what you discover.

Reviewing all this material I can see how readily past-and present-day descendants would be convinced that Thomas was born in Stanway. After all, I was previously persuaded it was so. The sheer number of genealogists who made the argument supported by peerage publications printed in the late 1800s and early 1900s makes it very difficult for amateur armchair family historians to contradict them, including yours truly. Plus, there is the overwhelming number of online postings on websites such as *Ancestry.com, FamilySearch.org, Myheritage.com, and LegacyFamilyTree.com* that show Thomas as being born into the elite Tracy line of Stanway. With such support for the assertion, there has been little reason not to accept it as accurate. On the other hand, just because it often appears in print or cyberspace doesn't mean it is accurate.

More Illuminating Illustrations of Muddled Research
Consider, if you will, the following illustration as to why some genealogical works must be taken with less than a grain of salt. Witness a book written in 1914 by Cuyler Reynolds that included a section on the lineage of the Tracy family of Stanway. Reynolds' book is entitled *Genealogy and Family History of Southern New York and the Hudson River Valley: A Record of the Achievements of Her People in the Making of a Commonwealth and the Building of a Nation, III.* Like Burke and other heraldry experts, Reynolds linked the family to Ecgbert (sic), who ruled England 800-839. The 25th generation of descendants includes one Richard Tracy, Esq., son of William Tracy of Stanway. Okay, so far Reynolds was consistent with multiple peerage sources. Notably, Reynolds made no mention of Thomas Tracy of Connecticut. That's good, but then he took a completely different tack, incredulously claiming that Samuel Tracy, another son of Richard, had several sons of his own one of whom was Stephen Tracy. Reynolds made it very clear that he was referring to our Stephen Tracy of Norfolk, Leiden, Plymouth, and Duxbury. Indeed, Reynold specified that the Stephen in the Tracy peerage he gave was a Pilgrim who came to Plymouth on the *Anne* in 1623.

What in the world would have led Reynolds to such an untenable supposition!? As we well know and have demonstrated there was no direct connection of Stephen to Stanway. Stephen was irrefutably from Norfolk, the son of Stephen Tracy, Sr. and Grandson of Roger Tracy of Norfolk.

Was it just inconceivable to Reynolds that a commonplace Tracy would have come to the colonies? Reynolds wasn't the only one who came up with a bizarre connection.

Alright you might say, maybe Reynolds was not really qualified to pen such an ambitious work of genealogy. Regrettably, you'd join me in being sadly mistaken. He was the Curator of The Albany Institute and Historical Art Society for ten years, Director of a New York State History Exhibit in 1907, and the compiler of the *Albany Chronicles*. The latter is described on one website as *"A compendium of information and lore arranged chronologically and according to mayoral administration. (That) includes fanciful biographies of each of the mayors of Albany that are full of errors!"* Well, you'll not get an argument for me regarding the inaccuracy of the content on the Tracy family in Reynold's publications.

A likely source for Reynolds was Henry Whittemore who had a similar theory about Samuel being the father of Stephen. He posed the idea in a book published in 1897 on *The Heroes of the American Revolution and Their Descendants*. Whittemore had impeccable credentials. He was the author of many history books and even has a library named after him at Framingham State University in Framingham, Massachusetts. Like Reynolds, Whittemore connected Stephen Tracy of Plymouth and Leiden to Richard of Stanway through his grandson Samuel. According to a footnote on the subject in Whittemore's book, he came up with the idea based on that mysterious *"old manuscript in possession of A. H. Tracy, of Chicago ___."* Here's the kicker. Whittemore noted that there is no mention of a Stephen in the manuscript he cited. That apparently wasn't a problem for him. Whittemore just shrugged it off and suggested that Stephen may not have been mentioned because he had gone to Leiden.

I haven't a clue as to the identity of A. H. Tracy of Chicago who had in his possession a *Pedigree of the Tracy Family*. But whoever he was he was also used as a source by Dr. Evert E. Tracy, M.D. in his book *Tracy Genealogy: Ancestors and Descendants of Lieutenant Thomas Tracy of Norwich, Connecticut 1660* published in 1898. Evert said that he based the theory that Stephen Tracy was a cousin of Thomas Tracy because Stephen was a son of Richard's grandson Samuel. Where did he come by this information? In a footnote in the Appendix Evert said it was in an old manuscript "*in the possession of Mr. A. H. Tracy, of Chicago.*" Well, that sounded familiar! Note that this contradicted Whittemore's claim that there was no reference to Stephen in A. H.'s manuscript. Wouldn't I love to get my mitts on a copy of that manuscript!

Richard Tracy did have a son Samuel who had a son also named Samuel who was born in 1568 at Stanway. Both Samuels moved at some point from Stanway to Clifford Priory, Herefordshire, England. It is located on the eastern border of Wales, some distance from Norfolk. This also poses a major problem for the validity of the theories of Reynolds, Whittemore, and Dr. Tracy.

Another bizarre claim had been made earlier in 1849 when Justin Winsor wrote his *History of the Town of Duxbury, Massachusetts with Genealogical Registers*. In this work Winsor lists Thomas as son of Stephen of Plymouth and Duxbury, Massachusetts and Norfolk, England. This theory defies logic. Stephen was born in 1596, Thomas in 1610. I suppose Stephen could have been a father at age 14, girls certainly could have borne a child at that age. But, all that is moot, as we know Stephen didn't marry until 1620 in Leiden, Holland. William Henry Upton observed in 1893 in his *Upton Family Records* that Colonel J. L. Chester "*pronounced Winsor's statement unfounded, and based on 'alleged' records which had no existence.*"

All the questions about the birthplace of Thomas remind me of the parody in Gilbert & Sullivan's *The Gondoliers*. You'll recall, I'm sure, that there are two gondoliers in Venice one of whom is a prince. But, because at a young age the prince was entrusted to the care of a drunken gondolier who mixed up the prince with his own son, no one knows who the true prince is. A tongue-in-cheek verse in the song "*I Stole the Prince and Brought Him Here*" goes "*Of that there is no manner of doubt – no probable, possible shadow of doubt – no possible doubt whatever!*" Wrong! There IS a dark shadow of a doubt! This is where we are as regards the birthplace of Thomas; anyone who says they know with certainty is barking up the wrong tree or has identified the wrong prince, as it were.

"The Fate of the Tracys"
In searching in vain for information on the manuscript on the Tracy pedigree held by the shadowy A. H. Tracy of Chicago, I came across a fascinating tale in the form of a proverb published in 1740 by Thomas Fuller, Doctor of Divinity, an English churchman and historian. Dr. Fuller related the proverb that *"The Tracies (sic) have always the wind in their faces."* The proverb comes from a curse put on the Tracy family as a result of the participation of William de Tracy of Toddington in the murder of Thomas Beckett in 1170, as mentioned above. It seems that William and other members of his family tried to make penance by going on a pilgrimage to the Holy Land, *"but were always driven back by contrary winds and violent gales."* Lest my close and distant relatives fear that the curse still applies to the family, the comments on the proverb by Fuller merit being repeated in full with English spellings. The quote is taken from page 552 of *The History of the Worthies of England.*

> *"The Tracies have always the wind in their faces." This is founded on fond and false tradition; which reporteth, that, ever since Sir William Tracy was most active amongst the four knights which killed Thomas Becket, it is imposed on Tracies for miraculous penance, that whether they go by land or by water, the wind is ever in their faces. If this were so, it was a favour in a hot summer to the females of that family, and would spare them the use of the fan. But it is disproved by daily experience, there being extant at this day in this county two houses, the one honourable, the other worshipful, growing from the same root; so that we see it is not now, and therefore believe that it was never, true. If you say that, after so many generations, this curse at last is antiquated; know that, according to popish principles, it deserved rather to be doubted of late, seeing*

> *no gentile family in England, since the Reformation, have more manifested their cordial disaffection to Popery by their sufferings and writings, as hereafter will appear."*

Note the playful positive spin Fuller put on the curse and the affirmation that it was lifted due to the important role that the family played in the Protestant Reformation. This was especially true of Sir Paul Tracy of Stanway. Fuller further made the case that the Tracys did well in spite of the curse by noting William Tracy's possessions as evidenced by the towns (hamlets) in Cornwall County bearing his surname: Woollacombe Tracy, Bovey-Tracy, Nymet-Tracy, Bradford-Tracy, Newton-Tracy, etc.

During the same search I found a 1905 reference to another Tracy pedigree. Supposedly, there were only two copies of this one. One was in the hands of the half-brother of the person making the claim and the other was in the Library of the British Museum. The catalogue of the museum is online. Unfortunately, a quick search turned up a blank. Oh well, another excuse to go to London!

Summarizing the Case for Aristocracy & Stanway
I wouldn't be surprised that this lengthy one-sided dialogue on the possible ancestry of Thomas Tracy hasn't left some readers more than a little confused or bored. And I'm not finished! In an attempt to clarify for me, as well as the reader, with sincere apologies to David Letterman for stealing his skit and for not being clever enough to keep the list to ten, here is a brief summary of the top 11 progressive steps involved in evolution of the claim that Lt. Thomas Tracy was a member of the well-known Tracys of Stanway.

1. A mysterious document *"Pedigree of the Tracy Family"* was written in 1843. It influenced the thinking of Judge Frederick Palmer Tracy and Chancellor Reuben Walworth as to the place of birth of Thomas Tracy in Gloucestershire. It was at one time in the possession of A. H. Tracy of Chicago, whoever he was. What ever happened to the document!?

2. F. P. Tracy surveyed Tracy family members in 1844 and 1857. He traveled to England in 1846. He examined local registers and records and apparently concluded that Thomas is the son of Paul Tracy of Stanway. Unfortunately, F. P. died before his research was published. His unpublished paper is apparently a part of a collection of Tracy papers at the Bancroft Library, University of California, Berkeley. The paper makes no obvious reference to a Thomas Tracy who could have been Lt. Thomas Tracy.

3. John W. Stedman cited the on-going research of Reuben Walworth and F. P. Tracy related to the family lineage of Thomas Tracy in 1859. Both Stedman and Walworth participated in the Norwich Jubilee in September 1859.

4. Reuben Walworth accepted the findings of F. P. Tracy and wrote in his book published in 1864 that Thomas was the son of Paul Tracy of Stanway. Walworth also cited *Burke's Peerage* to document the peerage of the Stanway Tracy lineage even though no edition of *Burke's Peerage* refers to a Thomas Tracy born about 1610 in Stanway.

5. Frances Manwaring Caulkins referenced F. P. Tracy and Walworth in the second edition of her *History of Norwich* published in 1866 noting that Thomas Tracy was born in Tewkesbury, England. In the first edition published in 1845, she did not know his birth place.

6. Charles H. Browning included Thomas in the peerage of the Stanway Tracys in 1883. No source was provided. Browning later recanted, acknowledging there was no evidence to support the connection with Stanway.

7. Matilda O. Abbey wrote in 1888 that F. P. Tracy conducted extensive research in England. She used his research to document that Thomas was from the Stanway Tracys.

8. Charles Stedman Ripley wrote *The Ancestors of Lieutenant Thomas Tracy* in 1895 which became a standard reference for supporters of the *Thomas-from-Stanway theory*.

9. Multiple genealogical publications repeated the *Thomas-from-Stanway theory* with several variations as to the identity of Thomas' father in the Stanway family of Tracys.

10. Prevailing current online genealogical postings on *Ancestry.com, Familysearch.org*, and other sites support the *Thomas-from-Stanway theory.*

11. Whittemore, Reynolds, and Evert E. Tracy linked Thomas to Stephen of Plymouth, claiming they both were born into the Tracy family of Stanway and are close cousins based on that old document in the possession of A. H. Tracy of Chicago. I've been unable to learn anything about A. H. Tracy or the document he held. Nonetheless, it isn't possible that Stephen was a son of Samuel Tracy, as primary documents show that he was the son of Stephen Tracy, Sr.

With the exception of item 11, I can see a rationale for believing the *Thomas-from-Stanway theory.* Yet, I'm not convinced.

Have you noticed how these days many politicians and government administrators ask their own question and then answer it when speaking to a reporter, thereby making sure that the question they want to answer is actually asked? I seem to recall that technique was perfected by Defense Secretary Donald Rumsfeld. Now everyone does it. So why should I be left out? Ergo, does all this research mean that Thomas Tracy is definitively not from the Tracy family of Stanway? No, it doesn't. Does it mean that he is definitively from another family line? No, it doesn't. Does it mean there is no definitive answer? Yes, it does. Is there circumstantial evidence that would strongly suggest that Thomas was from Norfolk? Yes, there is.

.

Prior to my current research, his connection to Stanway made sense even to me until I made a careful examination of the works of seven renowned genealogists. That research led me to an unexpected discovery and often ignored factor, namely; "Watertown", as in Watertown,

Massachusetts. Unlike Orson Welles' enigmatic "Rosebud", the importance of Watertown on this tale of Thomas Tracy is fully explainable and I'll try to do just that in the next chapter. As a certain politician might put say, "it's huge. Okay"?

7

WAS NORFOLK THE BIRTHPLACE OF LT. THOMAS TRACY?

Fledging family genealogists like me make mistakes. As I've mentioned, a 2009 publication of mine unequivocally states that Thomas was from Stanway. Could I have been wrong? Perish the thought! Yet, the more research I've done since then, the more I've become convinced that the *Thomas-from-Stanway theory* doesn't pass the smell test. To get this out of my system so I could sleep better at night, I decided that I needed to go back and recheck the few publications I had seen that had raised questions about Thomas' birthplace. I wanted to learn if there was a discernable pattern that might enlighten me or give me more clues.

Donald Lines Jacobus' Take on Lt. Thomas Tracy
My first move was to reexamine the genealogical writings of the late great Donald Lines Jacobus. I did this for two primary reasons. One was because of Jacobus' indisputable reputation as a distinguished genealogist. He is definitely someone worthy of paying heed. He was the founder and editor of *The American Genealogist* and is known as the Dean of American Genealogy. The second reason for taking another look at Jacobus was because of his extensive research on Lt. Thomas Tracy.

As far as I am aware, Jacobus made the first serious challenge to the multifarious attempts to link Thomas to Stanway. This was in 1939 when Jacobus published a seminal genealogical work. The short title is *The Waterman Family: Descendants of Robert Waterman of Marshfield, Massachusetts (Volume 1)*. It doesn't sound like this has anything to do with Thomas Tracy, but, trust me; it does in a big way. The Waterman and Tracy families in New England had very close ties. For starters, Thomas Tracy's daughter Miriam married Thomas Waterman. In his book, Jacobus included a section on *"The Thomas Tracy Family"* where he systematically laid out why Walworth and subsequent claimants of the Stanway birthplace theory are unsubstantiated. If not mistaken, they are, at minimum, uninformed as to the likelihood of Thomas Tracy's origin. It didn't escape my notice that Thomas Waterman's father, Robert, was born in Norwich, Norfolk, England. It probably didn't escape Jacobus' notice, either.

Jacobus' Repudiation of Walworth's & Ripley's Theories
Please forgive me for drawing heavily on quotes from Jacobus in the following discussion. It is just that he said it so much better than I ever could. I highly recommend that you go to the original source to grasp the full weight of his discussion about the dubious assertions in the literature pertaining to the birth place of Thomas Tracy. In volume I of *The Waterman Family* (pages 691-684) Jacobus methodically repudiated the theories of several genealogists about Lt. Thomas Tracy. He pointed out that while Walworth's theory that Thomas Tracy was the son of Nathaniel Tracy of Stanway had been widely accepted *"no evidence for it has been seen."*

In addition Jacobus led readers to doubt a claim made in 1895 by Charles Stedman Ripley that Thomas (born 1610) was the same Thomas who was the ninth son of Sir Paul Tracy of Stanway. A theory that was repeated by Dr. Evert E. Tracy in 1898 based on Ripley and F. P. Tracy. Jacobus also chided General Tracy Campbell Dickson for having observed that Charles Stedman Ripley was correct in saying that Thomas was from Stanway. Jacobus noted that *"No evidence and no reasons are presented for this dogmatic conclusion."*

In 1904, Henry R. Stiles repeated the theory of Walworth in his *History of Ancient Wethersfield* quoting a letter written in 1878 by Colonel Joseph L. Chester. Stiles wrote *"… it may be reasonably safe to accept the connection between the Eng. Family referred to* [Sir Paul Tracy of Stanway] *and Lieut. Thomas Tracy, on the authority of that eminent genealogist, the late Col. Joseph L. Chester, of London, himself a Tracy descendant, who in a letter dated 16 April, 1878, and addressed to Judge Owen Parry, of Pottsville, Pa., said 'I have never had the slightest reason to doubt the accuracy of our Tracy descent as given by Chancellor Walworth in his Hyde Genealogy'."* Jacobus commented on the Chester quote by saying that he was *"quite unable to share Colonel Chester's confidence in statement made by Chancellor Walworth unless supported by definite evidence."*

As I previously pointed out, Jacobus also noted that Walworth's alleged *"pedigree of Thomas was reproduced in an early edition of* Charles H. Browning's 1883 publication *"Americans of Royal Descent."* But, Jacobus then referred to a review by Browning printed September 7, 1904 in the *Boston Evening Transcript.* The review suggested that Browning had changed his view as he *"pointed out that no baptism of Thomas Tracy is found in the parish registers of Tewksbury, co. Gloucester, about 1610, and that no evidence that Nathaniel Tracy, alleged father of Thomas, every married."*

I was curious about the genealogists mentioned by Jacobus. Of course, I was already familiar with Walworth and Ripley. I had obtained copies of the works of Stiles and Evert E. Tracy, but I knew little about them as persons. And I had never heard of either Chester or Dickson. Hence, I wanted to know more about the identity of Evert E. Tracy, Henry Reed Stiles, Joseph Lemuel Chester, and Tracy Campbell Dickson. Who were these folks whose judgment Jacobus questioned? Were they fly-by-night family historians or were they serious genealogists? Here's what I found out.

Dr. Evert Evertsen Tracy, M.D. was born 1870 in Albany, New York. He was a descendant of my direct ancestor, Jonathan, son of Thomas. He practiced medicine in Albany and Ohio before settling in Prairie View, Illinois. I had referenced a history book by Dr. Henry Reed Stiles, M.D.

about Windsor, Connecticut. Born in 1832, I learned that he was a well-known physician who *Wikipedia* states "*wrote a number of highly regarded historical records and genealogical books.*" Joseph Lemuel Chester, born in 1821, was a genealogist for the U.S. Government assigned to review all English wills, as well as parish registers in England, before 1700. Each of these men had strong research credentials but Jacobus called them out on specific statements about Thomas Tracy for which they failed to provide evidence.

Before moving on to learn something about Dickson, I paused to explore why had Chester written to Judge Owen Parry about Thomas Tracy. In the letter written in 1878 referenced above Chester had used the phrase "*our Tracy descent.*" After a little digging on Ancestry.com and a Google search I discovered that the connection to the Tracy ancestry was through the mothers of Parry and Chester. Parry's father, Edward Owen Parry, married Susannah Tracy (1745-1827). Chester's father, Joseph Lemuel Chester, Sr. married Purdee Tracy (1789-1835). Both wives and mothers were descendants of John Tracy, son of Thomas.

The mention of Brigadier General Tracy Campbell Dickson by Jacobus made we want to know more about the General. He was born in 1868 and died in 1936. It so happens that the General's mother was Lucy Ellen Tracy. She was a descendant of Lt. Thomas Tracy's son, John. Dickson was an 1892 graduate of West Point and had a career in military ordinances. As a young Lieutenant he invented a rifle sight used by the Army. His later research profoundly impacted the technological and metallurgical advancement of gun manufacturing.

The career of General Tracy Campbell Dickson is certainly interesting, but here's the spooky part. He was born in Independence, Iowa. Coincidently, my father was born in Iowa (Sioux Rapids) and my family and I lived there many years later when I spent 12 wonderful and fulfilling, albeit brutally cold years at the University of Iowa. My years there were all the more meaningful because my father graduated from Iowa in

1929 with an undergraduate degree in speech. And my brilliant and beautiful wife received her Ph.D. from the University of Iowa in the College of Education, Division of Counseling and Human Development in 1995. My son and I are big Hawkeye fans!

Outside of presidential election cycles every four years, being associated with Iowa doesn't make one famous. But in the case of Tracy Campbell Dickson, his claim to fame came for his military weapons inventions when he was stationed at the Watertown, Massachusetts Arsenal Laboratory. How odd that his first success happened at the location of the first destination of Thomas Tracy. Even more strange is that when General Dickson retired he moved to Cleburne, Texas. While he was born in Iowa, he grew up in Cleburne. Curiously, Cleburne is the childhood home of my mother and uncle and maternal grandparents. As a wee lad, I spent many a happy vacation in Cleburne visiting my maternal Grandmother, Laura Melissa Garloff Martin (1877-1958).

The story got even weirder when I learned that the General's father, Captain Campbell Dickson (1836-1911), married a Tracy! Her name was Lucy Ellen Tracy (1847-1896). She was from Delphi Falls, New York. I knew that Captain Dickson was from Cleburne, so how did it happen that he married a women from New York? Two articles in the *Cleburne Times Review* by Pete Kendall in 2009 and 2011gave me the reason. The article told of young Campbell Dickson who had been born in New York but moved early at young age to Texas.

However, when the Civil War started he returned to New York to serve in the Union Army's 9th New York Calvary. Despite his lack of loyalty to his southern friends, he was well received upon his return to Cleburne after the war. The 1880 U.S. Census for Cleburne was 686 people, so it's not like his participation for the Union would have gone unnoticed. He opened the C. Dickson Hardware store. In 1882 he moved the store's location to East Henderson and Anglin Streets where it remained for 100 years. The building, as of 2011, still stands. He also helped bring the Sante

Fe Railway to Cleburne. My Grandfather, Uncle, and Cousin all worked for the railroad.

Can you believe that my Grandmother Martin lived at 307 S. Anglin Street which is only two tenths of a mile, a four minute walk from the Dickson store? Me neither. My parents married in Cleburne married in 1936. What a shame they were not aware of Lucy Tracy Dickson. Or maybe they were and just didn't know the family connection! My grandmother was a prominent woman in a small town. Could she have known Lucy Dickson without knowing her maiden name? Plus, how many times might my Grandfather John Martin or even my mother have gone to that hardware store? Captain Dickson and Lucy had six children, including General Tracy Campbell Dickson.

Isn't it interesting that the quest for finding the birth place of Thomas Tracy by Dickson, Chester, and Parry derived from their connection to him through their mothers? All of whom were descendants of Thomas through his son, John. Reuben Hyde Walworth's connection was through his paternal grandmother Jerusha Tracy (1723-1764) who was a descendant of Jonathan Tracy, son of Thomas.

Jacobus also cited William Henry Upton, M.A., LL.M., who wrote in 1893 that Colonel Chester was in the process of retracting his statement when he died. Regarding Walworth's assertion that Thomas Tracy was the son of Nathaniel Tracy of Tewkesbury, Upton wrote in a footnote "*I have always considered it very unfortunate that Walworth cited no authority for this statement.*" Jacobus apparently had no quarrel with this assertion by Upton. Upton was born in California in 1854. He practiced law in Walla Walla, Washington State. He was a member of the New England Genealogical Society. He apparently began to seriously engage in genealogical research after receiving a large number of family papers and documents. I couldn't find any connection of Upton with Thomas.

The Pitman Report on Lt. Thomas Tracy

The primary source used by Jacobus to refute the uncorroborated claims about Thomas's origin is a research report written by American genealogist Harold Minot Pitman. He is best known as an author as H. Minot Pitman. He was born in 1888 and died in 1970.The Pitman study is cited by Jacobus in the section he included on Thomas Tracy in his book on the Waterman family. Prior to beginning my research, I had not read the Pitman's study. Indeed, I had never even heard of it. Once it came to my attention, I didn't know if it was available. Since Jacobus made such a big deal out of the Pitman report, I knew that it was imperative for me to learn more about it.

After an online search, I discovered that the research had been commissioned by Henry Holton Conland. Conland was the publisher of the *Hartford Courant* newspaper. He was also an insurance executive in the city of insurance companies. My first question was why did Conland want to know? A search on *Ancestry.com* shows that his maternal grandmother was Matilda Jane Tracy (1827-1901) who was born in New Brunswick, Canada. So, it would seem that Conland was interested in his Tracy heritage through his maternal grandmother. She married William McGuirk and their daughter Matilda (1851-1931) married James Conland (1852-1903). Henry Holton Conland was their son. Even with all this information I've been unable to trace his direct lineage to Lt. Thomas Tracy.

One interesting tidbit I was able to dig up was that Henry's father, James Conland, was the personal physician of the author, journalist, and poet Rudyard Kipling. Finding that made me nostalgic reflecting on fond childhood memories of reading and re-reading *The Jungle Book* and one of my all-time favorite poems "*If.*" You know the one that begins "*If you can keep your head when all about you are losing theirs and blaming it on you*" and ends "*Yours is the earth and everything that's in it, and — which is more — you'll be a man my son.*" Powerful stuff, that. There is a short biography of Henry in the 34th edition of *The National Cyclopedia of American Biography*.

Whatever his motivation Henry Holton Conland requested Pitman to make an extensive search of Gloucestershire England probate and related records. I'm eternally grateful that he contracted for the research. I don't believe there has been any relatively recent study on Thomas that begins to approach the diligence of the Pitman study. His research resulted in an unpublished handwritten 22-page *Report on Lt. Thomas Tracy* dated February, 1938. Why it hasn't been published is beyond me. It would be very informative to Thomas Tracy family genealogists.

So where does one find a copy of this Holy Grail of Stanway skeptics and supporters alike? Ah, that would be the *New York Genealogical and Biographical Society Collection of the New York Public Library*. The report isn't available online, but for a modest fee an electronic copy can be yours for the keeping. Infinitesimally cheaper, I might add, than ordering the Dickinson paper from the private Morgan Library and Museum. I love public libraries! They are a truly wonderful American institution and becoming more important all the time as community centers, as well as resource centers. I was assigned to Mr. Maurice Klapwald, Assistant Manager, Interlibrary, Document & Research Services to help me out. It took a few weeks for him to locate and prepare the document for sending it to me as an email attachment. When it was ready there were complications in transmitting it to my email address. I had to have it sent to an alternative address I seldom use for the attachment to actually be attached. But Mr. Klapwald was very patient with me so all's well that ends well and I came into possession of the handwritten report.

The Pitman report includes seven pages of analysis and 15 pages of abstracts from documents such as the 1624 will of Sir Paul Tracy, the 1637 will of Sir Richard Tracy, and the 1639 will of Sir Paul's daughter, Alice. It also contains abstracts from the wills of other of Sir Paul's children, as well as extracts from registers and abstracts from other relevant documents. The "Sir" in Sir Paul Tracy comes from having been made a Baronet by King James I in June, 1611.

After printing the report and placing it in my eagerly awaiting hands, I was able to see for myself what Jacobus gleamed from the report. Note that the Jacobus reference to the Pitman report in his book *The Waterman Family* is a very succinct and pithy summary. It is really only one long paragraph. But, that paragraph is the bases for subsequent articles that reject a direct connection of Thomas to Stanway. To be sure, there aren't many such refutations but highly respected genealogists are included among the naysayers. The first question I had after reading it is why didn't other Tracy family genealogists writing after 1939 turn directly to the Pitman report, the original source of doubt? Were they not aware that is was available? Why haven't recent family genealogists used it as a source?

Pitman began his report on the origin of Thomas Tracy of Connecticut by stating that he had two goals in conducting the research. The first was to prove or disprove the "*the tradition which connects him* [Thomas Tracy] *with the ancient family of Tracy of Gloucestershire.*" In case that didn't work out, his second goal was "*that of discovering an alternative.*"

Pitman pointed out that he initially examined the pedigree of Sir Paul Tracy in the 1623 *Visitation of the County of Gloucestershire* (available on *Archive. org*). He noted that Sir Paul had 21 children. Among these were 10 sons, including one named Thomas. But Thomas was one of only five children mentioned in Sir Paul's will of 1624. He is listed along with his eldest brother Richard, two sisters, and his brother Nathaniel. Pitman inferred from this that Thomas was one of Sir Paul's youngest children. It was assumed that the others had probably married and left the household. The Thomas declared in Sir Paul's will would have been born between 1599 and 1615. Pitman wrote that this is well within the range of Lt. Thomas Tracy's birth commonly thought to be 1610.

However, there was one more piece of evidence that Pitman cited to help him reach an inconclusive conclusion about Thomas, son of Paul. The evidence he presented is so important that it bears quoting in full from page 2 of his report, as follows:

"…. *Thomas Tracy is mentioned also in the will of his sister, Alice Tracy, which was proved in 1645. In it she in no way implies that he had gone abroad but as the will was made in 1639, nothing can be built on this since it is not certain that he had left England. So far then it must admitted that no impossible obstacle has been proved to the theory Lt. Thomas Tracy was a son of Sir Paul Tracy's; on the other hand no definite confirmation has been found. The son of Nathaniel Tracy would definitely be too young.*"

Pitman included an abstract of Alice's will in his report. In it Alice mentioned three brothers: Paul, Alexander, and Thomas. Pitman was reluctant to draw the conclusion that Alice's brother Thomas was Lt. Thomas Tracy because *"she in no way implies that he had gone abroad but as the will was made in 1639, nothing can be built on this since it is not certain that he had left England."* Ah, but we now know that IT IS CERTAIN that the Thomas of Connecticut had left England in 1636 and arrived at Boston Harbor, three years before Alice's will. If Thomas, son of Paul, was in England at the time Alice's will was written, then he is not Lt. Thomas Tracy.

Granted we don't know what happened to Alice's brother, Thomas. Nor does her will say that he is in England in 1639. We do know that it would be extraordinarily strange for someone to have included a sibling in a will written in 1639 that was not living, if not in close proximity, then certainly in the country. I know that Jacobus was aware that Thomas of Connecticut arrived at the Massachusetts Bay Colony in 1636 because he made note of that in *The Waterman Family*. I'm speculating that after reading the Pitman report he also had concluded that the Thomas in Alice's will, son of Paul, could not have been Lt. Thomas Tracy because Lt. Tracy had been in the colonies three years when her will was written.

Having been unsuccessful in finding conclusive evidence to prove or disprove Lt. Thomas Tracy's connection to Gloucestershire, Pitman turned to plan B, i.e., possible alternatives (plausible, not fabricated ones). He approached this by looking at Thomas' corroborated profession as a shipbuilder, also known as a shipwright (he used the nomenclature ship-builder as a synonym of shipwright). For Pitman a viable alternative was to try and connect other English Thomas Tracys of the period living in the general vicinity of Gloucestershire who were shipbuilders. Pitman made sure that the reader understood that being a shipwright was a profession of skilled manual labor.

Being an appropriately cautious social scientist, Pitman observed that his research *"has been more successful in unearthing possibilities than in proving or disproving existent traditions."* The possibilities to which he referred aren't very encouraging. Pitman identified two Thomas Tracys who were shipbuilders of a compatible age with Thomas Tracy of Connecticut. One was from a yeoman family in Northam, Devon, England. The other was from Stepney, Middlesex, England. Pitman was unable to link either with Lt. Thomas Tracy or with immigration to the Colonies. Significantly, Pitman observed that shipbuilding seemed like an improbable profession that would have been encouraged by Sir Paul Tracy. I would add that Thomas being mentioned in Sir Paul's will Thomas suggests that he held favor with his father. This, to my thinking, makes it even more improbable that he would have apprenticed Thomas to a profession of manual labor.

Let me expand on that premise a tad more. Throughout my research on Thomas I've found numerous references to him as a *"ship carpenter."* This description has sometimes been used to suggest that a carpenter probably was not born into high social rank. That makes sense to me. But, Pitman took it one step further with his depiction of Thomas as a *"shipbuilder"* or *"shipwright"*. Being a ship carpenter and being a shipbuilder are two quite different professions. As a carpenter it might be assumed Thomas had skills that would be useful on a ship or·building a fort. He would still have had those skills as a shipbuilder. But, shipbuilding is a much more complex profession that would have involved a lengthy apprenticeship and not one to which many persons of the aristocracy would aspire. Pitman put it that *"shipbuilding is a manual occupation and not one that seems likely to have presented itself to Sir Paul Tracy as a suitable career for one of his sons."*

Truth be known, all I've written about Jacobus's analysis of Thomas' origin to this point is even more succinctly and convincingly argued by the man himself in *The Waterman Family* listed in the annotated bibliography. I encourage you to carefully read pages 691-694 and see for yourself. Both the Pitman report and Jacobus' *The Waterman Family* should be required reading for all of Thomas' descendants, especially those who cling to the dubious idea that he was from Stanway.

But, as my high school English teacher, Miss Attie Faughn was so annoyingly fond of saying: *"You can lead a horse to water, but you can't make it drink."* In fact, she said this so often with such seriousness that there isn't a student who was ever in her English class at Murray Training School who has gone through life without being haunted by this aphorism. As you probably know, that isn't original with Miss Faughn. It is credited to John Heywood who was an English playwright, poet, and maker of proverbs. He lived about 1497 to 1580.

I shudder to think that Miss (don't you dare call me Attie) Faughn's favorite adage was in full bloom in the early 1600s and undoubtedly crossed the lips of Thomas on numerous occasions. It goes back many generations but is documented as having been uttered in the anonymously written stage play *Narcissus: A Twelve Night Merriment* first performed at Oxford University in 1602.

No, Murray Training School was not a reformatory. It was the laboratory school for Murray State College (now University) where we students served as guinea pigs for budding teachers "in training". It was a great school!! Go Colts!! I thank you Lillian Lowry, teacher and mentor extraordinaire, for taking me and so many others under your illuminating wings. Although the school is no more, it lives through its graduates, many of whom have done wondrous things around the globe. And its heritage continues through so many others who stayed at home making valuable contributions to the local community.

Support for Jacobus & Pitman: Hunt, Peck, Detrick, Reed, & Greene

After Jacobus' brief but brilliantly crafted analysis of Thomas Tracy's origin based on the Pitman report in 1939, I searched for corroborating repudiations of F. P. Tracy and Reuben Walworth's original contention. It took a while, but I finally unearthed what I was looking for in an article written 26 years after Pitman's report. In 1965 John G. Hunt jumped into the "find Thomas Tracy's origin" squabble with a short paragraph in a two-page article in *The American Genealogist*. He pretty much repeated what Jacobus said. Hunt, a distinguished American Genealogist, also further disputed Dwight Tracy's claim that Lt. Thomas Tracy was of Stanway. Getting as much as possible into a two page article, Hunt suggested that Thomas may have been the same Thomas Tracy who was mentioned in a manuscript by Dr. Charles Edward Banks as having been rebuked twice for not attending the church of St. Peter Mancroft in Norwich, Norfolk, England in 1631.

Unfortunately, Mr. Hunt, who was the author of numerous genealogical studies, failed to enlighten the reader with the name of the Banks' book other than to mention that he found it in the Rare Book Room in the Library of Congress (LOC). That is not much help as Dr. Banks was the author of at least 239 genealogical works. In 1985 the view of Banks and Hunt were further supported by the noted American Genealogist, Meredith B. Colket, Jr. Colket also "*presumed*" that Thomas of Connecticut was the same Tracy who skipped church in Norwich in his book *Founders of Early American Families: Emigrants from Europe 1607-1657*.

During my research on Banks, I couldn't help but think of the frequent times I did research at the LOC on social security programs in other countries as part of my job as a senior research analyst with the Social Security Administration in our nation's capital in the 1970s. Had I known of the vast genealogical collection in the LOC, I could have spent a productive lunch hour or two or three using my government access to explore my family roots. Who am I kidding, in my mid to late-30s, I couldn't have cared less! Besides, I spent those precious "free" hours trying to hone my skills on job-related research. Nah, I wasn't that ambitious. Most lunch hours were spent strolling around the DuPont Circle area with colleagues and my favorite boss, my mentor, and my dear friend the amazing Dr. Max Horlick who, as of this writing, is a robust 98-year old. I owe more to him for my career than I could ever adequately express.

I digress again! Our Mr. Hunt tied Dr. Banks' hint that Thomas might have been the same Thomas in Norwich in 1631 and 1632 to Hunt's own observation that Thomas was a close associate with Major John Mason. (Major Mason played a critical role in the development of the Connecticut Colony, as discussed much later). Hunt said that the name "Mason" was common in Norfolk. He concluded from this that both Thomas and Major Mason may have been natives of Norfolk. I've got my doubts about this as the only reference I could find about the English home town of Major Mason is that he was a native of Ravensthorpe, Northamptonshire, England.

In 1973 Connecticut genealogist Brainerd Tracy Peck took up the baton and reviewed all the earlier efforts to link Thomas to the baronetage of Stanway. Writing in *The Connecticut Nutmegger*, published by the *Connecticut Society of Genealogists, Inc.*, Peck wrote a brief summary of the discussion of the origin of Lt. Thomas Tracy up to that point. He drew on the analysis of Pitman and Jacobus and dismissed the Walworth and subsequent claims. Another author to repudiate the Stanway connection is Nancy Backus Detrick who wrote in 1989 in *Hear-Saye, Quarterly Newsletter of the Saybrook Colony Founders Association,* an important but little known journal of the *Saybrook Colony Founders Historical Society.* She posited that Thomas Tracy of Saybrook and Norwich was most likely born in Norfolk, England. Her article was primarily based on the Jacobus book on the Waterman family.

From my humble perspective, one more nail in the coffin filled with unconfirmed theories about Thomas's lineage comes from a 1992 report prepared for the author's Cousin Bonnie Aloma Seto by genealogist

Paul C. Reed of *Lineages, Inc. of Salt Lake City, Utah*. He prepared a report that focused on Thomas' origin. More explicitly, it was aimed at *"reconciling discrepancies between American printed sources and records obtained in England by family members."* Reed noted that there are no less than seven different genealogical works linking Lt. Thomas Tracy to Toddington [Stanway], Gloucestershire.

Reed cited Jacobus' dismissal of Ripley's theory that Lt. Thomas Tracy could have been the son of Sir Paul Tracy. Reed also rejected Dwight Tracy's theory that Lt. Thomas Tracy could have been the son William Tracy of Stanway and Virginia. He concluded by observing that *"The origin of Thomas TRACY, the New England immigrant, is probably to be found in co. Norfolk, England, _____ from whence so many other New England immigrants ventured."* This concurs with Jacobus' conclusion that *"The probability is that our Thomas Tracy sprang from the Tracys of Norfolk County, England, and was related to Stephen Tracy of Plymouth."* I have been much influenced by these statements. They resonate with findings I have recently made about Thomas regarding *Watertown, Massachusetts* that I'll go into shortly.

The preeminent genealogist Dr. David L. Greene the then Editor of *The American Genealogist* seems to have had the last word to date on the subject. Writing in 1996, Dr. Greene published a brief article on the subject in the fall issue of *Hear-Saye*. He apparently was responding to query posted by Doris Palmer Buys of Oceanside, California in the spring issue of *Hear-Saye*. Ms. Buys had asked if the father of Lt. Thomas Tracy was Sir Paul Tracy, Nathaniel Tracy, or Sir William Tracy of Stanway. Dr. Greene responded by summarizing Jacobus' previously stated position that *1) Thomas Tracy was not the son or grandson of Sir Paul Tracy, 2) Thomas Tracy was almost certainly not a son of Nathaniel Tracy of Tewkesbury and a nephew of Sir Paul Tracy, and 3) Thomas Tracy was not a son of Mr. [not Sir] William Tracy of Virginia, another scion of the Tracys of Toddington.*

Greene explicated that the use of the nomenclature "Mr." in Connecticut was a term of gentility, noting that Thomas was never called

Mr. Tracy. Rather he was called "Goodman" Tracy before becoming Ensign and, later, Lt. Tracy. Greene argued that not to be addressed as Mr. indicated that he was not of aristocracy. Greene adds that *"The likelihood is that Lt. Thomas Tracy came from a solid yeoman family in England. Jacobus presents evidence showing clear associations between the family of Lt. Thomas Tracy of Saybrook and Norwich and that of Stephen Tracy of Plymouth Colony. Stephen Tracy's origin has been found in Great Yarmouth, county Norfolk, England."* Actually, that counts as a twofer, as the even more prominent genealogist Donald Lines Jacobus is tagged in the quote.

Unfortunately, once published or put online, historical perspectives, accurate or inaccurate, take on a life of their own. Witness a recent reprint of the above-mentioned Dwight Tracy's dubious article on William Tracy of Virginia and his son Thomas. It was reproduced in September, 2015 with the same title in the form of a 46 page book published by *Forgotten Books* of London. This, of course, only serves to prolong the myth. If only it had been forgotten!!!

To be fair to all those who have thought and think that Thomas was of aristocratic blood from Stanway, I must concede that they may not have had ready access to the arguments of Pitman, Jacobus, Hunt, Peck, Detrick, Reed, and Greene. To make sure I'm being clear about the sources which have help lead me to believe that Thomas was a native of Norfolk, I've listed below a chronological list of seven genealogical works that raise into question Thomas' heritage with Stanway and lean toward Norfolk County as his home in England:

> H. Minot Pitman genealogical research files, ca. 1932-ca, Bx.14, Folder 10, (Henry Conland File), "Report on Lt. Thomas Tracy", Feb 1938. The New York Public Library, 1938.

> Donald Lines Jacobus, *The Waterman Family: Descendants of Robert Waterman of Marshfield, Massachusetts Through Seven*

Generations, 1 (New Haven, CT: E. F. Waterman, 1939), 21-28, 616-629, 691-698.

John G. Hunt, "Fiction Versus Possibility in the Tracy Genealogy," *The American Genealogist,* October 1965, 41: 250-252.

Brainerd T. Peck, Pre-American Origins, Proven, Disproved, Questionable, *The Connecticut Nutmegger,* v. 6 (1973): 202-206.

Nancy Backus Detrick, "Corrections to the Thomas Tracy and Francis Griswold Lines," *Hear-Saye, Quarterly Newsletter of the Saybrook Colony Founders Association,* v. 9, No. 2 (Spring 1989): 7-8.

Paul C. Reed, *Research Report (#38083 – Seto),* Lineages, Inc., Salt Lake City, Utah August 2, 1993.

David L. Greene, Ph.D. "Lt. Thomas Tracy of Saybrook and Norwich: His (Unknown) Origin and (Unknown) Wife," *Hear-Saye, Quarterly Newsletter of the Saybrook Colony Founders Association,* XI, 3, Issue 39 (Fall 1996), 540-542.

While I've found these works to be extremely enlightening, it is more than plausible that other family genealogists have not discovered them. And, admittedly, they may not share the passion (obsession?) I have in trying to unlock the secrets of Thomas' birth place. It is unclear how much visibility the Pitman research received beyond the book on the Waterman family by Jacobus. Or how many Tracy family genealogists are even familiar with the section on Thomas in the Jacobus' book on Thomas Waterman. The articles by Peck and Detrick are in relatively obscure journals. And neither the Pitman nor Reed reports have been published. Having said that, both the Hunt and Greene articles are published in *The American Genealogist* and most genealogists are familiar with that respected journal. However, as they so often say these days in these types of situations "it is what it is." Should I be telling myself just to "deal with it?"

Disdain Redo – Sir John Tracy of Norfolk
Despite my disdain for the futile attempt of myself and of others to connect Thomas to hoity toity English baronetage and heraldry, I'm compelled to go off point and relate a little story about a Sir John Tracy of Norfolk County, England. Sir John was brought to my attention by Paul C. Reed in his report where he observed that there was a *"Sir John TRACY, of Stanhow, Norfolk"* who died in 1663 or 1664.

I must admit that when I first saw a reference to Sir John, I thought he might be a Norfolk link with the rich and famous Tracy family in Stanway. I couldn't stand to leave it hanging. It had to be investigated and so in 2012 I did something about it. For those of you have done the math and noticed that there is a 19 year gap between 1993 when I first set out on this journey and 2012, I can only plead that sometimes (read more and more often) it takes a while for my ideas to fester before coming to fruition. I have to wait for an idea to become one whose time has come, as it were. Admittedly, this one took an inordinate amount of time. I'm still waiting for others to mature! One must be patient with the elderly, don't you know.

Be that as it may, in July 2012, I tried to find someone to contact at the aforementioned town of Stanhow in Norfolk County. I didn't have much luck until I discovered I should have been looking for the town of Stanhoe. It is funny, as well as exasperating, how ending a name with a "w" instead of an "e" can lead to a wild goose chase. Once that was resolved, I located two local Stanhoe historians, Charles Butcher and Gillian Beckett, and sent them an email. They were quick to respond. They were quite familiar with Sir John Tracy and intrigued by the interest in an ancient local Knight by an American who lived so far away. I suspect that a request from a person with a Tracy surname added some credibility to the inquiry. They most graciously agreed to do some exploring for me, gratis, no less. I was curious to find out what they might know about Sir John Tracy to see if there was a potential connection to Thomas and Stephen, as well as to Stanway in Gloucestershire.

They reported that "*Sir John Tracy Kt. came here* [Stanhoe] *early in the 1600s and died in 1664* [the correct date is 1663]. *As he didn't buy any property here but simply rented a house suggests he hadn't intended to stay too long, maybe he had already planned the move. He did, however, have one son, in 1643, Robert and 8 daughters. Son Robert died in 1671, leaving no offspring and all his father's properties to his sisters all of whom were married. This of course meant there was no one of the Tracy name to inherit. This wasn't the only line of the family and the senior line lived in Gloucestershire at Stanway, a fine Elizabethan mansion which is still extant, though a bit altered.*"

Their report was later confirmed in a response to an email inquiry I made to the Norfolk Record Office in Norwich. An Archivist in the Office, Hannah Verge, affirmed that a search of a survey compiled in the 1980s had the following engraving: "*A large black nameless slab at the top of the name which shows a scallop shell only, covers the grave of Sir John Tracy, one time owner of a large manor in Stanhoe, who was buried here in 1663.*"

Charles Butcher was kind enough to search for and locate the tomb of Sir John in the Stanhoe *All Saints Anglican Church* built around 1300. He even took the time and effort to remove the carpet covering the tomb in the center aisle so he could make a photo to send me. It shows the engraving noted above. It's a bit blurry, but Charles' photo confirms the description. The scallop shell family crest is similar to that found at the Tracy family home in Stanway, Gloucestershire indicating a possible link to that family line.

I interpreted the report of Butcher and Beckett to mean that Sir John was probably related to the Tracy family at Stanway. However, since his only son had no offspring, the chances of him also being closely related to Norfolk native Stephen seemed very remote. As for a possible direct relation to Thomas, it depended on the doubtful Thomas' connection to Stanway.

I've squandered many perfectly innocent megabytes looking for the names of Sir John Tracy's parents without success. Good night, you'd think that somewhere there would be a family chart of the good Knight. I thought I had exhausted my resources and that it would remain a mystery until it isn't. Didn't Yogi Berra say something along those lines? Maybe I'm thinking of this little Berra ditty: *"I wish I had an answer to that because I'm tired of answering that question."* That is until I chanced upon a pedigree chart of the Tracy family of Toddington included in a heraldic history by John Burke published in 1841. Voila, there was Sir John Tracy of Stanhow (sic). He was the son of another Sir John Tracy who was knighted by James I in 1609. Therefore, John of Stanhoe, Norfolk is, in fact, directly connected to the aristocratic Tracys of Toddington.

I can't let this go without mentioning that one of Sir John's daughters, Catharine, married a man by the name of, and I kid you not, Butts Bacon. Actually, that's Sir Butts Bacon to you and me. He was the 1st Baronet of Mildenhall. That would make him the Baron Butts Bacon. I do so appreciate an amusing alliteration. In case you are wondering, he is related to Sir Francis Bacon.

Now let us proceed to a detailed examination of the significance that the Massachusetts Bay Colony settlement of Watertown plays in our saga.

8

THE SIGNIFICANCE OF WATERTOWN: A SETTLEMENT OF EAST ANGLIANS

It is quite feasible that Thomas, like Stephen Tracy, came to New England to be with a specific group of fellow travelers. In the case of Stephen the group was his religious community of Puritan Separatists and friends from Leiden newly settled in Plymouth and Duxbury. In the case of Thomas, at the beginning of his journey, I discovered that it was very likely a group of non-Separatists from East Anglia, particularly Norfolk, who initially went to the Massachusetts Bay Colony settlement of Watertown about ten miles west of Boston.

How did I come to this conclusion? Well to begin with, the observations of Pitman, Jacobus, Hunt, Peck, Detrick, Reed, and Greene seemed to support the theory that Thomas hailed from Norfolk. These are all highly esteemed genealogists and who am I to question their wisdom? On the other hand, they were not entirely persuasive. I needed more convincing evidence, but didn't really know where to turn. As luck would have it, I stumbled onto a significant aspect relative to his birthplace of which I had not been aware. It happened, as it often does, while I was looking for something else. Indeed, I can't count the times that I've made a serendipitous discovery in academic research, as well as genealogical investigation.

On Friday, January 29, 2016, I was browsing through some publications looking for material about Salem, Massachusetts where Thomas had gone soon after his arrival in the Bay Colony when I had one of those "ah ha" moments. An OH YEAH! A Woo Hoo moment! Hot damn! This was followed by a declaration of "Saucy Boucy" (private joke). In current vernacular it was what I often hear as a "that's what I'm talking about" moment. I was sitting in an easy chair in front of our ventless gas fireplace on a cold winter night reading *The History of Salem* by Sidney Perley. I had downloaded the book from the *HathiTrust Digital Library* onto my Kindle Fire HD. Suddenly, the following entry leapt out at me: *"And at the same meeting Thomas Tracy, a ship carpenter from Watertown, was received for an inhabitant '2 Mar. 1636-7, 'vpon a Certificate from duers of watter Towne', and was granted five acres of land."* The illuminating words here are Watertown and five acres of land.

I thought "steady on old boy" (I enjoy watching a lot of BBC productions on PBS!). I was so caught up in my moment of excitement that I failed to consider going to the original source to verify the record. I definitely should have done that because there was a shorthand entry after the record that has an important bearing on my story. I discovered my oversight only after making the auspicious acquaintance of Sean C. Tracy, a heretofore unknown distant cousin. I was unaware of Sean until earlier last year (2016). On March 12, 2016 I received a notice from *FamilyTreeDNA* that there was a DNA match with him at 37 markers (more about the DNA process later).

I sent Sean an email on March 12, 2016 and received a reply two days later. After hearing from him and doing a little calculating, I discovered that Sean is my 7th cousin. Sean has done and is doing excellent research on Thomas Tracy. He was kind enough to invite me to look at his extensive online postings. Unlike yours truly, Sean had the good sense to examine the Salem Town Records which are available on *Archive.org* in greater detail. He noted in his email that while Thomas was *"to have 5 acres of land"* it was available to him *only if he paid for it.* That was the content of the shorthand statement to wit: "*which he may have laid out when he hath a ticket from me* [Town Clerk] *that he hath paid me*". The actual record shows his name as *Tho: Trace* (sic). Hold on to that phrase "*only if he paid for it.*" I'll come back to it shortly.

Allow me to back up to the evening of my discovery and the critical reference to Watertown in the Salem records. After disturbing my wife who was deeply engrossed reading a novel by pondering aloud how could it be that I had not made Thomas' connection to Watertown before. In my defense, I want to point out that numerous genealogical works skip over the fact that Watertown was Thomas' first destination.

Despite the town clerk's mention of "*watter Towne*", most genealogical publications related to Thomas incorrectly record that he first arrived at Salem, Massachusetts. More often than not there is no mention of him ever having been in Watertown. In fact, doing a quick and dirty count I came up with a minimum of 10 widely read and trusted genealogical books and articles penned from 1888 to 1973 that make no reference whatever of Thomas ever having been to Watertown! For reasons best known to them, these authors like to start with Salem as his first residence. I was certainly thrown off track. Apparently, I'm not the only one!

Armed with the correct information from Sean and the Salem Town Records, I asked myself the following questions. Is there supporting evidence that Thomas's original destination was Watertown? If he did first try and settle in Watertown instead of Salem, why did he chose a backwater settlement 10 miles west of Boston to start his new life in the colonies?

The answer to the first question is yes! There is corroboration that his first destination was Watertown. In addition to the Salem Town Clerk's record, it is confirmed by the previously mentioned highly reliable *The Great Migration Directory: Immigrants to New England, 1620-1640* by Robert Charles Anderson. Back once more to January 29, I rose from my comfortable chair and pulled that treasured tome from my bookshelf, dusted it off, looked at the index, turned to page 340 and, voilà, there it was:

"Thomas Tracy: Unknown [place of origin], *1636* [arrival], *Watertown, Salem, Wethersfield, Saybrook, Norwich."* Goodness, how many times had I looked at that? Apparently, not enough times for it to register as being of any consequence.

As to why he chose Watertown, the answer is, for me, my friends, no longer blowing in the historic wind (thank you Bob Dylan, Noble Literature winner, for the allusion). Ironically, I had just finished reading two well researched books that discussed Watertown as the destination of groups of settlers from East Anglia. One book is entitled *Mobility and Migration: East Anglian Founders of New England, 1629-1640.* The other is *Divided We Stand: Watertown, Massachusetts, 1630-1680.* Both books are written by Dr. Roger Thompson, emeritus professor of American Colonial History at the University of East Anglia, Norwich, England. Good credentials, wouldn't you agree? Hmmm, I said to self. Watertown was settled by East Anglians. Thomas's first destination was Watertown. Ergo, Thomas is from East Anglia. I bounced this logic off my resident expert on logical reasoning, my wife Patsy, and she concurred that I might be onto something. For a change, I should hasten to add.

Notably, it wasn't only Watertown that was settled by Puritan parish families from Norfolk. Prof. Thompson observed that *"The great majority of people who left Great Yarmouth on the Norfolk east coast clustered together at Salem, Massachusetts".* Is it unreasonable to assume when Thomas was denied a land grant among his fellow Norfolkians in Watertown, he opted to take his chances with other Norfolk planters at Salem? Unluckily, that didn't work out so well either.

East Anglia

Now that I've brought it up, I'm compelled to take a moment to try and define East Anglia. The definition during TGM is a moving target since the counties so designated vary according to at least three factors. One is the 1630 to 1640 time period of TGM (even the range of years varies). A second is that it depends on which website one accesses. A third is one's selection of history books and articles. What is certain is that the name is derived from a tribe in Angeln, Germany, a small peninsula in present-day Southern Schleswig. The Kingdom of East Anglia in England dates from the early 6th Century. The first two kings were Wehha and Wuffa. This line of kings was known as the Wuffangas. I'm not pulling your leg. I think George Lucas should consider naming his next Star Wars film: *The Rise of the Wuffangas*. According to the tourist websites and most of the history books I've read, East Anglia is currently made up of the three counties of Norfolk, Suffolk, and Essex. Robert Charles Anderson says that no matter how it is defined, most of those who came during TGM were from those three counties. That works for me.

Professor Thompson's research covered what he called "*Greater East Anglia*." This included Essex, Suffolk, Norfolk, Lincolnshire, and Cambridgeshire. He put the number of immigrants from this expanded definition at 2,138 for the period 1630-40. According to *Wikipedia*, East Anglia refers to the counties of Norfolk, Suffolk, and Cambridgeshire plus the city of Peterborough which is in Cambridgeshire. Nothing about English governmental divisions is easy! Regardless, Norfolk is always included in the definition of East Anglia. Moreover, East Anglia is well represented in the Massachusetts Bay area. Boston is in Suffolk County bordered by Essex County to its north and Norfolk County to its south.

Watertown, Massachusetts – Norfolk Legacy
As for Watertown specifically, Professor Thompson explained that the settlement had three stages of growth: The first was in 1630. The second was from 1634 to 1636. The third was in 1637. Thomas arrived with the second wave. All three waves were dominated by immigrants from East Anglia, beginning with immigrants primarily from Suffolk with the Winthrop Fleet in 1630 and followed with immigrants largely from Essex beginning in 1631. Then there was a big wave from Norfolk in 1636 and 1637. Dr. Bernard Bailyn Harvard University Professor Emeritus of Early American history wrote in 2012 that almost all people of Watertown "*were derived from a thirty-five-mile-wide band from norther Essex to southern Suffolk.*"

Watertown was first known as Saltonstall Plantation. It was so named because it was founded by Sir Richard Saltonstall who was an assistant to Governor Winthrop. Saltonstall came with Winthrop on the *Arbella* (also spelled *Arabella*) arriving at Salem, Massachusetts on June 12, 1630. Soon after his arrival, Saltonstall led a group of settlers from Norfolk who had also sailed on the *Arbella* up the Charles River to what is now Watertown. It was the fourth town in the *Massachusetts Bay Company*. Remember that Governor Winthrop encouraged groups of families, kin, and whole Puritan non-Separatist communities to move to the colonies. According to Prof. Thompson it was essentially an immigration of extended families. He points out that many English communities had a mistrust of people from other English regions. So, there was an inclination for whole groups from a specific community to immigrate together rather than mixing with people from a different community.

If a community could bring their minister with them, that was so much the better. This, in fact, is what Saltonstall did. He brought the Reverend George Moses Phillips with him to be installed as the first Minister of Watertown. Rev. Phillips had been the vicar of Boxted, Suffolk, England. He was a native of Raynham, Norfolk. Phillips remained the Watertown minister for 14 years until he died. Phillips was with familiar faces as about one in five allotments of land at Watertown were occupied by families from the Boxted Area.

One thing about the men from Norfolk who settled Watertown that caught my eye when reading Prof. Thompson's account is that as early as 1631 the community under Rev. Phillips' leadership had been credited with an early enunciation of a familiar refrain, namely: "*No taxation without representation.*" Apparently, only four years earlier East Anglians had resisted an effort by King Charles I to get his subjects to "*lovingly, freely, and voluntarily*" give him money with little in return. It's hard to believe they would turn down such an opportunity to please the King, but they did. There are the usual disputes that accompany claims on who said an iconic saying first, but, it was definitely an East Anglian-Norfolk-Watertown attitude long before there was any thought being given to dumping English tea into Boston harbor.

Sir Saltonstall stayed only a year, returning to England. He came back to Connecticut in 1635 to establish a colony at the mouth of the Connecticut River, which became the Saybrook Colony where Thomas also lived for several years before being one of the founders of Norwich, Connecticut.

Unfortunately, the names of people from Norfolk who came to Watertown in the 1636 wave were not entered on ship manifests. One explanation for this is that there was no need to write down the names of passengers who were linked by kinship or neighborhood to the original 1630 wave that were mostly from Essex and Suffolk. Okay, so it's a weak explanation, but it's the best I've found. The thing is that the lists for numerous ships during The Great Migration don't exist, have been lost, or were never recorded. And this includes ship manifest records for Thomas. While his name isn't recorded on a ship manifest, he was definitely in Watertown in 1636. This would have given him an opportunity to be among friends and kin, probably from Norfolk. As Sean C. Tracy pointed out to me, he very likely *"arrived in the company of other immigrants who already knew him."* Thomas' traveling companions may well have been from the same congregation or community. Sean shares the view with me that his appearance in Watertown in 1636 lends credibility to the idea that he was from Norfolk.

An additional indication that Watertown would have been a preferred destination for anyone from Norfolk County is that ALL the planters in the 1637 wave who came to Watertown were from Norfolk. That wave consisted mostly of older people. While the largest contingency from Norfolk to Watertown was in that year, there were most certainly others from Norfolk in the 1636 group, along with Thomas. It should also be noted that there were at least 64 inhabitants of the city of Great Yarmouth alone who are known to have migrated to New England during the Great

Migration. They were only a small part of an exodus of several thousand immigrants from East Anglia in the 1630's who sought to create a "Bible Commonwealth" utopia in the Massachusetts Bay area.

By way of summation, it is well documented that Thomas' first destination was Watertown. Watertown was the primary destination of East Anglians, particularly whole communities from Norfolk. In my mind, this is a strong indication that Thomas was from Norfolk.

Please forgive me dear reader and dear cousins for my obsession with the birthplace of Thomas. Now that I have it out of my system, I want to take the measure of the man, but not for his social status at birth. Rather I want to focus on his contributions to his community and to early Connecticut history. Let us proceed to chapters 9 to get a glimpse of what he accomplished in Wethersfield and Saybrook and chapter 10 where he really shines in Norwich.

9

LT. THOMAS TRACY IN SALEM, WETHERSFIELD, & SAYBROOK

At long last, I'm actually going to get to the nitty gritty of the life and times of Thomas Tracy. The focus in this chapter is on Thomas in Salem, Wethersfield, and Saybrook. However, for comparative purposes I first want contrast the motivations of Stephen and Thomas, as I conjecture them to have been.

Stephen came to New England because of deep religious convictions, a longing to be with people with whom he had built lasting friendships in Leiden. Stephen desired to live and worship free from the shackles of a society that stifled the right to be different. In the new world he could worship as he wished. He was in an environment that shared his values as a Puritan, a Pilgrim, a "Saint", an "Old-Comer", and a "Forefather." It was not an environment suitable for everyone, especially anyone who was different or who didn't live by the prevailing social and religious norms. Holding views contrary to the English Anglican Church was accepted in Plymouth, expressing different views from those of the Puritan Church in the colony were not. Openly challenging religious or civic authority in the Plymouth Colony often led to watching people going about their daily activities in the commons with your feet bound and your head and arms locked in a stock!

Thomas also came to the New World as a Puritan seeking religious freedom, but his journey contrasts sharply with that of Stephen. Thomas was not a Puritan "Saint" and his quest seems to have been more dominated by a goal of personal advancement. He certainly was committed to life in a religious community, but religion was more tangential to his life than the dominant focus that it was in Stephen's life. The more I looked into his life, the more I appreciated his obvious passion to wander with the goal of continually improving his lot in life. As I did the research on him a verse from a J. R. R Tolkien poem came to mind; namely, *"Not all those who wander are lost."*

Brief Residence in Salem, Massachusetts Bay Colony

I've established that Thomas' first destination when he arrived in 1636 was Watertown. He apparently *"got no satisfaction"* in that settlement because it is recorded that he was in Salem in March of 1637 less than a year after arriving at Boston Harbor. My first thought was that perhaps he wasn't granted as much land in Watertown as he expected. In fact, there is no record of any land grant to Thomas in Watertown. However, as I thought about possible reasons for his leaving Watertown, I recalled reading about the problems of a scarcity of land within the newly established towns in the Massachusetts Bay Colony. As early as 1635, all the settlements in the Bay area were being constrained by family plots that were placed close together for security reasons.

I remembered also that Winthrop's government required that every man live within half a mile from their farms and the meeting-house (often the tavern) which was fortified and equipped to repeal sustained attacks. The restriction of where a man could live was a policy that probably did not sit well with independent-minded planters. Moreover, many planters wanted to expand their property which was difficult under the prevailing law. The situation got worse as the population grew. Soon there was a severe space situation in all the original seven plotted communities, including Watertown. Actually, the same scenario was playing out in the Plymouth Colony.

I couldn't help but ponder if there wasn't some more definitive information out there in cyberspace or in solid state library material that would help to clarify the potential impact on the possible unavailability of land for Thomas in Watertown. I turned to a source that I've only recently begun to utilize. This is *The Great Migration Newsletter*, edited by, can you guess? Yes, that's correct, the proficient and prolific Robert Charles Anderson. The *Newsletter* has been in publication since 1992. In a 2002 issue I found an article on land grants in Watertown. The article sheds light on why Thomas might have decided to go to Salem.

In particular, the article explains that Watertown was facing a shortage of land. It notes that on November or December of 1635, it was *"agreed by consent of the Freemen (in consideration there may be too many inhabitants in the Town & the Town thereby in danger to be ruinated) (sic) that no Foreigner coming into Town, or any family arising among ourselves, shall have any benefit of commonage, or land undivided but what they shall purchase..."* Consequently, by the time Thomas arrived then next year in 1636 the only way he could obtain land in Watertown was to purchase it. Being a ship's carpenter, it is unlikely that he could have afforded such an acquisition. This may well have been a reason for Thomas to cast his lot with the folks in Salem located 25 miles northeast away from the "crowded" Boston area.

Recall that land in Salem was also available to Thomas *"only if he paid for it"* and the Salem Town Clerk provided no record that a payment was ever made. Thomas may not have known that Salem imposed the same requirement as Watertown that land had to be purchased. There was no free land grant option available for him in either settlement. I know that I'm repeating myself, but it is important to bear in mind that it would have been difficult for a ship's carpenter to afford buying five acres of land in Salem.

I recently ran across a different speculation as to why Thomas could not afford to purchase land. It was put forward by a Tracy family genealogist who recently communicated with me on *Ancestry.com*. Based on information from her late husband, a descendant of Thomas, she thinks Thomas might have been an indentured servant. That would not have been unusual. Indentured servants typically made arrangements to have the cost of their transportation to New England covered in exchange for a specified number of years of servitude to their sponsor. There was also the option to "buy out" their contract whenever it became economically possible. If Thomas was indentured, it would be another indication that he wasn't from a wealthy family and that he couldn't afford to purchase land at either Watertown or Salem.

A Few Words on Salem, Massachusetts

I want to stray away from Thomas for a moment to say a few words about Salem. Of course, thanks to multiple renditions of Witchcraft in books, plays, and movies, the first thing anyone thinks when they hear a reference to historic Salem is the witchcraft hysteria of 1692. Consider, however, that the town was first established in 1626. That's nearly 70 years of history of social and economic development that are typically eclipsed by this admittedly troubling facet of life in the Colonies. I got quite exasperated by looking for online information on Salem that didn't focus on witchcraft and witch trials!

I was able to find that when Thomas went to Salem, London merchants were falling all over themselves trying to get a piece of the mercenary action in the colonies. Furs, in particular, were bringing top dollars and when a company had their own settlement the opportunity for big profits was greatly enhanced. In 1628 the New England Company received a grant on behalf of the Plymouth Council for New England under the guise of launching a profit-making settlement. They chose the Salem location to set up housekeeping. While the pretext was to generate revenue for Plymouth Council stockholders, the principle investors in the New England Company were more interested in creating a haven for disgruntled Puritans. Towards this end, the Company sent in John Endecott 1628 as Governor. The thing is that there was already a group of settlers in Salem, but the company that had sponsored them had failed. Nature abhors a vacuum, enabling Endecott and his companions to waltz right in and take over. Endecott then arranged for Salem to be settled by a different company of London merchants.

In 1629 three hundred Puritans joined the company's fledging settlement at Salem. One fascinating aspect of the settlement for me is that, similar to the planters at Watertown, the Salem Company was dominated by immigrants from East Anglia. The original settlement was called by its Indian name Naumkeag (fishing place) but it was renamed Salem in 1629 from the Hebrew word Shalom, meaning peace. Curious, what! Or, as W. S. Gilbert put it in the comic opera *Patience*, "*The meaning doesn't matter if it's only idle chatter of a transcendental kind.*"

In 1630 the London Company reorganized and selected John Winthrop to replace Endecott as Governor. One look at Salem is apparently all it took for Winthrop to decide to relocate the colony's government seat approximately 20 miles southeast at the mouth of the Charles River at a place which is now the home of baked beans and the Red Sox. Endecott decided to stay in Salem where he held virtually every important public position. Yet, he is mostly known by today's school children as the man who planted the Endecott Pear Tree in Danvers, Massachusetts which is still living and bearing fruit. Too bad Winthrop moved the government to Boston; I like the sound of the Salem Sox. Salem baked beans or Salem cream pie, not so much.

Endicott's church in Salem held Separatist views, which as we know, sought a complete break with the Church of England. Whereas, the Boston church held to the "Nonconformist" or non-Separatist view that the Church should be reformed from within. Endecott had an adverse relationship with the prevailing religious beliefs in Boston and rubbed salt in the wound by giving refuge to the renowned Separatist Roger Williams who had arrived as an unwelcome immigrant in Boston in 1631.

Despite his support of the unorthodox Williams, Endecott was famous for his intolerance of religious diversity. My heart tells me that the prevailing narrow-mindedness repulsed Thomas and contributed to his quickly changing his mind about living in Salem. My mind tells me, no. It was the fact that he couldn't purchase land. After arriving in Salem about February, 1637, by mid-May of that year we find him in the frontier settlement of Wethersfield in the Connecticut Colony. Wethersfield was a non-Separatist community located in a very rural setting miles away through hostile Indian Territory. So, why choose Wethersfield?

Move to Wethersfield, Connecticut Colony & the Pequot War
Although there was no Internet, social media, radio, or TV, to spread the news about what was happening around the colonies, people did get news, albeit typically late. It came by word-of-mouth or in broadsheets (a piece of paper with written or printed information on one side). News was critical to knowing the status of relationships with Native Americans, as well as trade, civil strife, religious disputes, and political situations. It was also essential to those who were on the lookout for better circumstances and living conditions. The development of Wethersfield and the promise it held for adventurers would have easily been known by Thomas, especially because of his connections with the East Anglian men in Watertown who founded Wethersfield.

I've mentioned the crowded conditions of Watertown, Salem and other settlements around Boston. These circumstances encouraged the formation of many new settlements in distant locations. Due to the lack of adequate space in Watertown in 1634 a group of ten disgruntled and venturesome men decided to leave the jurisdiction of the Massachusetts government. They wanted to seek their fortunes in a distant place in the southwest Connecticut wilderness on the Connecticut River. It was described as *"a brave piece of meadow"* which they named Wethersfield after a village in Essex County, England (East Anglia). The land was so choice that a group of Watertown neighbors in Cambridge also coveted it. They were much chagrined when they learned that the Watertown planters had beat them to the land patent. Some from the village of Cambridge came anyway, but there was bad blood between the two groups that lasted many years.

You'll recall an earlier discussion of John Oldham who came to Plymouth on the *Anne* with Stephen Tracy. Oldham's sister married Jonathan Brewster, son of William Brewster of the *Mayflower* and Plymouth. Remember Oldham had been cast out of the colony because of his rebellious disposition. He comes back into our story as the leader of the Watertown group who settled Wethersfield. Of the ten founders of Wethersfield under Oldham's leadership, six were East Anglians. Over the next two years, numerous Watertown proprietors, including more East Anglians, joined their friends in Wethersfield followed by an influx of planters from all over Massachusetts and Connecticut.

Even though Oldham had left Plymouth under duress for Connecticut, Plymouth Governor Winthrop kept track of his movements. Winthrop recorded in his journal of September 4, 1633 that John Oldham and three others went overland about 160 miles to Connecticut to trade. The local sachem gave them beaver and hemp *"which grows there in great abundance."* I couldn't find a reference to what Oldham gave in exchange for the fur and hemp. Incidentally, after hundreds of years of growing valuable industrial hemp in the United States, its production came to a screeching halt when it was classified by the U.S. Congress as marijuana under the Controlled Substances Act of 1970.

Hemp farming became illegal as the production of synthetic fabrics and fibers skyrocketed. And we began to import millions of pounds of industrial hemp. In fact, in 2016 the U.S. imported two billion dollars of industrial hemp! Thanks to federal legislation in 2015, industrial hemp is about to make a comeback as a valuable crop, led by Kentucky farmers.

It will provide nutritious edible seed, oil, hair care, clothing, fabric, and insulation to name a few vital uses. This has nothing to do with our story, but it promises to be a huge economic boost for my Old Kentucky Home. Enlightened pragmatism of the John Dewey kind! That's what has made America different and great!

End of commercial, back to the story. Is it a coincidence that Thomas left Salem for Wethersfield? I have my doubts. Recall that Wethersfield was established in 1634, two years before Thomas arrived at Watertown. So he certainly would have known about it when he was in Watertown.

Initially, Salem apparently had more appeal to Thomas than Watertown. Salem, after all, was not far away, much safer from Indian attacks, and home to many planters from East Anglia and Norfolk. But he left Salem practically before the mud on his shoes had time to dry. Throwing caution to the wind, he embarked upon a long trek of about 120 miles through hostile Indian Territory. So, that's what, a four day walk, at best? Undoubtedly he took the well-trod Old Connecticut Path, a Native American Indian trail that led westward from the Massachusetts Bay area to the Connecticut River Valley. It was the primary route for the settlers who had left the Massachusetts Bay Colony to found the more democratic communities of Windsor, Wethersfield, and Hartford in 1635. Hopefully, Thomas had a horse, but that would have been an expensive luxury. In 1638-39, the three communities united in an independent commonwealth, adopting a democratic constitution.

His journey to Wethersfield through Connecticut would have been made even more perilous by the fact that the Connecticut Colonists had been fending off attacks by the Pequot tribe since 1634. The Pequot were understandably piqued by the incursion of the English from Plymouth and the Massachusetts Bay Colony into the fertile Connecticut Valley. In as much as that was the location of Wethersfield, the town was in the direct line of fire. Indeed, the Pequot had periodically laid siege to nearby Fort Saybrook from September, 1636 to April, 1637. During one attack in October 1636, sachem Sassacus led a raid on Saybrook that killed 30 settlers.

Another incident indicative of the growing problems with the Indians happened earlier on July 20, 1636. It was on that date that John Oldham was killed during a trading mission at Block Island, Rhode Island. His death came at the hands of the Narragansett, but the Narragansett convinced the English that he had been killed by the Pequot. The deception was aimed at getting the English to wage war against the Pequot who were the Narragansett's ancient enemy. Had the Narragansett gotten their hands on a copy of Machiavelli's *The Prince*!? The English must not have been familiar with the age-old ploy. The gullible English bought the sham lock, stock, and barrel and turned their wrath against the Pequot.

The event that triggered a formally declared war with the Pequot by the Connecticut Colony occurred on April 23, 1637. It was then that a large force of Pequot warriors attacked English settlers at Wethersfield. Six men, three women, and twenty cows were killed. Two young girls were kidnapped, but were later rescued for a ransom arranged by the Dutch out of New Amsterdam. As a result of the brutality at Wethersfield, the Connecticut General Court declared war on the Pequot on May 1, 1637. Following the declaration of war a tax levy was imposed on towns along the Connecticut River. The communities of Hartford, Windsor, Springfield, and Wethersfield had to pony up money, food, and soldiers. Wethersfield was taxed £124 ($276,000 in 2016). The town was also required to provide 48 bushels of corn, of which 24 bushels were to be prepared as biscuits, a bushel of beans, 30 pounds of butter, two bushels of oatmeal, 150 pounds of beef, and one hog. Most significantly for Thomas who had just arrived in the frontier town, Wethersfield had to provide 26 soldiers.

Thomas surely must have known he would literally be walking into a war zone by going to Wethersfield. I don't know the precise date he arrived, but it was after the May 1 attack because on May 16 he was apparently conscripted into the Wethersfield militia. I say apparently because there is no primary documentation that he was one of 18 men from Wethersfield initially conscripted toward reaching the town's quota. He is, however, listed as being a probable member of the total number of 26 recruits from Wethersfield as noted in *The Memorial History of Hartford County, Connecticut 1633-1884, II, Town Histories* by J. Hammond Trumbull.

A downside to looking at family in an historical context is that it isn't always about the wonderful things your ancestors accomplished. Some events in which ancestors were involved are disturbing. The skeleton in the closet, as it were. Such is the case of Thomas' possible experience with the short-lived Pequot War. A 90 man militia from Wethersfield, Hartford, Springfield, and Windsor was placed under the command of Captain John Mason of Windsor. Mason and his troops were responsible for the Massacre at Mystic. This tragic event occurred on May 26, 1637. The English were joined by 200 Narragansett and 70 Mohegan allies in attacking a fortified Pequot village near the Mystic River and present-day Groton. It was a surprise attack that took advantage of the absence of several hundred Pequot warriors who were on their way to stage a siege at Hartford. The attack at Mystic was merciless, even genocidal. Over 500 men, women, and children in the Indian palisade were killed. Thomas might have been a participant in the raid. The war officially ended in 1638. Captain Mason was promoted to Major following the Mystic River Massacre.

Years in Wethersfield – Including Marriage
Thomas is recorded as one of the first settlers of Wethersfield. But since the town was founded in 1634, about three years before he arrived, he is not considered to be a founder. In 1641, at age 31, Thomas married his first wife. Her name and age are unknown. She is often recorded as Mary. It is frequently, but erroneously, alleged that she was Mary Mason, widow of Edward Mason. This occurs in numerous historic and contemporary publications and online postings. There is no documentation to support that his wife was the widow Mason.

We have Dr. Dwight Tracy to thank for calling it to our attention that the widow Mason never remarried. He cited the *First Book of the Land Records of Wethersfield, Connecticut* that show the widow Mason died a widow between March 22, 1650 and February 20, 1659. Dr. Tracy reported this in the *New England and Historic Genealogical Register* in 1907! This hasn't prevented the claim from continuing to be made even by normally reliable sources. For example, the *Society of Colonial Wars in the State of Connecticut* lists seven family pedigrees traced back to Thomas listing his wife as Mary Mason. Moreover, at least one lineage entry into the *National Society of the Sons and Daughters of the Pilgrims* shows the wife of Lt. Thomas Tracy as the widow of Edward Mason.

I've been unable to find much material on Thomas during his stay in Wethersfield. I did find enough to know that he was a stalwart member of the Weathersfield community as he was appointed to several posts of honor. Among these was his appointment by the Connecticut General Court to serve as a juror from Wethersfield in 1644. In December of that year there is a record of a Robert Beadle of Wethersfield stealing a *"sack"* from Thomas. Beadle stole several other items from other folks. His hand was branded and he was *"severely"* whipped for his transgressions. Thomas' home in Wethersfield was located on the south side of the main road through town. His property in Wethersfield was not destined to last. A book written in 1904 described his land as having been covered by the Connecticut River for more than 200 years. Although Thomas was obviously successful in Wethersfield, in 1647 he relocated his family along with friends and neighbors downriver to Fort Saybrook Colony.

Relocation to Fort Saybrook, Connecticut Colony
Fort Saybrook or Old Saybrook as it is called these days is about 40 miles south of Wethersfield at the mouth of the Connecticut River. Its location on the river made it an important trade site. First settled in 1624 by the Dutch, they later abandoned it to focus on strengthening their settlement in New Amsterdam. In 1635, the English occupied the vacated area and constructed Fort Saybrook and established the *"Colony of Saybrooke"* (sic).

The colony was established by Governor Winthrop's son, John Winthrop the Younger. Doesn't that sound so much more regal than "Junior"? The colony was named in honor of two prominent English Protestants. These were William Fiennes, 1st Viscount, Saye & Sele (that's all one title!) and Robert Greville, 2nd Baron Brooke (ditto). Both "Lords" were close chums of the Protestant Lord Protector Oliver Cromwell. It was rumored that Lords Saye and Brooke, as well as Cromwell, intended to visit Fort Saybrook. It never happened because events associated with the English Civil War kept them all too occupied. Cromwell died in 1658 at age 58 of complications from malaria and urinary infection. The Passing of "*Old Ironsides*" as he was known to friend and foe alike was welcomed and none too soon for those who wanted to restore the monarchy. Cromwell has the dubious distinction of being among the few in history who was executed posthumously!! His bones were burned and the ashes were dispersed hither and yon when they were fired from a cannon.

Incidentally, if you, like me, thought that the term "Redcoat" for British troops originated during the Revolutionary war, you'd also be wrong. It originated during the English Civil War in the mid-1600s when the Parliamentarians formed the "New Model Army." The Parliamentarians sought to reduce the King to a Constitutional Monarchy. They and their supporters were known as "Roundheads" because they cut their hair very short. It was a term of derision.

The Royalist supporters who wanted reigning King Charles I and all future monarchs to maintain authority over Parliament were called "Cavaliers." I couldn't find out how they wore their hair. I gather, however, that is wasn't trimmed using a bowl! Oliver Cromwell was a leader of the Parliamentarians. For those readers who want to delve more into the intriguing story of Cromwell and the English Civil War, I highly recommend a book by Charles Harding Firth entitled *Oliver Cromwell and the Rule of the Puritans in England*.

Now, where was I? Oh yes, Thomas' motivation for moving from Wethersfield to Fort Saybrook is not entirely clear from the sources I've been able to find. One factor mentioned is an unstable social and political environment in Wethersfield. This could have been a reason but Thomas' move may have had more to do with the fact that Saybrook was sold to the Connecticut Colony in 1644. The sale followed the exodus of the three Connecticut River towns of Hartford, Windsor, and Wethersfield from Massachusetts in 1638-39. I noted earlier that these communities formed an independent commonwealth with a democratic constitution. This was the beginning of Connecticut.

The purchase of Saybrook expanded the Connecticut colony. Moreover, the sale opened up the colony for settlement and provided folks like Thomas with a great opportunity to purchase more land. Thomas and others from Wethersfield jumped at the chance. This included the Wethersfield military leader Major John Mason. For whatever reason Thomas had for moving his family to Saybrook, he is listed among the original 40 grantees of land in the Saybrook town records of 1650. Incidentally, the Wethersfield military leader Lt. Robert Seeley had been appointed commander of Fort Saybrook in 1637. Captain Mason replaced him in in that position in June, 1647.

The Saybrook Colony had a history of confrontations with Indians, especially the Pequot tribe. I mentioned previously that they had attacked Fort Saybrook periodically over a span of eight months in 1637 during the Pequot War. The fort survived the war, but ten years later in the winter of 1647 it burned to the ground. The origin of the fire was unknown, but it doesn't seem to have been the misdeed of the Pequot.

In seeking information on Thomas during his stay at Saybrook, I was informed by an Administrative Assistant at the *Old Saybrook Historical Society* that the fire in 1647 destroyed all records. Fortunately, I had purchased a book while visiting Preston, Connecticut in 2014 written by

Harriet Chapman Chesebrough (1819-1897) and published in 1984 that reported that Thomas and his family were living in the fort when it burned. Chesebrough wrote that *"Lieut Thomas Tracy's family of three little ones"* escaped the fire. Ooookay smart guy, you justly ask, if all records were destroyed in the fire how did Chesebrough, whoever SHE was, know that? Moreover, if the author died in 1897, which she did, why was the book not published until 1984?

Excellent questions *mes amies*! I also wondered as much. Let's take the first question first. Chesebrough herself explained that some fragments of the Saybrook records were re-recorded by the town clerk who went with the others to Norwich. And, she was able to review those reproduced records. Plus Chesebrough had access to family Bibles, Old Wills, and legendary stories, along with various secondary sources. We'll just have to give her the benefit of the doubt that she ran across a reference to Thomas and his children in one of these documents. As to the posthumous publication date, at her death she left a two-volume manuscript that her husband passed along to the *Acton Library Association* and from there made its way into a publication long after his and her deaths.

After escaping the fort fire, Thomas settled on the east side of the Connecticut River opposite Saybrook, now known as Lyme. Putting his carpenter skills to good use he participated in the construction of a *"new dwelling house"* at New Fort Hill. He and Stephen Post were added to the commission to build the house on March 20, 1649. Thomas's surname is spelled *"Traisy"* in the Connecticut Public Records in this one instance. The dwelling was completed in 1652. At about that time the Dutch had second thoughts about the advantage of controlling river traffic on the Connecticut and hostilities with the English interlopers ensued. Thomas and Jonathan Rudd were responsible for putting the cannons into place to ward off potential Dutch attacks on the new fort. To my knowledge, the Dutch never tested the strength or accuracy of the weapons.

Thomas Hooker & James Fitch

In 1646, a year before the fort fire, a stimulating event took place at Fort Saybrook. The renowned minister Thomas Hooker (1586-1647) came to town to make a speech and ordain James Fitch into the Congregational Church. The event was attended by an assembly of local notables in the Great Hall of Fort Saybrook. Thomas is documented as being present at the assembly. Hooker is known as the *"Father of Connecticut"* because of his role in leading the formation of the colony after dissenting with Puritan leaders in Massachusetts. Hooker and his supporters felt that church reform was going too slow. Hooker was also more of a champion of universal Christian suffrage than were his fellow ministers in Massachusetts. He preached that church doors should be open to all, not just the selected "Saints" which prevailed elsewhere in the Colonies.

Hooker's religious and government views were a significant inspiration for the *"Fundamental Orders of Connecticut."* This document grew out of the dissatisfaction of planters in the Massachusetts Bay Colony *"River Town"* settlements along the Connecticut River consisting of Wethersfield, Windsor, and Hartford. The planters in these communities sought self-rule. After a long process of deliberation by a government appointed commission, on January 24, 1639 the *Fundamental Orders* were adopted and Connecticut became a self-ruled entity. Both Hooker and now Major John Mason are credited with being among the writers of the Orders. This is the Connecticut document that is often cited as the world's first democratic constitution because it established a representative government. Hence the Connecticut nickname of *"The Constitution State."* If you ever wondered, as I did, why that motto is on Connecticut license plates, now you know.

Before you and I get carried away by the thought that the newly formed Connecticut's representative government was truly representative, I should point out that in 1679 a state statute required voters to have 50 shillings of assessed property. One shilling was one-twentieth of a pound, so 50 shillings is 2.5 pounds. In 1679 a pound was worth about $209.

Ergo, 50 shillings would have been equivalent to $522 of assessed property. I suspect that amount was sufficient to impose an insurmountable restriction on quite a few potential voters, limiting voting rights to a less than fully represented population. The effort to restrict voting rights to a select few is not a new idea!

While the Fundamental Orders provided for local self-rule, in 1650 a code was compiled by Roger Ludlow resulting in the first codification of Connecticut laws. It began with a bill of rights and outlined the duties and powers of every colony, town, and official. It is called, can you believe, *Ludlow's Code*. Some prefer to not call attention to Ludlow and refer to it as the *Code of 1650*. I find it intriguing that while the *Fundamental Orders* made it possible for Connecticut to have self-rule, the towns in the Colony lost their self-rule because the Orders established a central government. For those of you who would like to explore this paradox in more depth I recommend that you read *The Connecticut Town: Growth and Development, 1635-1790* by Bruce C. Daniels published in 1979.

Interestingly, Thomas Hooker is indirectly tied to Norfolk, England through his close association with John Haynes (1594-1653/4). Haynes was a one-term Governor of the *Massachusetts Bay Company* in 1635 and the first Governor of Connecticut in 1639. He served eight terms in that office. Hooker and Haynes arrived in New England together on the *Griffith* in 1633. Haynes is of particular interest to me because he was a long-time resident of Norfolk, England. Indeed, he was the Lord of the Manor in Hingham, Norfolk, known as the hot-bed of Puritanism. It is located 16 miles southwest of the city of Norwich. Abraham Lincoln's ancestors were from Hingham.

I'm trying hard not to read too much into the association of Thomas with planters who were from Norfolk. However, it is difficult to imagine that he wasn't influenced by their strong stances on religious reform and government self-rule. Thomas was, after all, a close friend and colleague of Major John Mason. Moreover, both Thomas and Mason were members of Rev. Fitch's Congregational Church in Saybrook and Norwich. And, as we shall see, all three men were founders of Norwich. All would have likely been influenced by Hooker and Haynes. All three were civic leaders in Saybrook and Norwich.

Lest I forget, the explanation for dual years such as 1653/4 is because the Pilgrims regarded March 25th as the beginning of the new calendar year. This resulted in posting dates in January, February and March with two years (such as 1653/4). The first year is the year as computed by the Pilgrims. The second year is the year as computed by the modern calendar.

Thomas & the Mohegan Sachem Uncas
During the years Thomas spent in Wethersfield and Saybrook, he became a life-long friend of the Mohegan Indians who sided with the Colonists in their struggles with the Pequot, Narragansett, and other tribes. He had a particularly strong relationship with Uncas, the Mohegan sachem. The Mohegan were Pequot Indians who broke away from the main tribe to form their own tribe following a dispute between Uncas and the Pequot sachem Sassacus. One facet of the dispute was that Uncas favored collaboration with the English. Uncas named his breakaway tribe the Mohegan, meaning *Wolf People*.

Because of similar sounding names, the Mohegan are sometimes confused with the Mohican. I'm sure you are familiar with James Fennimore Cooper's *"The Last of the Mohicans."* Well, you should also read Michael Leroy Oberg's *"Uncas: The First of the Mohegans"* published in 2004. I wouldn't suggest waiting for the movie, although I think it would be great idea. I'd love to work on a script to give me a chance to highlight the role of Thomas in the life of Uncas. I'm thinking Leonardo DiCaprio or Brad Pitt would make a good Thomas.

Much has been written about sachem Uncas and his pivotal role in the settlement of Eastern Connecticut. Most of what I've read is complementary. The occasional criticism of him appears to be lumped together with general censure of the conduct of Indians of the time. To get a good sense of his pedigree, character, and activities, link to *www.nativeamericamohegans. com.* Another excellent historical perspective on Uncas is a 1904 book edited by Forrest Morgan entitled *"Connecticut as a Colony and as a State, or One of the Original Thirteen."*

I recently came across an online monograph written by Arthur L. Peale in 1930 entitled *"Memorials and Pilgrimages in the Mohegan Country."* Peale, a Norwich, Connecticut Scoutmaster, notes that on July 4, 1842 the citizens of Norwich expressed their gratitude to Uncas with a granite obelisk on his grave at the Royal Burying Grounds of the Mohegans. The author also mentions the Memorial to Major James Mason and the Founders of Norwich, Connecticut. The cornerstone to the monument was laid in 1859 during the 200th celebration of the founding of the town. It took until 1871 before the granite memorial was erected with the names of all the founders, including Thomas and his son, John.

The Peale monograph includes the following poetic tribute to the Mohegan tribe and to the city of Norwich by A. G. Chester whose full name is Anson Gleason Chester. Chester often corresponded with Edgar Allen Poe.

The City of the Kings

Where the red Mohegan's wigwam stood beneath the friendly shade,
Where, with tomahawk and arrow, through the wilderness, he strayed,
Where he skimmed the sparkling river, where his dusky children grew,
'Mid the music of the robin, and the incense of the dew,
Where he smoked the fragrant calumet and lit the council fires,
Standeth now the crowded city, with its many roofs and spires.

The Siege of Fort Shantok

The friendship between Uncas and Thomas was cemented during a famous incident in the spring of 1645 when Thomas was living in Saybrook.

Uncas and members of his Mohegan band were under siege by Pessachus, sachem of the Narragansett. The siege took place at Fort Shantok on the Pequot (now the Thames) River near present day Montville, Connecticut. The Mohegan had a nearly impregnable fort at that location. Catching wind that Uncas was in the fort, the Narragansett surrounded it. The intent was to starve out the Mohegan and force them into surrendering so they could get their hands and hatchets on Uncas.

A Mohegan warrior managed to escape through enemy lines to seek help from the settlers at Fort Saybrook under the command of Lt. Robert Seeley. Lieutenant Seeley must have had considerable confidence in soldiers named Thomas because he responded to the plea for help by sending Thomas Leffingwell, Thomas Tracy, and Thomas Minor to paddle up the Thames River with provisions for the beleaguered Mohegan. The three amigos had to sneak past the hostile Narragansett surrounding the Mohegan. After receiving the provisions, the Mohegan let their enemy know that they could not be starved out by displaying a large piece of beef on a pole. Upon seeing that the Mohegan had supplies, as well as evidence of the presence of the English, the Narragansett departed and the siege was lifted.

There are numerous variations of the telling of this episode, so be advised that I've chosen the version I like the best! Even the histories that list Thomas as one of the two or three men who rescued Uncas tend to list Thomas Leffingwell as the leader. There are a number of such histories. I'm relying on the expertise of two prominent researchers who participated in a Harvard University project on *American Indian Economic Development* in 2004. The authors, Kimberly G. Burgess, Ph.D. and Katherine A. Spilde, Ph.D. mention the three Thomas' noted above as coming to the Mohegan's aid.

The posting of the event on *Wikipedia* lists Thomas Tracy and Thomas Leffingwell as the two heroes. A third testimony is given in an 1851 *History of the Indians of Connecticut* by John W. De Forest commissioned by the Connecticut Historical Society. De Forest notes that "*it is probable, although not certain*" that Tracy and Miner (sic) accompanied Leffingwell. An article written 1902 by Edward Livingston Taylor in the scholarly publication *Ohio History Journal* adds Thomas Minor as a participant. Minor later was a founder of New London and Stonington, Connecticut.

Before writing this narrative, I hadn't given any thought as to why the Narragansett were so dead set to see the Mohegan dead. It turns out that there was a history of bad blood between the tribes, especially between Uncas and sachem Miantonomoh of the Narragansett. Uncas had bested Miantonomoh in a battle in 1643 taking him prisoner and, after gaining permission from the English, the Mohegan executed Miantonomoh. Uncas didn't do the deed, but apparently he ordered one of his brothers to do it. The Narragansett blamed Uncas and swore revenge and for years unsuccessfully tried all manner of devilish tactics to kill Uncas. He lived to be about 85 dying of natural causes in 1682 or 1683. Fort Shantok is now a Connecticut State Park.

New England Confederation
Once again in the course of preparing this narrative, I ran across information that would not have occurred to me to examine beforehand. I'm referring to an event in May of 1643 when four of the colonies came together to draft *the Articles of Confederation of the United Colonies of New England.* This led to the formation of a confederation appropriately named the *United Colonies of New England.* It is also known as the *New England Confederation.* A major purpose of the confederation was to join forces militarily to protect the colonies from attacks by French, Indians, and the Dutch. It was also established to help resolve disputes among the colonies related to trade, boundaries, and religion. It was established in Boston by delegates from Massachusetts, Connecticut, New Haven, and Plymouth. Rhode Island was excluded from participating because of its "heretical" views. I found the Confederation to be of interest because of its role in laying the foundation for our current form of government. It is also fascinating to me because it gives me a framework to help understand the historical context of Thomas' life.

At the time of the creation of the Confederation, the Saybrook Colony was not part of Connecticut. So, it did not participate as a Colony in its establishment. However, the General Court of Connecticut made sure Saybrook was represented. Two of the delegates from Connecticut chosen to attend the first meeting of commissioners in September, 1643 were from Saybrook. This included George Fenwick, Governor of the Saybrook Colony. Soon after the Confederation was established, Saybrook ended its autonomous status when Governor Fenwick agreed to sell it to the Connecticut Colony. That action in 1644 takes us back to the migration of folks from Wethersfield to Saybrook looking for new opportunities in an expanded Connecticut Colony, including Thomas and family.

Despite the ambitions of the New England Confederation its authority was weakened due to a lack of mechanisms for enforcing decisions made by the commissioners. Massachusetts, the strongest member, often ignored them all together. The Confederation's influence declined further when a merger between New Haven and Connecticut in 1662-65 made them strong enough to also pick and choose which Confederation dictums they would follow. The power of the Confederation was temporally revived in 1675-78 in response to King Philip's War. It was formally dissolved in 1684. While the confederation did not last, it left a legacy that was to have a significant impact on future generations of Americans as the *Articles of Confederation* were the first effort to form a union with a representative centralized government structure for mutual defense and benefits.

Thomas in Saybrook Colony, Connecticut
Politics, war, and economic struggles aside, life in small settlements like Saybrook, while difficult, was ostensibly not quite as somber and bleak as is often made out in movies and TV shows. I'm referring to film like *The Scarlet Letter* and *The Crucible*. Community festivities, games, and celebrations were common in the colonies. Clothing was more colorful than the black and drab colors often portrayed in the media. A Massachusetts minister commented in 1896 on life in Saybrook in the 1600s noting that there were decorative gardens for pleasure, as well as for raising vegetables

and *"a goodly store"* of apple and cherry trees. The same minister listed the Tracy name as being on his roll of *"unpretentious but wholly honorable"* names.

It hasn't been particularly difficult to find material on Thomas. Unlike having to dig deep to find information on Stephen, material on Thomas is readily obtainable. In fact, I've been amazed at how much there is in print about the fellow. A primary reason for this is Thomas' involvement in highly visible historic events in Connecticut. He was active in many military, civic, judicial, and government initiatives. In Saybrook, for example, he was one of five men selected by the Saybrook commissioners to settle a dispute involving the distribution of land outside the town into quarter sections. This occurred on January 4, 1648. On that day it was recorded that there were 48 proprietors living in Fort Saybrook and Lyme.

On the same day Thomas and four other men were *"ordered and empowered"* by the town to take a survey of the *"Out Lands"* of Lyme. The intent was to divide them into several quarters to provide people with a more *"comfortable subsistence."* Once divided into quarters, Thomas and 19 others contributed a total of £2,800 ($466,000 in 2016) to take possession of the land to dispose of as they saw fit. The land was used for corn, pasture, stone, timber and *"the like."* Thomas also paid £150 ($25,000 in 2016) for land in the Oyster River Quarter where he built a home. The Oyster River Quarter is now the village of Westbrook. It is *"a quaint shoreline community nestled on the banks of Long Island Sound between New Haven and New London."*

This was the first of many recorded land surveys over the years in which Thomas participated in several towns to lay out land or settle boundary disputes. Some 16 years later in September, 1684 Thomas and Matthew Griswold were asked by the town of Saybrook to come back from Norwich to resolve a land dispute. This related to a disagreement concerning the original dividing line between the Potapaug Quarter and the town boundary that had been marked over a decade and half before. They were given full authority to make the final decision. By that time both Thomas and Matthew Griswold had long been residents of Norwich.

It demonstrates how highly respected Thomas was as a surveyor and a person who would make an impartial, fair ruling.

Among the many mentions of Thomas in Saybrook, there is a record of him, Francis Bushnell, and Stephen Post being approved as property appraisers for William Waller and John Clark, Jr. in May, 1653. He is also recorded as being present at a town meeting in Saybrook on January 7, 1655. There is a record of him being a witness to a deed recorded in the Saybrook Land Records between John Clarke of Saybrook and Thomas Birchard of Martha's Vineyard on November 1, 1656. To me, this last event is more significant than it appears at first glance. It suggests that activities involving people who lived far apart was not as much of an impediment to social and commercial interaction as one might think.

Beware, dear reader. I'm deviously planting the kernel of an idea that the geographical distance between Thomas in Saybrook and Stephen in Duxbury would not have prevented them from knowing of each other's presence in the colonies. If Thomas knew a person from Martha's Vineyard 160 miles from Saybrook, there is no reason he could not have known of another Tracy from Duxbury, 130 miles distant.

Thomas and his first wife, whose name has been lost to history, had seven children. The first two were born in Wethersfield. They were John, born in 1642, and Thomas, Jr., born in 1644. Their other five children were born in Saybrook. They were Jonathan, Miriam, Solomon, Samuel, and Daniel. Their births were 1646, 1647, 1650, 1652, and 1654, respectively. Jonathan is my 6th Great Grandfather. It is not known when or where Thomas' wife died, but it appears to have been in Saybrook after the birth of Daniel. At least one source has her death as February 20, 1659. This date comes from the Family Data Collections, which, as I mentioned at the beginning is a dubious source but it may close to the correct year.

For all we know, his wife could have gone with her family to Norwich. She could have remained a housewife with no reason to have been recorded in town records. Chesebrough says that she was buried in *The Ancient Cemetery* at Saybrook Point. If so, she probably died before the move to Norwich. Regrettably, Chesebrough didn't provide a source. But, recall that she did have access to numerous primary records. Diane Hoyt, Administrative Assistant of the *Old Saybrook Historical Society*, informed me that a construction project led to moving the burials in *The Ancient Cemetery* to the *Cypress Cemetery* in about 1870. I checked with the Cypress Cemetery Trustee, J. H. Torrance Downes, to see if there is any record of a Tracy. He told me that early burials were in unmarked graves until 1685 and that there isn't any record of any Tracy in *Cypress Cemetery*.

Now, let's explore some of the historic and religious circumstances during the time of the purchase of land from the Mohegan which led to the establishment of the settlement of Norwich in 1659. This will set the stage for a discussion of the roles Thomas and his son, John, played in making a successful venture of the purchase of land from the Mohegan known as the "Nine-Mile Square" land grant.

10

THOMAS – A FOUNDER OF NORWICH

Around 1658 or 1659, a group of men from Saybrook joined together to submit a patent to the Connecticut General Court to purchase land from sachem Uncas and the Mohegan Tribe. Uncas apparently needed funds to fuel his fight with the Narragansett. The land, twenty-eight miles to the northeast, was seen as very desirable property that was ideal for a new planation. It is very probable that the initiative originated with Major John Mason. Major Mason is described as being *"stern, self-reliant, honorable, and honored."* His character might well be questioned based on his rationale for the Mystic Massacre, but his strong leadership skills were ostensibly deemed suitable to an unstable environment. His hostility toward Indians was discerning as he had a friendly relationship with Uncas and the Mohegan which enabled him to strike a deal to buy land from them.

Historians also credit Reverend John Fitch as playing an instrumental role in negotiating the purchase. Fitch is described as *"learned, zealous, beloved by Englishmen and Indians."* Of course, Mason and Fitch weren't the only ones with an inside track with the Mohegan. As we know, both Thomas Leffingwell and Thomas Tracy had a strong association with Uncas and the Mohegan Tribe.

Major Mason described the coveted Mohegan land as *"brooks and mountains well-watered and fertile."* At a bi-centennial celebration of the founding of Norwich one speaker gave the following flowery description of the land: *"__ this beautiful Mohegan plain; they had climbed Wawequo's hill; had traced the Shetucket and the Yantic, form their confluence in the Pequot, far into the back country; had admired the waterfalls, never so wild and picturesque as then; had estimated their power for grist-mills and saw-mills, had examined the forests, fisheries and soil; and were ready to return to the other side of the Connecticut ___."*

My wife and I drove through Norwich several years ago. It is a very pretty city with broad beautiful rivers. Major Mason's reference to brooks is very much an understatement. In fact, three rivers flow into the city's harbor: the Yantic, the Shetucket, and the Quinebaug. The Thames flows south from their confluence to Long Island. These rivers must have been a big part of the attraction given their beauty and bounty. Even 200 years later, one writer observed that the rivers in Norwich were widely known for their lavish abundance of fish. There were large quantities of shad, alewives, bass, mackerel, eels, oyster, lobsters and even sturgeon. As late as 1729, there were reports of catching 20,000 bass within a few days. Who would pass up an opportunity to own that!? I understand that the three rivers are now annually stocked with fish.

Norwich's Shetucket River is described in one book as running from the mouth to the crotch of the Quinebaug. That's a phrase I was unfamiliar with. It seems that the crotch is a bend in the river. There is actually a contemporary site in Windham County, Connecticut known as *"Crotch of the River."* I don't know if it has any special qualities other than being a bend which one can, presumably, go. It won't be at the top of my buckets list of places to visit. I can go around the bend at home, thank you very much.

The sale of the land was negotiated with Uncas and his sons Owaneco and Attawanhood. Owaneco succeeded his father as sachem when Uncas died in 1683. Attawanhood was also known as Joshua Uncas. An agreement was reached between the Mohegan tribe and 35 Colonists. Shortly, I'll explain the importance of the fact that 33 of the 35 purchasers were from Saybrook Colony. Significantly, two of them were from Plymouth Colony. An application was filed with the Connecticut General Court on May 20, 1659 for a land patent (grant) to purchase Mohegan. The sale was completed on June 6, 1659. The land consisted of nine-square miles and sold for seventy pounds ($12,800 in 2016). Not surprisingly it is known in history books as the *"Nine-Mile Square"* or the *"9-Mile Square"* land purchase.

The new plantation site was surveyed in the fall of 1659. I haven't any proof, but it seems highly feasible that Thomas, who was called upon multiple times for his skills as a surveyor, was involved in the original survey of Mohegan. The village green was laid out, house lots assigned, and a few homes constructed. The following spring owners brought their cattle and goods from Saybrook. According to the *Vital Records of Norwich 1659-1848*, the plantation was known as Mohegan until 1662, although the first reference to Norwich appears to have been in a General Court Record in March, 1661 regarding property taxes. The name is believed to have been taken from the ancestral English home of one of the prominent settlers, William Backus, Sr., who is my 7th Great Grandfather through another line. Over the years several other towns emerged on the land. Once known as the *"City of the Kings,"* the modern town of Norwich is known as *"The Rose of New England."*

By the by, it isn't unusual for anyone who had ancestors living in New England in the early to mid-1600s to have multiple relatives from innumerable family lines, along with thousands of distant cousins. The small population and relatively (no pun intended) close proximity to each other meant that intermarriage between family friends was quite common. While not polygamists, most men had serial marriages with two, three, and more wives over their lifetime. This was often due to short lifespans of women, relative to those of men, who bore way too many children under unsafe conditions. Although, many men also died off before reaching old age from illnesses, diseases, accidents, and the occasional Indian arrow or musket ball.

Both widows and widowers were expected to remarry to keep families intact and to maintain the stability of the community. In fact, it was illegal for men or women to live alone unless there was a very compelling reason. This *"twisting of family cords"* as it was known, could not easily be broken and one's neighbor was most often a relative. Hence, I, like many others, have more than a few grandparents from the period who are closely related. It was probably a good thing that the Great Migration brought in fresh blood and different DNA!

The group of 35 purchasers whose names are listed on the *Society of Founders of Norwich* website includes 49-year old Thomas and his 17-year old son, John. At least eight of the founders were born in Norfolk, Suffolk, and Essex, England. Thomas' good friend, Lt. Thomas Leffingwell, hails from the village of White Coine in Essex near the southern border of Norfolk County. The 35 proprietors were identified as *"wheelwrights, and millers, and merchants, and surveyors, and shoemakers, and brewers, and tanners, and cutlers, and stone-cutters, and carpenters, and farmers."*

I should mention that Thomas Leffingwell is well remembered in Norwich. The *Leffingwell House Museum* in that historic city is named after him. The museum was originally built as a two-room house in 1675 by Stephen Backus. Stephen is my 6th Great Grandfather. The house later belonged to Thomas Leffingwell who obtained permission to run it as an Inn in 1701. I'm not sure how long it was in the family, but I do know it was managed by Christopher Leffingwell during the Revolutionary War. The museum website says that he was *"invaluable as supplier of provisions for the Revolutionary forces."* Check it out online at: *http://www.leffingwellhousemuseum.org/history/*. The museum is owned and operated by *The Society of the Founders of Norwich*.

Thomas Leffingwell and Thomas Tracy were very close associates, participating together in numerous community activities and missions. Their association extended long after they had departed. A book written in 1897 by two of Thomas Leffingwell's descendants, Albert Leffingwell, M.D. and Charles Wesley Leffingwell, D.D., make this very clear. Its title is *The Leffingwell Record: A Genealogy of the Descendants of Lieut. Thomas Leffingwell, One of the Founders of Norwich,* Conn. In the book there are 174 references to various members of the Tracy family. One chart shows that four grandchildren of Lt. Thomas Tracy married four grandchildren of Lt. Thomas Leffingwell in the early 1770s. A daughter and son of Solomon Tracy, a son of John Tracy, and a son of Daniel Tracy all married children of Thomas Leffingwell, Jr.

As for the deed between the Mohegan and the 35 proprietors, it is worth citing in its entirety. For one reason it is interesting in its own right. An even better reason is because it highlights the role of Thomas. There were only two witnesses to the deed and they are Major John Mason and Thomas Tracy. I think that this speaks volumes as to Thomas' status in the Saybrook settlement, as well as his relationship with Uncas and the Mohegan. Here is the deed of June 6, 1659 in full.

> *"Know all men that Onkos, Owaneco, Attawanhood, Sachems of Mohegan have Bargained, sold, and passed over, and doe by these presents sell and pass over unto the town and Inhabitants of Norwich nine miles square of land lying and being at Mohegan and the parts thereunto adjoining, with all ponds, rivers. woods, quarries, mines, with all royalties, privileges, and appurtenances thereunto belonging, to them the said inhabitants of Norwich, their heirs and successors forever--from thence the line run north north east nine miles, and on the East side the aforesaid river to the southward the line is to join with New London bounds as it is now laid out and to run east two miles from the aforesaid river, northwest nine miles to meet with the western line.*

In consideration where of the Onkos, Owaneco and Attawanhood do acknowledge to have received of the parties aforesaid the full and just sum of seventy pounds and doe promise and engage ourselves, heirs and successors, to warrant the said bargain and sale to the aforesaid parties, their heirs and successors, and them to defend from all claims and molestations from any whatsoever.

In witness whereof we have hereunto set out to our hands this 6th of June, Anno 1659.

Onkos, Owaneco, Attawanhood

Witness hereunto, John Mason, Thomas Tracy"

Each Mohegan signed with an Indian version of an early emoji. Uncas signed by drawing Arms and a Heart. Owaneco sketched a Turkey and Attawanhood depicted a Rabbit. They were not great art, but still legally binding. Unfortunately, the deed doesn't show Thomas' signature.

Interestingly, a *"partly mutilated"* copy of this deed is housed in the British Museum in London under *"A collection of deeds and other exhibits in the case of the Mohegan Indians."* Another deed between Uncas and his son, Owaneco, giving land to Thomas Tracy and Thomas Leffingwell is also housed in the museum. The museum wasn't established until 1753, so one wonders how they came by these documents.

While the Mohegan/Norwich government administration was well-planned and well-organized, for many years the community had no merchants and no shops. The town plotting did not follow Winthrop's *"wheel and spoke"* design. There was not even a central area other than the "commons." Houses were scattered hither and thither. For food and goods people were primarily reliant on what they could raise themselves with the occasional buying or trading spree upriver in Hartford or downriver in New London. Another interesting feature of the settlement is that the

Indians were not immediately chased off the land they had previously owned. In fact, wigwams were initially randomly located all over the place. The attempt of integrating Indian and English cultures did not last as apparently the life styles were too far apart to be compatible. Eventually, the Indians were invited to leave and actually forced to relocate elsewhere.

The original planters in Norwich were a tight knit and exclusive group. For example, voting in the community was restricted to the 35 men who participated in the purchase and their lawful heirs. One also had to be a member of Rev. Fitch's church to be in good standing and eligible to vote. We tend to think that our early ancestors cherished their personal liberty above all else, but in this instance, perceived community needs prevailed. One example of this was that individuals had to obtain permission from the Townsmen (elected from the group of 35 and their heirs) before property could be bought or sold. The tight control of the local government must have been viewed as being a bit over the top by people who came from outside to settle in Norwich, at least for the first few years. Transients who wandered into the community were unwelcomed and were hastily hustled out.

The land included in the *nine-mile square* is now home to several towns. Besides Norwich there are the communities of Bozrah, Sprague, and Lisbon. The original purchase also included a nine-mile long strip of land east of the Quinebaug, Shetucket, and Thames Rivers called the "*Long Society*." This area became the present location of the towns of Preston and Griswold. Thomas's sons, Thomas, Jr. and Jonathan, played instrumental roles in the establishment and development of Preston. The Tracy family continued to have a large presence in Preston for centuries. This is confirmed in two books published by the Preston Historical Society. One titled *Early Homes and Families* published in 1998 lists the homes of 16 Tracy families. Another is *Preston in Review* published in 1971. It covered Tracy families in the early years of the settlement. I obtained copies of these little gems from the Preston Town Hall when my wife and I visited there in 2008.

Reverend James Fitch of Saybrook & Norwich

I hadn't planned on doing any research on the good Reverend James Fitch, but his name kept reappearing over and over again as I read about Saybrook and Norwich. He is important to the story of Thomas because he was one of the original 35 proprietors of Norwich and because he was Thomas' minister in both Saybrook and Norwich. As mentioned, most of the proprietors of the *"Nine-mile square"* from Saybrook were members of his church, the First Church of Christ (Congregational). Fitch continued on as the minister and spiritual leader in Norwich for many years. It was a difficult time to be a minister as statements from religious leaders of the time point to the period of 1660 to 1740 as years of spiritual decline in New England. The primary culprits, according to some sages, were the *Cambridge Platform* and *"half-way covenant."* Both of these divisive tenets were endorsed by the Rev. Fitch and his flock in the Norwich Church. Thomas, as a long-time member of this church, no doubt held similar views.

I learned that *The Cambridge Platform* was a doctrinal statement for Congregational Churches that was adopted in August, 1648 by a majority of ministers in Connecticut and Massachusetts. It upheld the local church governance practiced by the Puritans and Pilgrims that made the congregation the focal point of authority, rather than the Colonial government. This means that there was a clear separation between church and state. I find this to be of particular interest in as much as it seems to be a harbinger of the Constitution written 141 years later in 1789. The doctrine was opposed to central authority outside the settlement and supported local government, church authority, and community compliance. Local civic leaders were expected to intervene when someone was found guilty of blasphemy, idolatry, heresy, profanity, or contempt for what was said in the pulpit.

From my readings, I gather that the Connecticut Government and Governor weren't all that keen on this policy and they made their displeasure known to those who thought otherwise. There were strong sentiments among government leaders for more centralized authority which was typical of the teachings of the Presbyterian Church and John Calvin. Bear in mind, this was long before the concept of the separation of church and state was law. As a result, for government officials and many church leaders, centralized authority meant that the state – which was the church – held sway. One can see why the Cambridge Platform was viewed by many with trepidation.

If it is not already painfully obvious, theology is not my strong suit, so take this discussion with a grain of salt. Nevertheless, I'll continue on undaunted as though I actually know what I'm talking about. This is not because I intentionally want to mislead you. Rather, my goal is to give you some idea of the complexity I found doing the research on the emergence of the competition between church and state and how it helped to define Thomas and his generation of *Connecticut Nutmeggers*.

Parenthetically, a *Nutmegger* is a nickname for people from Connecticut. Its origin is not known, but is believed to have something to do with Yankees peddlers selling nutmeg in colonial times. Why the enchantment with nutmeg? The early settlers in New England believed it to have properties that warmed you up and held off head colds and stomach aches. Nutmeg was so important that with the *Treaty of Breda* in 1667 the Dutch traded Manhattan to the British for its last nutmeg producing island, Run Island in the East Indies, as well as for land in South America that produced sugar.

Aside from the surprising prominence of nutmeg, the point I'm trying to make is that the Rev. Fitch defied the central authorities on the issue of state and church authority. He proclaimed that his church would bow to no ecclesiastical authority but God and the congregation's own judgement. Fitch and his congregation supported the concept of a *"free church."* Free didn't mean free as you and I might understand it. It meant that the local church was autonomous in forming a local covenant with their congregation. It also meant that the local church had the authority to define who could be a member, how members were allowed to act at home and in public, and how they were to relate to one another.

It was not an inclusive approach in which people were "free" to worship as they wished or where they wished. I must admit that the stance of Rev. Fitch is somewhat perplexing to me. Especially given that he was ordained by Thomas Hooker who was known for his support of inclusivity through the doctrine of the Universal Christian Church. Moreover, the Connecticut Colony distinguished itself from the Plymouth Colony on its preference for inclusivity over exclusivity. I'll leave that conundrum for you to figure out at your leisure.

Apparently, by 1662, the position of the Norwich First Congregational Church on the level of local authority had gained some traction. This led to an initiative referred to as the *Half-Way Covenant*. Taking my information from *Wikipedia*, this was an attempt to counter the perceived drift away from the original religious purpose of the settlements. As the first-generation settlers began to die out, the second generation was more inclined to have less religious piety and a desire for more material things. Well, that's a shock! In addition, many in the second generation were being admitted to churches without demonstrating that they had had a conversion experience. They were not recognized "Saints." The half-way covenant provided a partial church membership for children and grandchildren of church members with a number of conditions related to voting and baptism. Suffice it say that not all Puritans agreed with this approach and that its divisiveness was a factor for years.

Thomas' Move To and Life in Mohegan/Norwich
As mentioned, Thomas' first wife might have died at some time before the petition was made to purchase Mohegan. Early on in my research I thought that her death might have been a motivation for Thomas to move from Saybrook to Norwich, but I'm now convinced that he would have gone to Norwich regardless. I think his loyalty to James Fitch, Major Mason, the church, the many friends he had who went to Norwich, and

the opportunity for more and better land, would have motivated him to leave Saybrook.

Before he moved to Norwich, on November 1, 1660 Thomas sold *"several parcels of lands"* in the Oyster River Quarter to one of Saybrook's founders. The buyer was Captain Robert Chapman. The sale included Thomas' *"house, orchard and land adjoining thereunto, of forty acres more or less."* It also included a meadow of 24 acres, another meadow of two and a half acres at Pouchaug, five acres of upland valued at £150 ($28,000 in 2016), and title and claim to lands at Hammonasset valued at £160 ($30,000 in 2016). Thomas took this sizable bounty and headed off for Norwich with his six sons and one daughter. Thomas was about 50 years old.

Some of the properties he sold are a little confusing. A search for the location of Pouchaug, Connecticut, for example, shows that the small town of Pauchaug is located nearly 40 miles northeast of Saybrook and 10 miles in the same direction from Norwich. Pouchaug apparently is a different area near the Oyster River Quarter. The only reference to Hammonasset is Hammonasset Beach located about 16 miles southwest of Saybrook. The man had accumulated a lot of property or as they would say hereabouts, it was a "right smart" amount of land!

The group of families left Saybrook in the spring of 1660 in shallops sailing along the Long Island Sound to the mouth of the Thames River at New London. They stayed overnight at New London. They sailed the next day up the Thames passing *"the chair of Uncas"* at Fort Shattuck where the great sachem sat during the Narragansett siege 15 years earlier. At that point (Shattuck Point) a group of Mohegans, in their birch canoes with Uncas at the lead, joined the planter platoon and accompanied them to the confluence of the Shetucket and Yantic Rivers, disembarking near the falls.

With the lucrative sale of his Saybrook and surrounding property, Thomas' could clearly afford to build a nice house in his new digs. His original home in Norwich was built on a lot consisting of nine acres with 34 rods on the south side of Town Street (now East Town Street). A rod is 16.5 feet. That would make his front yard 561 feet or 187 yards. That's an expansive front yard! His property extended from the six-acres owned by Christopher Huntington to Thomas' East to Simon Huntington's property on the west.

There was a brook running between Thomas and Christopher's property. Based on Google maps, I'm guessing that the brook may have been the Bobbin Mill Brook. Opposite Thomas' property were four-acres owned by John Bradford, son of Plymouth Colony Governor William Bradford. I believe that this property boarded East Town Street which is now the northern border of the Norwichtown Historic District. Later, Thomas' son, Solomon, built a second home on the same lot. Thomas' son John had 12 acres in Mohegan, one of the largest lots. A 1795 map of Norwich shows the location of the homes and businesses of several of Thomas's descendants.

On the same map, the homes of Daniel, Samuel, and Dr. Philemon Tracy are shown. Also displayed is the property of Mundator Tracy (known as *"an accomplished young gentleman"*) who owned two homes. The map also locates the *Tracy & Coit Store* and a house owned by, who else, Tracy and Coit. And a blacksmith shop owned by Samuel Avery & his son-in-law Major Thomas Tracy (1769-1828) which they purchased in 1791. I'm grateful to Louise Leake, Genealogist, *The Society of Founders of Norwich*, for the map.

Upon finding the list of Tracy property owners, I naturally wanted to know more about the store and blacksmith shop. For that I turned to Mary E. Perkins' 1895 publication: *Old House of the Antient Town of Norwich, 1660-1800: With Maps, Illustrations, Portraits and Genealogies*. Before you question the accuracy of my spell check software, *"antient"* is an obsolete English word for ancient. Perkins provides incredible details on the location of Thomas' property and more about the Tracy family in Norwich. She mentions Thomas 28 times and refers to all Tracys 267 times. The *Tracy & Coit Store* was a general store, carrying most everything. It was started in 1790 by Uriah Tracy (1753-1832) and Joseph Coit. Uriah, Great Great Grandson of Thomas, is also notable because in 1790 he purchased the house of Norwich's native son and hero gone rogue, Benedict Arnold. Uriah lived in that house the remainder of his life.

I find it interesting that Thomas' neighbors, Simon and Christopher Huntington, were natives of Norwich, Norfolk, England. Is it another coincidence that two of Thomas' neighbors were from what I'm assuming was his home county of Norfolk? It doesn't escape my attention that another neighbor in Norwich, John Bradford, had grown up as a neighbor of the Stephen Tracy family in Duxbury. Nor that after John Bradford died his widow, Martha Bourne Bradford, married Thomas Tracy! I'll come back to the ramifications of these relationships.

Two years after he died, in 1687, Thomas' lot in Norwich was sold to Israel Lathrop. In 1688, Thomas's son Daniel bought a third of the original lot from Lathrop and sold part of that to his brother Solomon in 1692.

Division of Commons
The first division of the common lands in the nine-square mile took place in April, 1661. Included in Thomas' portion was the "*Indian Graves*" wherein lay many Mohegan ancestors. Sachem Uncas was laid to rest in that graveyard on his death in 1682 or 1683. Giving the grave site to an Englishman, even one as well respected by the Mohegan as Thomas, was an abomination in the view of the tribe. The planters agreed with the tribe. The gravesite was returned to the Mohegan. Thomas was compensated by the town with eight acres of pasture land. He was also allowed to retain part of the original allotment, namely; "*Six and one half acres of upland more or less, in the little plaine (sic) by the Indian Graves, abutting Indian land....*" At the death of Thomas this property was given to his son Dr. Solomon Tracy. When he died in 1693, it became the property of Thomas' youngest son Daniel who kept it until his death in 1671.

Fast forward to an article published in *The New York Times* of March 8, 1998 "*Norwich Plan Yields to Burial Ground.*" The article provides the skinny on a Norwich city proposal to build a multi-million dollar communications and technology center on the site that included the remnants of the Indian grave site. By then, most of the grave site was the location of a large Masonic Lodge. Protests from the Mohegan convinced city officials to back off on desecrating the remaining paltry 1/16th of an acre left as a graveyard. Although the Mohegan had no legal basis to prevent the construction, the city officials acknowledged that the tribe had a moral claim on the sacred grounds. But, the fight did not end there.

It took until 2006 for the Mohegan Tribe to fully reclaim some of the original acreage with a 3.4 acre site. The tribe was able to restore *The Royal Mohegan Burial Ground* where possibly thousands of Mohegans are buried dating back to the 1600s. An article in *The Washington Post* of June 22, 2007 entitled "*Mohegans Restore Ancient Burial Ground*" related the story of how the Mohegan bought and demolished the Masonic Lodge and conveyed the burial ground into a park-like setting.

Wouldn't Thomas be pleased as punch to know that his giving up the sacred land in 1661 withstood the onslaught of modernization and people who for 415 years had little or no respect for the hallowed land of Indian ancestors? I like to think he would! Currently there are about 2,000 members of the Mohegan tribe. There is a 700 acre Mohegan Reservation located on the Thames River at Uncasville, Connecticut. I recently met a woman from the Norwich area and mentioned my connection to Thomas and his relationship to the Mohegan. She immediately said "*oh yes, the Mohegan Sun Casino!*" The casino alone takes up 240 acres of the Reservation. So much for historical appreciation of the Tribe's part in the creation of Norwich!

Thomas Tracy, Jr. & Jonathan Tracy
I knew that Thomas and his son, John, had done well in acquiring land in Norwich, but I was interested in knowing about what his other sons had managed to attain. Both Thomas Tracy, Jr. and my direct ancestor, his

brother Jonathan Tracy, were founders of nearby Preston, Connecticut. Jonathan was the first Town Clerk of Preston. At that time a Town Clerk was known as the *"Keeper of the Ordinary"* or *"Ordinary Keeper."* Doesn't either of those titles sound so much more gratifying than Town Clerk? I mean, wouldn't you rather be someone who "Keeps the Ordinary" in a community than a mere clerk? No offense to all you clerks out there who do great work.

I had a fairly good idea of the land holdings and success of Thomas, Sr., John, and Jonathan. I wondered, though, how well the other sons had fared. On this, I'm afraid, I haven't had much luck. I was able, though, to learn a little more about property that was owned by Thomas Tracy, Jr. I found a story that relates that Junior owned a farm not very far from land owned by Owaneco, son of Uncas. Both Owaneco's and Junior's lands were located east of the Shetucket River.

Apparently the properties were a tad too close. On May 10, 1679, despite the long and friendly relationship between the families, Thomas, Jr. took Uncas and Owaneco to court charging that members of their tribe had killed Junior's swine when they were caught eating corn in Owaneco's field. I gather the issue was not that the swine were in the wrong, but that they had been killed rather than corralled and returned to Thomas, Jr. As a consequence, Junior was considered to have been *"damnified"* which seems to mean abused or offended. So, Uncas and Owaneco were ordered to give Junior satisfaction by handing over 100 acres of land. Guess who was appointed to lay out the 100 acres for Junior? You have it, Lt. Thomas Tracy and Lt. Thomas Leffingwell. I have to wonder if this had any impact on Thomas' relationship with Uncas and Owaneco.

Thomas was continually expanding his property ownership. In 1667 Thomas Tracy and Thomas Leffingwell petitioned the General Court to approve the purchase of an additional 400 acres of land that lay east of the Shetucket River outside the boundaries of Norwich. Again, it was land that belonged to Uncas. Uncas apparently agreed to the sale with the

Court's approval. It has been inferred that since both Thomas and Thomas Leffingwell made the request of Uncas, the sale might have been another way for Uncas to repay them both for bringing food to Uncas during the siege by the Narragansett in 1645. Caulkins cautioned that this may not be true as both Thomas Tracy and Thomas Leffingwell were very involved in public affairs that may account as compensation for other services. The General Court approved the land grant petition and instructed Thomas and Thomas to divide the land equally between them.

One other record I found provides good evidence of Thomas' special relationship with Uncas. I'm referring to Uncas' will of February 29, 1675. In the will Uncas bequeathed Thomas 5,000 acres of land appraised at 560 pounds ($103,800 in 2016 currency). That's no meagre gift. Only one year later in 1676 Thomas was one of 16 beneficiaries in Norwich of a large tract of land bequeathed by Joshua Uncas, son of sachem Uncas. The land was Joshua's hunting grounds. Today a small part of the land is in the capable hands of the non-profit *Joshua's Tract Conservation and Historic Trust*. It is a 4,000 acre preserve in Mansfield, Connecticut providing the public with trails, as well as education, training, and scientific study of nature. Well played!

Thomas's 2nd & 3rd Wives

As noted earlier, there was legal and social pressure for widowers and widows to remarry as soon as possible after the death of a spouse. Since the rules were made by men, this was especially true for widows. Although it isn't known for sure when Thomas became a widower, it is known that it was before 1680 because that is the date of his marriage to his second wife. He was age 70. This marriage was to Martha Bourne Bradford, the "relic" (widow) of John Bradford. She had been a widow for four years. I'm guesstimating that because she was age 62 there was less pressure for her to remarry. I'm also conjecturing that the General Court gave her some slack about having to remarry soon after her husband died as she was past childbearing age. Martha was born in Kent, England in 1614 and was raised in Marshfield, Plymouth, Massachusetts. She was the daughter of a Deacon in the local church in Marshfield. Martha lived for only three years after she tied the knot with Thomas in Norwich, dying in 1683.

Thomas' third and last wife was Mary Foote. A native of Colchester, Essex, England, she was the daughter of Thomas' friend, fellow East Anglian and fellow Wethersfield settler, Nathaniel Foote. She married Thomas three years after she was widowed from her third husband. Given that she was only age 57 when she married Thomas, she had had a string of bad luck with spouses staying alive. Her first marriage had been in 1642 to John Stoddard who died in 1664. Her second husband was John Goodrich. She married him in 1674. He died in 1680. Thomas became her fourth spouse in 1683, marrying her in Norwich. She died in 1685. Most probably she died before Thomas whose death occurred on November 7, 1685 because there is no mention of a surviving widow in his will.

Thomas' Positions of Responsibility in Norwich

In the abbreviated annotated bibliography at the end of this discourse you'll find some of the multiple books, articles, and family stories that attest to the fact that Thomas was a prominent leader in Norwich. I want to make special mention of three books that have been indispensable in discovering the plethora of his civic and professional activities. These are the two volumes of the *Public Records of Connecticut* compiled by J. Hammond Trumbull and the *History of Norwich, Connecticut* by Miss Frances Manwaring Caulkins. Many of Ms. Caulkins citations of Thomas are drawn from the public records. I had to carefully review each mention of Thomas in these works and compose a list of every reference so that I could see where they overlapped. The list has also been critical to preparing a separate, much condensed, document with specific citations.

If you want to get a good feel for the depth of Thomas' presence in Norwich search for Thomas Tracy in these three sources (don't forget to also search for Tracey, Traisy, Trass, and Trasy). The public records are available online free at *archive.org* and the Caulkins book is available free online at *Hathitrust.org*. Most of the following litany of Thomas' role as a surveyor, Juror, Deputy to the Connecticut General Court, Constable, Justice of the Peace, community leader, and his military responsibilities are taken from the books noted in the previous paragraph.

I have only two major reservations regarding the accuracy of Caulkins' accounts of Thomas. The first is that she neglected to mention that his first destination upon his arrival at Boston Harbor was Watertown, Massachusetts. She only said that his name was enrolled by the Town Clerk at Salem. I have to blame someone for my not paying attention to the fact that Salem was not the first, but the second plantation he went to after his arrival. I suppose that I'm being too harsh on Ms. Caulkins because most books didn't report Thomas' first place of residence as Watertown, preferring to skip over it for Salem. Why did they do that?! Did they not know? Did they think since he was in Watertown for such a brief time it wasn't worth noting? That doesn't seem right, as he was also in Salem for only a brief period. The omission is very puzzling to be sure.

As you are by now no doubt tired of hearing, the fact that Thomas' first destination was Watertown is critical in speculating that his place of origin was East Anglia. I was misled by Ms. Caulkins and some otherwise mostly reliable works. I have only myself to blame for being too lazy to check more reliable sources until I got involved in writing this narrative.

My second bone to pick with Ms. Caulkins is that she perpetuated the myth that Thomas married the widow of Edward Mason. She did qualify that observation with *"supposedly."* Her restraint in making an unequivocal statement is very refreshing and encourages me that her other observations are mostly accurate.

After moving to Mohegan/Norwich, it didn't take long for Thomas to be called upon by the Connecticut General Court to help with an incident in the new settlement. It seems that soon after the Saybrook group had arrived at their new plantation, some Narragansett Indians *"did in the dead of night shoot eight bullets into an English house.*" This prompted the General Court in September, 1660 to assign Thomas Tracy, Thomas Leffingwell, and three other men to find the Narragansett sachem and demand that they turn over the offenders so that they could be prosecuted and justice be served. I don't know how that worked out, but it does show the Court's confidence in Thomas to participate in executing such a dangerous assignment.

Thomas and Thomas Leffingwell were also the first deputies elected to the Connecticut General Court from the new plantation of Mohegan/Norwich in October, 1661. The election of deputies was done on a semi-annual basis, but for the first 11 years, with two exceptions, only four people were elected: Thomas Tracy, Thomas Leffingwell, Hugh Calkins, and Francis Griswold. Thomas was elected 21 times to represent Norwich at the General Court. He actually went to 27 sessions. The addition six sessions were extra meetings. Another indicator of his status as a respected person is that Thomas, Francis Griswold, and Thomas Adgate were chosen in 1662 by the Townsmen to form a Court of Commission to try all cases to the value of 40 shillings.

Appointments of Thomas Tracy by the General Court and General Assembly
Below is a mostly chronological list of the appointments of Thomas to a long series of activities.

Thomas was clearly admired for his talent as a surveyor. He was appointed over and over again by the Connecticut General Court to lay out land boundaries and to resolve boundary disputes. One such appointment came in May, 1661 when "*the General Court appointed a committee of three, Matthew Griswold, Thomas Tracy, and James Morgan, to try, that is, rectify the bounds of New London.*" This relates to disputes over land with the Indians in that area. It is described in great detail by Caulkins.

In 1665 Thomas was teamed with John Gallop and Thomas Minor to lay out lands for Robin, an Indian who lived near the Mystic River. (I can't help but observe the use of single names of Native Americans of the period such as Robin, Uncas, and Attawanhood. The Native Americans were way ahead of Adele, Prince, Madonna, Bono, Beck, & Sting!! Cher, of course, has Native American lineage, so she's right in step with her ancestors).

Another appointment by the General Court to survey land took place in October, 1666 when Thomas, Francis Griswold, and James Morgan were asked to find suitable land for the Pequot who were living in Cosattuck just outside the town limits of Stonington. This story is related in the *"Public Records of the Colony of Connecticut"*. The surveyors were to assess a suitable new place two or three miles square for the Pequot to live. While the Stoningtonians (?) showed no respect to the Pequot in forcing them out of town, they did pay for any improvements that the Pequot had made to Cosattuck before chasing them off. I couldn't find if this was done as a good gesture by the prejudice people of Stonington or if the General Court forced them to pay. Am I being too skeptical in thinking it was most likely the latter?

Thomas Tracy and Francis Griswold were appointed by the General Assembly on October 13, 1664 to survey 500 acres of land for Major Mason in an area north of Norwich called Pomakuck (now known as Lebanon, Connecticut). The Connecticut General Court of October, 1667 appointed Thomas, Robert Chapman, and Thomas Minor, among others to go to Narragansett country on June 11, 1668 to *"take a view of the said country and consider what places may be fitt (sic) for plantations_____."*

Thomas and Francis Griswold were also asked by the General Court to survey land allocated to one of Major Mason's sons on May 20, 1668. The land, 300 acres, was part of the original *nine-mile square* area. That same year, Thomas was appointed with Sergeant Thomas Leffingwell to survey a land grant for Major Jeremiah Adams. Major Adams had been a Puritan minister in Chelmsford, Essex, England. He was an original proprietor of Hartford, Connecticut.

Four years later on May 9, 1672, Thomas and Thomas Leffingwell were assigned to conduct a land survey for Major Mason and a Mr. Hawkins. In the same year Tracy and Leffingwell were also asked to lay out the land grant for William Pratt. Later, Thomas and Francis Griswold, two of the 25 freemen in Norwich, were asked by the General Court of Connecticut to *"warne (sic) the Indians of Qunabaug (sic) not to hunt within Uncas his limits."*

Another assignment in 1668 was when Thomas and Francis Griswold were appointed to lay out a hundred acres of land for Cristouer (sic) Huntington. Also in 1668-69 Thomas was appointed by the Court of Election (General Assembly) to measure two hundred acres of land at Wisquades for Benjamin Brewster near present day Preston and Ledyard, Connecticut.

In 1669, Thomas, John Post, and Thomas Leffingwell were assigned to survey 200 to 300 acres of land for the Mohegan sachem, Owaneco, the eldest son of Uncas. The land was within the *Nine-mile square* near the Shetucket and Quinebaug Rivers. Owaneco was in danger of losing his position as sachem because he did not possess enough land to accommodate his subjects of 20 to 30 families. The settlers of Norwich wanted to help him retain his position by giving him the land. In return, Owaneco and the members of his tribe agreed to abstain from working, hunting, fishing or doing any "servile" labor on Sundays.

In July, 1669 Major James Mason entrusted Ensign Thomas Tracy to take a letter to John Winthrop, the Younger who was then the Governor of Connecticut. The letter relates some news from England regarding the possible dissolution of Parliament and military preparations of the French at land and sea. Ensign Thomas was appointed as Town Constable in 1670. This position was also held by his son Solomon in 1681 and by Thomas, Jr. in 1684. In 1671, Ensign Thomas Tracy, Sergeant Thomas Leffingwell, and Hugh Calkins were appointed by the town as Commissioners. Thomas was appointed Commissioner by the General Court along with Reverend James Fitch in 1678.

In 1675 Thomas was appointed with five others by the General Court *"to put a value upon all the lands in the sererall (sic) plantations.* He was also one of the many men chosen to sign bills to pay military wages. Thomas was appointed to the prestigious position of Justice of the Peace in Norwich in 1678. Twice, in 1680 and 1683 he was elected Townsman. The Townsmen were two to six people elected each year who were charged with enforcing town rules. They called public meetings to discuss offences to laws, morality, public order, and the like. They were also responsible for settling small cases. During this period, people were quick to take disputes to court. The Townsmen helped to filter out certain cases, reducing the burden of the court. I'm not sure when he was first elected as a freemen, but he is listed on the role of freemen for Norwich on October 9, 1669.

Thomas' Military Rank
In the legions of histories and genealogies on Thomas that I've read, he is almost always referred to as Lieutenant Tracy. There are some exceptions. These are usually found when there is no honorific used at all until late in his life. A few times he is mentioned as Ensign Tracy. Ensign was the lowest military rank in the colonies. It seems that he became an Ensign in autumn of 1663, at age 53. The first reference I can find where he is called Ensign Tracy is October 8, 1664 when the General Assembly appointed him and Francis Griswold to survey a farm near Norwich granted to Major Mason. This is recorded in the *Public Records of the Colony of Connecticut* and repeated by Jacobus in *The Waterman Family*. In the previous 12 mentions of him in the *Public Records* there is no reference to him as Ensign. In fact, his name is recorded three times in March 1663 with no mention of him as Ensign. I infer from this that he became an Ensign sometime between March and October, 1664.

Following October, 1664 he is referred to as Ensign on April 20, 1665 and again on October 11, 1666 when he was made a member of the *"trainband"*, the 1st Company of Connecticut. He was still referred to as Ensign Tracy as late as October 10, 1672 when he and Thomas Leffingwell were appointed by the Court to conduct a survey for William Pratt. They submitted their report on May 8, 1673. It was signed by Ens. Thomas Tracy and Thomas Leffingwell. Hence, Thomas was still an Ensign in May, 1673.

Promotion to Lieutenant at Age 63
According to Jacobus and the Society of Colonial Wars, Thomas was promoted to Lieutenant in August, 1673 when he was 63-years old. The promotion was made with the New London Dragoons which was formed to repeal any invasion by the Dutch and Indians. Along with James Avery and John Denison, Thomas was ordered to be prepared in case military action was required against the Dutch. The 1673 date is substantiated in the *Second Supplement to the General Register of the Society of Colonial Wars* published in 1911. Given his appointment to Lieutenant at a late age, it appears to me that his promotion was made to give him more authority as an older man serving in what was equivalent to a "*rear guard*" patrol. Later in 1673 Lt. Thomas was appointed as Muster-master who inspected arms and ammunition.

Speaking of "*trainbands*" they were originally established in England to organize groups of civilian militia. The tradition was widespread throughout New England. In general all able-bodied men between the ages of 16 and 60 were required to participate in trainband activities. Each man had a musket, bandoliers, rest (for the musket), powder, and shot. Yeah, I had to look up the definition of bandolier. It is just a broad belt for holding bullets. It is worn over the shoulder just like the Mexican soldiers do in a Clint Eastwood western movie. Many militia men also had a sword and once in a while, a pike. The trainbands often held training exercises on the village "*commons*" and locals would come out to watch and make it a festive occasion. The commons in Norwich was also referred to as "*ye green*", "*ye meeting-house green*", "*the Parade*", "*the Training Field*", and "*the Plain.*"

I have no problem with the fact that Thomas was not a military hero. Indeed, for ten years he held the lowest military rank possible and that came only at age 53. I only made it to Special 4th Class in my three years in the Army, so I'm all about sympathizing with the rank-and-file. The problem for me is that historians and genealogists regularly gloss over the fact that he had very limited military experience. He is routinely referred to as Lieutenant regardless of the period of his life being addressed. Incongruously, long before he was a Lieutenant or even an Ensign, historians and family genealogist refer to him as Lt. Tracy.

For example, more than one reference I've found related to the names of the original proprietors who settled Norwich in 1660 lists all thirty-five men. Thomas is shown as "*Lieut. Thomas Tracy*". But we know he wasn't even an Ensign until 1663. Other histories also refer to "*Lieut. Thomas Tracy*" before 1663. This is found in books written in both the 19th and 20th Centuries. To their credit, there are some writers, albeit a woefully few, who when mentioning Thomas Tracy before 1673 make a parenthetical note of ("later Lieutenant"). Even the 35 names of original proprietors on the website of *The Society of the Founders of Norwich* show Lt. Thomas Tracy. It makes perfect sense because he was a Lieutenant. To the casual observer, however, the implication is that he was a Lieutenant when he helped found the settlement. When, in fact, it was another 13 years before he became a Lieutenant.

This innocent but misleading information really muddies the water for the few of us who see some importance linked to when he was actually give a military rank. It's significant because the literature erroneously gives the impression that he was a lieutenant while engaging in many of his worthwhile activities. For years, I certainly was led down that garden path. It just isn't so. I doubt if I am the only person who had mistakenly inferred from the literature that he earned the rank of lieutenant based on his participation in the Pequot War. Further it had crossed my mind that he was awarded land in Saybrook because of his military rank and friendship with Captain (later Major) Mason. Clearly that was not the case. Actually it is reassuring to know that Thomas earned his acquisition of land and his appointments to prestigious positions because of his character and contributions to his community, rather than as spoils of war.

King Phillip's War

I first became aware of, and interested in, King Phillip's War while doing research on my ancestor, James Travis. I'll say more about him momentarily. As far as I know he had no connection to Thomas, but I hadn't realized that Thomas was also involved in the war until undertaking the writing of my story.

King Philip's War is also known as Metacom's War or Metacom's Rebellion. It started in 1675 and ended in 1678. It was named after the Wampanoag sachem Metacom. How is it that I had never heard of this conflict so critical to early American history? It is the deadliest war per capita in American history. Five percent of the English population and perhaps as much as 40 percent of all Indian tribal members were killed.

The conflict began because Metacom (King Philip) was fed up with the English settlers taking their land and destroying their culture. He and his mignons set out to get rid of the English intruders with their greedy ways once and for all. To increase his chance of success in the endeavor he enlisted the Narragansett as allies. They weren't difficult to convince given all the agony their people had suffered at the hands of the planters. For their part, the English interpreted the uprising as a sign of God's displeasure with them. Ironically, the Puritan church leaders were also upset with the second generation of settlers for many of the same reasons the Indians were. English ministers were very concerned that their flocks were becoming increasingly greedy, lacking of piety, and paying less attention to religious practices.

When the dust of war had settled the Indian tribes who challenged the English had been almost completely eradicated. Most of those who hadn't been killed were sent as slaves to the Caribbean. Only a few remained and only recently have descendants of the Wampanoag begun to restore their native language and culture. It was not until 2015 that the Federal Bureau of Indian Affairs granted the Mashpee Wampanoag the right to reclaim a portion of their ancestral land (and, of course, construct casinos!). Descendants of the Narragansett fared somewhat better, being given Federal recognition in 1880 and being included in the Indian Reorganization Act of 1934.

It came as a revelation to me that in July, 1675 during the King Phillip's War, three trainband officers from Norwich assisted in an unsuccessful expedition into Narragansett territory to try and convince them not to join King Phillip. My high school classmates would have reacted to this revelation with the old English and still used local colloquialisms "well, I'll swan!" or "well, I'll declare!" The three appointed men, led by Captain Wait Winthrop, were 65-year old Thomas Tracy, 75-year old John Mason, and 63-year old Thomas Brewster. Were they sent because they were senior negotiators or expendable old men? I think that they were accompanied by younger men, so it is probable that they were included because of their seniority and familiarity with the Narragansett. The next year, Thomas and John Bradford were appointed to the position of Commissary and Quartermaster in Norwich.

James Travis and the Siege of Brookfield, MA
I said that I had done some previous research on King Philip's War. And some readers may recall that I wrote a story about one episode about James Travis, another of my paternal 7th Great Grandfathers. He was an English Puritan who lived through a famous attack by the Nipmuc tribe at Brookfield, Massachusetts. My self-published Amazon book was written for the young reader in my extended family. The title is *James Travis and the Siege of Brookfield, 1675*. It isn't just about the siege; it tells what life was like in Puritan village settlements.

Now I interrupt our story for the following commercial message: *The book is available on Amazon.com, Booksamillion, betterwoldbooks.com, books.rediff.com, tower.com, and a host of others. Old torn-up used copies can even be bought on eBay. So, if you are curious, don't let me stop you from helping to enhance my retirement income and buy a copy or two or more!!*

I know, I know, I have no shame. Before the New Hampshire's Presidential primary on February 9, 2016, I would have said that at my advanced age nobody cares how shameless I am. But, look, Bernie Sanders is only a year younger than me and he has won the adoration of millions of young people by saying all manner of things that at one time would have put him in a home (and I don't mean the Whitehouse). Good for Bernie! He's legitimized the views of old folks! If only I could get him to endorse my book!

More of Thomas's Accomplishments in Norwich
End of commercial, back to the story. In 1673 Thomas' skills were put to use when he was appointed to a committee with four other men charged with building a new meeting house high on a rocky peak overlooking Norwich. The construction began in 1674 and completed in 1676. In case I've left any doubt as to Thomas' prominence in Norwich, I'll cite an account of him included in a book written in 1846: *"He was a gentleman of importance in the colony. He was appointed a Deputy in 1662-3 – auditor of the accounts of J. Rogers and Leut. Smith on the corn rate for the expense of the Charter, 1663. He was a thorough business man. The name has been uniformly respectable."*

More evidence that Thomas was a revered founder of Norwich is expressed in the following exert from a poem entitled *The Inland City* written in 1851 by Edmund Clarence Stedman in 1909 commemorating the 250th anniversary of the founding of Norwich, Connecticut. It contains the following lines:

> *"Tales of the after time, when scant and humble*
> *Grew the Mohegan band,*
> *And Tracy, Griswold, Huntington and Trumble,*
> *Were judges in the land."*

When Thomas died in 1685 he left an estate of 500 pounds ($98,400 in 2016 currency) and 5,000 acres of land. He is buried in the Old Burying Grounds in Norwich Town. His legacy did not cease with his death as both he and his children left an indelible mark on the history of Norwich and the Connecticut Colony, as well as the embryonic United States. It is fair to say that Thomas was a self-made man who was among the very first immigrants to live the American dream. His children followed suit.

Recall that Thomas and his first wife had seven children, six sons and one daughter. Much information is available about the first four sons and the husband of Miriam, including their progeny to the present time. Much less is known about the last two sons. Here's a brief encapsulation of the lives of the children.

- John Tracy (1642-1702). John, at age 17, was also one of the 35 original founders of Norwich, Conn. He was a very prominent citizen of Norwich. He married Mary Winslow, niece of Massachusetts Governor Edward Winslow.
- Thomas Tracy, Jr. (1644-1721). Thomas was a founder of Preston City, Conn. He was an outstanding citizen in that community.
- Jonathan (1646-1711). Jonathan was also a founder of Preston City, Conn. He was the first Keeper of the Ordinary or Town Clerk of Preston.
- Miriam Tracy (1648-1732). Miriam was the wife of Thomas Waterman who, at age 15, was one of the original founders of Norwich. This happened because he was the charge of John Bradford, husband of his aunt, Martha Bourne Bradford. She married Thomas Tracy after her husband died.
- Solomon Tracy (1650-1732). Dr. Solomon Tracy was a well-respected physician, one of only two doctors in Preston.
- Daniel Tracy (1652-1728). Little is known about Daniel other than he lived in Preston and that he was known as a man of fashion, the owner of 23 ruffled shirts.
- Samuel Tracy (1654-1693). Little is also known about Samuel. He apparently died without issue.

Thomas' Family Line & Some Recent Descendants

Thomas' services to the establishment and prosperity of Norwich entitle his descendants membership in the *Societies of Colonial Wars and Colonial Dames*, as well as *The Society of The Founders of Norwich*. I'm very pleased to say that after a vetting by the latter society's genealogist, Louise Leake, on January 27, 2016 I was accepted as a direct descendant of Lt. Thomas Tracy through his son, Jonathan.

This might be a good point to list who begat whom in my direct ancestry to Thomas. I've listed only those wives who are direct ancestors and blood relatives, as follows:

Thomas Tracy (1610-1685)	+ (Unknown) – His 1st wife
Jonathan Tracy (1646-1711)	+ Mary Griswold (1656-1711)
David Tracy, Sr. (1687-1770)	+ Sarah J. Parish (1692-1729)
David Tracy, Jr. (1721-1777)	+ Abial Baker (1718-1770)
Solomon Tracy (1759-1849)	+ Lucretia Hall (1757-1849)
Joseph Tracy (1793-1855)	+ Polly (Mary) Haven (1797-1859)
Otis Augustus Tracy (1836-1926)	+ Margaret Amelia Dye (1845-1892)
James Albert Tracy, Sr. (1872-Aft. 1929)	+ Rita Booth (1874-1964)
James Albert Tracy, Jr. (1901-1985)	+ Alma Lee Martin (nee Miller) (1912-1986)

Most of my cousins reading this account (you know who you are) are descendants of one of three children of Otis Augustus and Margaret Amelia Dye Tracy: James Albert Tracy, Sr. (1872- 1929 or after), Alvin Otis Tracy (1881-1969), and Levin Melvin (Jack) Tracy (1884-1962). There are also descendants of two half-cousins out there somewhere, a result of Otis' second marriage to Elizabeth Viola Noland (1864-1934). They had one daughter, Wanda Tracy (1896-1919), and one son, Joseph Loring Tracy (1906-1992). If you read this CONTACT ME!

All in all Otis and Margaret had eleven children (hence the name "Levin" for their last child). Then there were the two additional children Otis had with Elizabeth Noland. Much of my family research time has been focused on looking for descendants of the siblings of my Grandfather; James Albert Tracy, Sr. It clearly was not a tight knit family that stayed in touch with each other. Or if they did, you can't prove it by me. I'm happy to say that this is not the case with my generation. Over the past 20 plus years, I've been very close to my 1st and 2nd cousins by blood and by marriage despite living far apart. They have indulged me in my quest for family history and even found cemeteries with family ancestors for me to wander through. The periodic family reunions, large and small, have been wonderful bonding experiences. Thanks guys for including me and Patsy in your lives!!

I'm also happy to say that I have had reasonably good luck in locating descendants of the last two children born to Otis and Margaret: Alvin Otis and Levin Melvin (Jack) Tracy. Alvin was a successful Percheron horse trader in Ohio and Arizona. Jack had an extremely successful career in raising and selling produce in California and Arizona. He co-owned the *Tracy-Waldron Fruit Company* and owned *Sunshine Farms* in Yuma and Phoenix. My Grandfather James Albert Tracy, Sr.'s last known residence was in San Francisco. He had a law degree from Drake University but primarily made his living as a real estate agent in Iowa, Nebraska, and Colorado before moving to San Francisco in the mid-1920s to work as an attorney for his younger brother, Levin. He disappeared in 1929, last seen boarding a ship in San Francisco harbor bound for Alaska. Countless efforts to discover what became of him have proved to be fruitless. It has been an impenetrable "brick wall."

Five of Otis and Margaret's children were daughters. Four were born in Wood County, West Virginia and one in Washington County, Ohio. One daughter remained single and stayed in Washington County. Three married and lived in other counties in Ohio. And one simply vanished without any trace of records. Of the remaining sons, William Henry Tracy (1868-1952), was a prosperous farmer in Morganton, North Carolina. Two others have proven too elusive for me to track down. Nor have I been able to contact descendants of Otis and Elizabeth's two children.

In recent years have I been fortunate to have found and corresponded with and even met some relatives of Alvin Otis and Levin Melvin. They have all been very gracious in helping me fill in the gaps. A few have become good friends. Despite the fact James Albert Tracy or J.A. Tracy, as he liked to be identified, was an attorney at Levin Melvin's business, the Tracy-Waldron Fruit Company in San Francisco in the 1920s; he seems to be virtually unknown to Levin's descendants. But that's a whole other story!

11

DID THE FAMILIES OF THOMAS AND STEPHEN KNOW OF EACH OTHER?

Could Thomas and Stephen Tracy have known each other? Or, more probably, known OF each other? I've given a great deal of thought to both possibilities. In the interest of full disclosure, as one often hears these days, I would like for it to be true. I admittedly have a bias. I won't be able to prove it, but maybe I can make you thoughtfully stroke your chin and say *"hmmmm, you just might be onto something there, you wild and crazy guy."* To borrow a phrase from another Martin!

Let's examine this by looking at some telltale numbers and facts. We know that Stephen was baptized in 1596. That he was originally from Norfolk County, England. That he went to Leiden, Holland with the Puritans and came to Plymouth in 1623 at age 27. That he relocated to Duxbury. That he went for a visit to England circa 1654 and died there in 1655. As for Thomas, it has been shown that he was born about 1610; that the place of his birth in England has never been verified; that his first residence in the Massachusetts Bay Colony was in Watertown in 1636 at age 26. That He was briefly in Salem, Massachusetts before taking up residence in Wethersfield. He relocated to Saybrook, Connecticut. Then he moved to the new settlement of Mohegan (Norwich).

While it is often suggested that Thomas was from Gloucestershire County, England, I've tried to make the case that it is more reasonable that he came from East Anglia, probably Norfolk. I know that some will argue that if Stephen was really his cousin, Thomas would have initially gone to Plymouth instead of Watertown. Fair enough. My response is that the two might not have known each other in the old country. Thomas was 14 years younger than Stephen. Admittedly, the odds of them meeting in the colonies before Thomas lived in Saybrook aren't in their favor. On the other hand, being aware of each other once Thomas moved to Saybrook is well within reason. I say this because of the documented back and forth movement between the Plymouth Colony and the Saybrook Colony of people with whom they were both well acquainted.

They were both of mature ages when interaction, such as commercial trade and military actions, between the two colonies was quite vibrant. Thomas was age 34 in 1644 when he moved to Saybrook. At that time, Stephen was age 48, living in Duxbury since 1634. The two men would have had good chances to have known of each other's presence in the colonies from 1644 up to the time Stephen went to England in 1654. Using the Martin Tracy method of calculation, I come up with a ten-year period during which two healthy, mature, socially and economically active, and distinguished Puritan men with the same surname could have been aware of each other. In fact, the two were the only known heads of family named Tracy in New England.

Meeting face-to-face seems unlikely because there is no evidence that Thomas traveled to the Plymouth Colony or that Stephen ventured to Saybrook Colony. But, at the risk of being repetitious, it is certainly reasonable to assume that they were familiar with people who knew them both. I've been able to identify several of their mutual friends who traveled regularly between the two colonies. I recognize that simply because they knew the same people, doesn't mean they were aware of each other, especially because they lived relatively far apart. Then again, did I mention that there were only two families with the Tracy surname in New England? It would be pretty strange if all the men going back and forth from Plymouth and Saybrook colonies that they knew in common would never have mentioned Stephen to Thomas or Thomas to Stephen.

As I tried to think this through, the first obstacle that came to mind was that a 130 or so mile separation between the residences of Thomas and Stephen might have been an insurmountable distance. I am well aware of the limited modes of transportation and dangerous travel of the time. I soon discovered, however, that it was not at all uncommon for men to travel between the colonies of western Connecticut and the Plymouth Colony. There was a significant amount of commerce between the Connecticut communities of Hartford, Wethersfield, Saybrook, New London, and Windham, as well as between all these communities and those in Plymouth, Duxbury, and Marshfield, Massachusetts.

Alas, I had a problem. Although there was commerce between the colonies when Stephen live in Duxbury and Thomas resided in Saybrook, could I find evidence that would unquestionably link men who knew them both who traversed between the two colonies? I must admit to doubting if this could be done. How was I to unravel the web, untie the knot, untangle the web, solve the Rubik's cube, and any other appropriate metaphor?

I believe I can make a good argument for linking the families by discussing two Johns. These are John Bradford and John Tracy. I'll start with John Bradford, son of William Bradford III and grandson of Governor William Bradford II. I'll follow with John Tracy, son of Thomas. Let's explore a little about these two Johns in an attempt to show the interrelationships between their families and the two colonies.

John, Son of William Bradford

The first John of interest is John Bradford who was born in 1618 in Leiden two years before the first wave of Pilgrims left Holland for New England on the *Mayflower*. He was the son of the soon-to-be Governor William

Bradford and Dorothy May Bradford. His mother drowned while the *Mayflower* was anchored in Plymouth harbor.

It took me many months to figure out the importance of John Bradford in this Tracy saga. For starters, at age 76, I'm not the sharpest knife in the drawer which is my excuse for overlooking clues that were right in front of my distinctive Norman/French ancestral nose. It should have been obvious to me that there were family connections between the Plymouth and Saybrook Colonies. To use a southern colloquialism; if it had been a snake, I'd have been bitten.

I had made an error in not paying sufficient attention to finding out more about the 35 men who founded Norwich. I overlooked the significance of the fact that most, but not all, were from Saybrook. It had not occurred to me to check if any of the purchasers were from outside of Saybrook Colony. More specifically, could any of them been from, say, far away Plymouth Colony? Now, wouldn't that be *something special*, as Saturday Night Live's Dana Carvey's Church Lady might put it?!

I recalled seeing a number of sources that listed the 35 men, including the website of *The Society of the Founders of Norwich*. But a quick check of this and other sources revealed only a list of names of the proprietors. I still didn't know where the men were from, so the list didn't help to establish a connection to the Plymouth Colony. Then, while going over the list of men on the Founders website, I got excited when I saw two familiar names: John Bradford and his wife's nephew, Thomas Waterman. That's it, I thought. These two men, actually one man and one teen, are the missing link because both were from the village of Marshfield in the Plymouth Colony about 130 miles to the east. I was really stoked!

Linking John Bradford of Plymouth Colony to Saybrook Colony
Now the burning question became how did John Bradford get involved in a Saybrook request for a land patent? It seems I'm not the first and only one to have posed this question. On Friday, February 27, 2016, I was once

again sitting in my favorite chair in our humble abode with the ventless gas fireplace ablaze re-reading my Kindle Fire edition of the *History of Norwich, Connecticut* by historian Frances Manwaring Caulkins. It so happens that 150 years ago Ms. Caulkins was way ahead of me. The question she posed was: how did John Bradford learn about the Saybrook group seeking to purchase land from sachem Uncas? She suggested that the answer lay in the person of Jonathan Brewster. I must say I hadn't seen that coming. If I had made this statement orally to friends in Western Kentucky, they would likely have expressed uncertainty that they heard correctly by uttering "do what?" meaning "what did you say?" Please do listen closely and stay with me as I try to connect the links in this chain as laid out by Ms. Caulkins!

The first link relates to the Brewster family. Jonathan Brewster was born in Scooby, England in 1593. He was the son of Pilgrim William Brewster. Jonathan was three years older than Stephen. He accompanied his father when the Separatists went to Leiden, but was not with him on the *Mayflower*. He stayed behind in Leiden with the other members of the Puritan congregation, including Stephen and family. Jonathan left Leiden one year earlier than Stephen, coming to Plymouth on the *Fortune* in 1621. He later settled in Duxbury where Stephen also lived. In sum, Jonathan Brewster was no doubt well acquainted with Stephan Tracy based on their close living proximities in the small Puritan communities in Leiden and Duxbury.

A second link is that William Brewster and Governor William Bradford were very close friends. Brewster was Bradford's mentor in Scooby, Leiden, and Plymouth. Their sons, Jonathan Brewster and John Bradford were also friends despite an age difference of 25 years. Don't forget that both the Bradford family, like the Brewster family, was also well acquainted with the Stephan Tracy family.

A third link relates to Jonathan Brewster's penchant for adventure and commerce. He was known for his frequent ventures along the Connecticut River engaging in trade. In about 1649 he established a trading post at the mouth of the Poquetannock Creek, mercifully later known to those of us who are language challenged with the less tongue twisting name of Brewster's Neck. The site was originally located in New London, Connecticut but it later became part of Preston. Jonathan's travels and trading store could have exposed him to traders from Saybrook.

A fourth link connects Jonathan Brewster to sachem Uncas, a mutual friend of Thomas Tracy. Jonathan had acquired Brewster's Neck from sachem Uncas. Some years earlier Uncas had contacted Jonathan to alert yet another of his and Thomas' mutual friends, Major John Mason, of a pending Indian attack.

A fifth link ties Jonathan Brewster to John Mason and John Bradford, Saybrook Colony purchasers of the *nine-mile square*. Both of whom were well acquainted with both Thomas Tracy and Stephen Tracy.

Additional Links between the Two Tracy Families
Okay, time to switch to bullet points, a favorite tool of teachers and trainers the world over. I hope to add more credence to the Brewster-Bradford-Mason-Uncas-Saybrook-Plymouth-Duxbury connection to the families of Stephen and Thomas Tracy. This summary, I hope, will help illustrate that there is every reason to assume that the two Tracy families would have known about each other, if not directly, then through their mutual friends and acquaintances. Here we go:

- Jonathan Brewster knew Stephen,
  - Both lived in Leiden at the same time.
  - Both lived and Duxbury at the same time.
- Jonathan Brewster probably knew Thomas or of him.
  - Both were friends of John Mason, sachem Uncas, John Bradford, & John Mason.

- Jonathan plied up and down the Connecticut River as a tradesman during the years Thomas lived in Saybrook and Wethersfield.
- Others from Saybrook who would have known Thomas may have traded at Jonathan's Trading Post at Brewster's Point on the Thames River.
- Jonathan Brewster also knew John Bradford
  - The two boys were sons of good friends William Brewster and William Bradford.
  - The two boys lived in Leiden, Holland at the same time in a very close knit community.
  - They both lived in the Plymouth and Duxbury at the same time.
- John Bradford knew Stephen
  - Stephen and the Bradford family had known each other in Leiden.
  - Stephen lived next door to the Bradford family in Plymouth for seven years.
  - Stephen lived next door to the Bradford family when both families moved to Duxbury.
- John Bradford knew Thomas before the move to Norwich in 1660.
  - John Bradford moved from Duxbury to Marshfield in 1653.
  - Stephan was still in Duxbury in 1653.
  - Thomas was in Saybrook in 1653.
  - John Bradford and Thomas knew each other as purchasers of the *nine-mile square* at Mohegan.
  - All but two of the 35 purchasers were from Saybrook, except for John Bradford and his nephew, Thomas Waterman. They were from Marshfield.

It is more than reasonable to assume that John Bradford found out about the purchase of the *nine-mile square* from Jonathan Brewster or Uncas or even, though less probably, from Thomas Tracy. It is also more than plausible that both Bradford and Brewster would have assumed that there was some connection between their Tracy friends, Stephen and Thomas. The name was unique in the colonies. Therefore, Thomas and Stephen would have at the minimum been aware of each other through mutual friends.

All this means that John Bradford (age 44) and Thomas Waterman (age 14) would most likely have traveled from their home of Marshfield, Massachusetts to attend a meeting in Saybrook, Connecticut in 1658 or 1659 to discuss the *nine-mile square* grant proposal. Here's how a conversation between John Bradford, Thomas Waterman, and Thomas Tracy might have gone at that meeting using contemporary language:

> John Bradford: *Goodman Thomas Tracy! What a pleasure it is to meet you at last and to join you in this exciting investment. I can't thank you enough for all that you, Major Mason, and others have done to make a deal with our mutual friend Uncas and the Mohegan Tribe. I'd love to talk more about it with you. But before we do, I want to introduce you to my wife's nephew, Thomas Waterman. Thomas lives with us in Marshfield.*

> Thomas Tracy: *Captain Bradford, the pleasure is all mine. And what a handsome young fellow your nephew is. He is most fortunate to have such a wonderful uncle.*

> *I'm so sorry about the death of your father last year. I know it is of little consolation, but the Governor certainly lived a full, productive, and Christian life. His leadership and legacy will continue to shape our society for years to come. He'll be greatly missed.*

> John Bradford: *Thank you, that is very thoughtful of you. I appreciate it. Let me express my condolences for the loss of your wife. I only recently learned of her death. My thoughts and prayers are with you. I also want to tell you how much I miss your cousin Stephen. He and I went through a lot together at Leiden. And he was our cherished neighbor in Plymouth and Duxbury for many years. He was such a*

stalwart figure in the community. His untimely and shocking death while traveling in England was a huge loss to the colony, as well as to his family.

Thomas Tracy: *Thank you for your kind thoughts and prayers for my wife. They are most welcomed. My dear wife would have been excited about relocating to Mohegan. While the children and I miss her terribly, we know that she is in a better place. Most of Reverend Fitch's flock is participating in the land grant, so it will be comforting to be in Mohegan with old friends, family, and our church led by our much loved Reverend Fitch.*

Thank you also for your kind words about my cousin Stephen. He had worked so hard to get to where he was as a leader in the Plymouth Colony. He was 14 years older than me and left Norfolk for Holland with the Pilgrims at a very young age, so I really didn't know him well in the old country. It is so gratifying to hear that he was so successful and well-liked in Plymouth Colony.

Tell me young Thomas Waterman, are you going to join in the purchase of the Mohegan land? You know, my son, John, is only two years older than you and he'll buying into the patent.

Thomas Waterman: *Oh yes, Goodman Tracy. Uncle John has advised me that it would be a good investment. Since the death of my father a few years ago, Uncle John and Aunt Martha have been so good to me. I'm looking forward to moving to Mohegan with them. I understand it is a beautiful and bountiful place with many opportunities for young men.*

Thomas Tracy: *That's wonderful. I'm sure you and my son John will be the best of friends, as I know your uncle and I will be. John, I assume that you and your wife will be moving to Mohegan after the deed is finalized and that young Thomas here will be coming with you.*

John Bradford: *Yes, my wife Martha and I have loved living in Marshfield and the Plymouth Colony close to family. However, we'd like to strike out on own and get in on the beginning of building a new community. We're quite excited about it.*

Thomas Tracy: *I hear you. At my age, I hope this is the last new plantation that I move to. I'm getting a little long in the tooth to keep breaking new ground. We better get back to the meeting. It has been so nice to meet you both. John, please give my regards to your wife upon your return to Marshfield. May God keep you both safe on your journey home.*

This fanciful dialogue is the creative part of creative nonfiction. I have documentation of most of the facts in this dialogue, but I have taken some poetic (prosaic?) liberties. What is factual is that John and Martha Bradford and their nephew, Thomas Waterman, were among the original 35 purchasers of Mohegan and the only two from the Plymouth Colony. And that Stephen and John Bradford knew each other quite well.

Before moving on to the other John, there is another fascinating fact that links the Bradford-Tracy families together. It also demonstrates the link between Plymouth Colony and Norwich. In 1668 the factual young man in the fictitious dialogue, Thomas Waterman, nephew of John and Martha Bourne Bradford, married Thomas Tracy's daughter, Miriam. After Thomas and Miriam married and got their own digs in Norwich, John and Martha brought John's nephew, Thomas Bradford, from Plymouth to live with them in Norwich. Thomas Bradford was a son of William Bradford IV and had inherited land in Norwich. John and Martha had no children of their own. And, of course, Thomas Tracy married John Bradford's widow, Martha.

John, Son of Thomas
Now let's see how the life of John, son of Thomas helps lay to rest any argument that distances between towns in the colonies would have lessened

the chance that the Tracy families would have been aware of each other. John Tracy was Thomas's first child born in Wethersfield in 1642. By age 18 he was doing pretty well for himself as one of the 35 original proprietors of Norwich which entitled him to some choice acreage in Norwich. That's certainly of interest, but here's the kicker, on June 10, 1670 at age 28 he married Mary Winslow. Now this is extremely interesting and not just because I was born on June 10 a few years later! It is fascinating because the marriage took place in Marshfield, Plymouth Colony, 110 miles northeast of Norwich.

Another factor adding fuel to the fire is that John's wife Mary Winslow was the daughter of Josiah Winslow, a brother of Plymouth Governor, Edward Winslow. That's pretty high society. How might have John gotten acquainted with the niece of a Governor who lived so far away from him? Glad you asked another great question. Would you believe that Mary Winslow was also the niece of John's stepmother, Martha Bourne Bradford Tracy? Recall, if you will, that Thomas Tracy married Martha Bourne Bradford in about 1680. This is ten years after his son John and Mary Winslow married. To me this suggests that these two families, one in Norwich and one in Marshfield, were well acquainted with each other. By 1673, at the latest, John and Mary had moved to John's hometown of Norwich.

Let's muddy the murky waters a tad more. We've established that John Tracy, son of Thomas, married a Winslow who grew up over a hundred miles from his home in Norwich. Do you remember who Stephen Tracy gave power of attorney to when he went to England? It was John Winslow, Stephen's *"loving friend."* John Winslow was the brother of Edward Winslow and Josiah Winslow. This makes him the uncle of Mary Winslow, bride of John, son of Thomas. Is that not intriguing if not confusing? Therefore, Thomas is linked to the Winslow family of Marshfield through the marriage of his son John to Mary Winslow. Stephen is linked to the Winslow family of Marshfield through his friendship with her Uncle John Winslow.

Stephen's family in Duxbury was separated from the Winslow family in Marshfield by five miles, an easy walk and even easier horse or buggy ride. To be fair, Stephen's connection to the Winslow family is 15 years before John's marriage. But, come on, man! How could there not have been an awareness among Winslow family members and both Stephen and Thomas of each other's existence?

In sum, John Tracy son of Thomas Tracy of Norwich married Mary Winslow of Marshfield. Mary was the niece of the woman who would become John Tracy's stepmother who was also the niece of John Winslow who was a dear friend of Stephen Tracy. I hope I'm not the only one that sees a distinct pattern here!

If, for some strange, reason Thomas and Stephen were unaware of each other before Stephen went back to England in about 1654, there is every reason to believe the families would have been aware of each other after the purchase of Norwich. There was just too much interaction among both Tracy families and their friends and acquaintances for there not to have been knowledge of each other's existence.

Review of Relationships

Time now for a final review of what I think I know, acknowledging that I may have said more than I know! The families of Lt. Thomas Tracy of Massachusetts and Connecticut and Stephen Tracy, Jr. of Massachusetts probably knew of each other's presence. It is possible that both were natives of Norfolk County, England. Stephen, who was about 14 years Thomas' senior, arrived at Plymouth in the summer of 1623 on the "*Anne*." Thomas's first destination after arriving at Boston Harbor 13 years later in 1636 was Watertown, Massachusetts. Watertown was predominantly settled by groups of people from Norfolk. Thomas lived in Weathersfield and Saybrook when Stephan lived in Plymouth and Duxbury. Thomas later was a founding father of Norwich, Connecticut. Both were very prominent men with numerous shared acquaintances and friends.

While both Lt. Thomas Tracy and Stephen Tracy, Jr. probably share a common English ancestry, Thomas has received much more attention by historians and genealogists. Indeed, the life of Lt. Thomas Tracy and many of his prominent descendants is very well known and much publicized, although, as I've tried to demonstrate, not always accurately.

As we've seen, the historical attention on Thomas is, in part, a result of the numerous attempts to link him to the aristocracy of the Hanbury-Sudeley-Tracy family line of Stanway House in Gloucestershire. Copious publications show Lt. Thomas Tracy as being from Stanway, ranging from assertions that he was the son, grandson, or nephew of Sir Paul Tracy, Nathaniel Tracy, or William Tracy. Such suppositions are also found in the vast majority of postings on *Ancestry.com* and *FamilySearch.org*. However, as news commentators and politicians have recently become annoyingly fond of saying, "at the end of the day", there is no viable evidence to support this. I'm saying that Thomas most likely came from Norfolk. That's my story and I'm sticking to it until one or several of you prove me wrong. It wouldn't be the first time I've been mistaken, or the last.

12

DNA & SUMMARY OF THE PURITAN TRACYS OF NEW ENGLAND

Using yDNA Testing

Throughout the text I've made several allusive references to DNA testing. Now I'll try to explain how DNA has influenced my research, especially regarding my genetic connection to Thomas Tracy. I've had my DNA tested twice by two different companies, specifically yDNA tests of male chromosomes. My first test was in 2006 with *The Genographic Project* conducted by National Geographic. My second test was in 2015 by *23andMe*. I had the second test done because data analysis for purposes of assessing individual and family ancestry had dramatically improved over that nine-year period.

Two other testing services that are worth exploring are *AncestryDNA* and *FamilyTreeDNA*. The data from both my tests were transferred to *FamilyTreeDNA* for purposes of comparison with other data sets from multiple DNA testing companies. Comparisons are made possible by a free service from *FamilyTreeDNA* named *Ysearch*. Ysearch has been extremely helpful in my connecting with distant cousins who are into Tracy family genealogy. More information on this very useful service is online at: http://www.ysearch.org/.

Recently *23andMe* merged with *Myheritage.com* which increases the opportunities to link with other tests. In addition *LegacyFamilyTree.com* offers many online webinars that make using the data much more effectively. Despite all the help, much of what can be concluded about genetic data is way over my head, but testing sites make every effort to make it as simple as possible.

One fun result of the tests identifies where one's ancestors lived from 40,000-45,000 years ago to the present. My DNA data show that within the past few hundred years, 99.9% of my ancestors are European. This is broken down to 44% British and Irish, 37% Broadly Northern European, 15% French and German, 2% Broadly Southern European, 2% Scandinavian, 0.3% Finish, 0.6% Iberian and 0.1% Broadly East Asian. I'm amazed at having even an inkling of East Asian DNA, but the rest makes sense. Did I mention that the tests also show that I have more Neanderthal variants (320) in my DNA than 96% of all *23andMe* customers? Some 2.4% of my DNA is traced to some Neanderthal who happened upon a humanoid and had an offspring. Boy does that explain a lot!!

Another cool fact is that my yDNA can be traced to only one area of Russia. That place is Samara Oblast (State) which in 3,800 BCE (Before Common Era) was home to my ancestors, the Yamnaya people. Here's the ironic part, in the mid-1990s and 2000 my wife and I made several trips to Oktyabrsk and Togliatti, Samara. The travel was in conjunction with social work and women education programs through the School of Social Work at Southern Illinois University. One of the projects, Russian/American Summer University (RASU) was sponsored by USAID. Another was with the Togliatti Social and Economic College. A description of RASU was included in a 2003 book entitled *Models of International Collaboration in Social Work Education* edited by Y. Asamoah, L. M. Healy & M. C. Hokenstad. What are the odds that my only exposure to Russia would be in my ancient ancestral land of Samara?

That's all in good fun, but the primary purpose that I took the tests was to see if my yDNA matched the yDNA of other men with the surname Tracy whose ancestry could be traced to Thomas and Stephen, especially Thomas. In this I have been quite successful. Up until two days ago as of writing this section on March 21, 2016, I had found six males who match my yDNA at 37 markers, all of whom are direct descendants of Thomas Tracy through his son, John. Two are my 8th cousins and two are my 8th cousins 1x removed (a difference of one generation).

As I mentioned earlier, on March 12, 2016 I received an email from *FamilyTreeDNA* that a new connection had been established with Sean C. Tracy at 37 markers. I was to discover later that he is my 7th cousin. As it happens, he, too, is a victim of *Cognatio Genealogia Indagatio Insectum (CGI)*. The research he's conducted and written about is well documented and thoughtfully presented. I'm glad to report that his studies have led to very similar conclusions as mine, particularly regarding the origin of Thomas Tracy. I'm looking forward to continuing to share information with him in the ongoing quest to know more about both Thomas and Stephen.

To be sure, the identified six men with yDNA matches at 37 markers are not my close relatives, but the matches do show that each of the six of us carry yDNA similar to each other. Since we all can trace our ancestry to Thomas, the odds are that he is a shared ancestor. If only I could persuade Henry Louis Gates to do a search of my ancestors on the PBS production *Finding Your Roots!*

One DNA test did reveal that I'm also related to the world class chef, Mario Batali. He was the chef who prepared the meal at the final state dinner held by President Obama and First Lady Michelle Obama for the Italian Prime Minister and his wife. In true Italian style the first course, after canapés, was pasta. In this case it was *Sweet Potato Agnolotti: "A velvety pillow of paper-thin pasta" stuffed with sweet potatoes, garnished with nutmeg and parsley, and topped with browned butter and sage.* Yum! No need for a second, third and fourth course for me! A little garlic bread to go with the pasta and I'm good. It's cool to be a relative the great chef, but makes no sense at all, much to my wife's chagrin; I can't boil an egg properly. I can brew a proper English breakfast cuppa!

My Line of Descendants of Thomas Tracy
My direct line of descendants of Thomas Tracy left Connecticut after 1756, moving to Berkshire County, Massachusetts. From there my family line is traced to Pawlet County, Vermont; Jefferson County New York; Wood County, West Virginia; Washington County, Ohio; Buena Vista County, Iowa; Kimble County, Nebraska; and Morgan County, Colorado. My immediate family lived in various parts of the country: Colorado, Idaho, Florida, Ohio, before settling in Calloway County, Kentucky. Given my own history of living in numerous places in the United States and abroad, I'd say there might be something to the notion that my Tracy family line is afflicted with a genetic wanderlust code, all part of the DNA!

Summary
So there you have it, a true confession of an addicted yet proudly not recovering victim of the infectious *Cognatio Genealogia Indagatio Insectum (CGII).* Have I adequately answered my original question of who got what, when, and how? Well, not entirely. There are always more questions and I hope I've raised a few new ones. I hope that you have found the stories to be interest and that I've elevated your desire to know more. As for me, I know that my quest to unlock a few of the mysteries of what made Thomas and Stephen tick has vastly increased my appreciation for early American history. It has given me a great deal of respect and great admiration for these two individual's sense of adventure, courage, and dedication to civic duties, as well as their love of family, community, and the common good.

Stephen clearly fits the mold of the stereotypical portrait of your garden variety Plymouth Colony Puritan. From the time he left Norfolk

County, England as a young man to cast his lot with the Puritans in Holland to when he became a Pilgrim and prominent leader in Plymouth and Duxbury he played by the rules in a society that was free to worship as they pleased. Even though, to be sure, those same rules did not apply to people with deviant religious views or who were not fully accepted into the church. Nevertheless, you have to hand it to him; he made a good life for himself and his family by overcoming incredible hardships, learning to farm, and being profoundly engaged in the religious, economic, and social development of the fledging colony.

Although Thomas was also a Puritan, he seems to have been driven more by his search for a place where he could prosper than by seeking refuge for his religious practices. While he was skilled as a carpenter, he rose way above the relatively low status of that honorable trade by learning how to survey property lines, how to befriend accommodating Indians, how to fight the ones who threatened those he loved, and how to support his family as a successful surveyor, farmer, and land owner. He gradually won the respect of his fellow travelers which led to his many elections to the General Court and other prominent positions of authority and respect, especially in Norwich. He and his children left an indelible mark on the history of Norwich and the Connecticut Colony, as well as the embryonic United States.

I believe it is fair to say that Thomas was a self-made man who was among the very first immigrants to live the American dream. I like to think that he preferred a life path in keeping with Ralph Waldo Emerson's admonition *"Do not go where the path may lead, go instead, where there is no path, and leave a trail."* That is how he lived his life, as a trail blazer. Thomas' life reflects that he believed in a mixture of self-reliance and civic involvement. I'm sure he would have been very comfortable as a fellow Rotarian adhering to the motto of "Service Above Self."

I must confess to having a much greater sense of pride in my paternal heritage knowing that I carry the DNA of these brave and illustrious men.

I hope that my much beloved son, granddaughters, sister, cousins, and members of my extended family share my enthusiasm for the legacy of our ancestors. And that the multitudes of those of you who are also linked to Thomas or Stephen do as well.

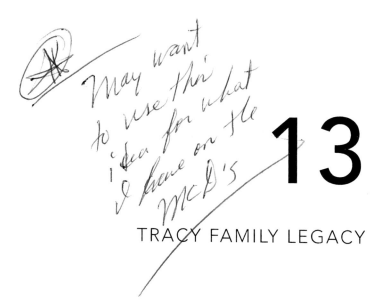

May want to use this idea for what I have on the MCD's

13

TRACY FAMILY LEGACY

BUT WAIT, THERE'S MORE, as the obnoxious commercial announcer with the loud, irritating voice shouts from the TV screen. One more thing before you put this book on the shelf, the dust begins to settle on the cover, and the booklice begin to enjoy a meal. While I'm convinced that Thomas and Stephen were not of English high society, rather that they created their own legacies. They laid the foundation for many of their descendants who have also left a permanent imprint on American society. The list includes lawyers, ministers, community advocates, national leaders, artisans, politicians, businessman, military officers, and even fellow Rotarians. I'll take the liberty of identifying a select few descendants of Stephen Tracy's son John Tracy and his daughter, Sarah Tracy Partridge. I've also listed some of the descendants of Lt. Thomas Tracy's sons. Most of those listed are descendants of Thomas Tracy, Jr., John Tracy, and Jonathan Tracy. Jonathan is my direct ancestor.

I made a diligent effort to find interesting male descendants of Thomas. I focused on males because it is so much easier to search for family members with the surname Tracy. While it was relatively easy to find descendants of Thomas, Jr., John, and Jonathan, this was not the case with his other sons, Samuel and Daniel. Samuel was "without issue" as they say, so that was a dead end. Daniel is marginally mentioned in histories of Norwich, so I don't think he was very prominent and I've been unsuccessful in identifying a notable descendant. Thomas' son Dr. Solomon Tracy seemed promising as a primogenitor of interesting descendants, but I could find only one descendant of note. The descendants I did manage to find are listed below, mostly, in chronological order.

Stephen Tracy, Jr. Descendants

Direct Descendants of Stephen Tracy's son John (1633-1718)
Reverend Stephen Tracy (1749-1822) was the first minister of the Congregational Church in Partridgefield (Peru), Berkshire, Massachusetts 1772-1776. He helped to recruit soldiers and raise resources for the Revolution. He was later the first pastor of the First Congregational Church in Norwich, Massachusetts from 1779 to 1781. He was also a state representative in 1804. For a brief period in 1812 he was a missionary to Rhode Island where he conducted family genealogical research. He was a strong opponent to the War of 1812.

Reverend Joseph Tracy (1794-1874) was a graduate of Dartmouth and pastor of Congregational Churches in Vermont. He was a well-known theologian with numerous influential publications. *Wikipedia* describes him as *"a Protestant Christian minister, newspaper editor, historian and leading figure in the American Colonization Society of the early to mid-19th century. He is noted as a typical figure of the New England Renaissance."*

Benjamin Franklin Tracy (1830-1915) was a lawyer, soldier, judge, and Secretary of the Navy 1889-1893. His *Wikipedia* entry says *"Tracy was noted for his role in the creation of the "New Navy", a major reform of the service, which had fallen into obsolescence after the Civil War."* He is, therefore, known as the *"Father of the Modern American Fighting Navy."* Had I known this as an 18-year old when I graduated high school, I might have gone into the Navy instead of the Army. That way I would not always be on the losing end of the annual Army-Navy football classic in Philadelphia. I personally witnessed the 43-12 drubbing by Navy in 1959. Not much has changed over the subsequent years.

Dr. Roger Sherman Tracy (1841-1926) was the Uncle of Evarts Tracy highlighted next. Roger graduated from Yale in 1862 and received a M.D. degree from Columbia University in 1868. He was most noted for his work in sanitation, authoring numerous books on the subject, including the *Handbook of Sanitary Information for Householders* (1884), *The Essentials of Anatomy, Physiology, and Hygiene* (1884). He was also the author of *The White Man's Burden: A Satirical Forecast* (under the *nom de plume* of T. Shirby Hodge) in 1915. This is a science fiction story set in 5,000 CE in which the White race is living in chaos in North America while the Black race lives in a Utopia in Africa. It was endorsed by W. E. B. DuBois who said *"I have read this book with interest and recommend it to my friends. It has a fine lesson in its breast which is voiced in the concluding lines: The White man's burden is himself."* I bought a copy in early spring 2016. It isn't great literature but it relates a very imaginative story with eerily spot on predications of technology in life as we know it. I highly recommend you check it out.

Evarts Tracy (1868-1922), brother of Roger, graduated from Yale University in 1890. He was a renowned architect and head partner of the New York architectural firm of *Tracy and Swartwout*. The firm designed many well-known buildings, including the U.S. Post Office, the Federal Building, the Cathedral of Saint John in the Wilderness, and the Court House in Denver, Colorado. The firm also designed the George Washington and Victory Memorial in Washington, D.C. and the Missouri State Capitol. The papers of Evarts Tracy, Roger Tracy and other Tracy Yale University graduates contained in the *Tracy Family Papers 1794-1937* collection are housed in the *Manuscripts and Archives of Sterling Memorial Library*, Yale University, New Haven, Connecticut. Evarts is of special interest to me since my father grew up in Colorado and received his Master's in Speech at Denver University. He would have been astonished that so many well-known public buildings in the city were designed by a distant relative.

Howard Crosby Tracy (1866-????) was an 1887 graduate of Yale University. He earned a LL.B. from Columbia in 1889. He was a partner with Wolcott G. Lane in the New York City law firm of Tracy & Lane. He served several years as a member of the Republican city committee of Plainfield, New Jersey.

Direct Descendants of Stephen Tracy's Daughter Sarah (1621-1708)
Ulysses S. Grant (1822-1885) was the Commanding General of the US Army and 18th President of the United States. Connections like this to famous people are a little misleading. Given the small pool of people who settled the colonies, almost anyone who lived there at the time has famous or infamous descendants. Descendants of maternal lines are harder to find, so I thought I would throw this one in since Grant is connected to Sarah Tracy Partridge.

Lt. Thomas Tracy's Descendants

Direct Descendants of Lt. Thomas Tracy's son Thomas Tracy, Jr. (1644-1721)
Ebenezer Tracy (1744-1803) owned a large cabinet making business in Norwich, Connecticut. He is best known for his Windsor chairs that are still sought after by museums. Chairs built by him and his son are held by the Metropolitan Museum of Art, the Connecticut Historical Society, and the Winterthur Museum in Delaware. The Leffingwell House Museum in Norwich also has some original Windsor chairs.

John Tracy (1763-1864) was an American lawyer and politician. He was elected Lieutenant Governor of New York, serving from 1833 to 1836. He was also a Regent of the University of the State of New York. In 1846 he was a delegate to the New York State Constitutional Convention from Chenango County and was chosen its President. After the convention of 1846, he withdrew from political life.

Phineas Lyman Tracy (1786-1876), the brother of Albert Haller Tracy mentioned below, was a Whig from New York who served in the U.S. Congress, 1827-1833. He was a graduate of Yale University.

Albert Haller Tracy (1793-1859) was a Democrat in the U.S. House of Representatives from New York and a member of the New York State Senate. *Wikipedia* notes that he was elected as a "Democratic-Republican." I had to look that up! It was the political party of Thomas Jefferson and James Madison. It was formed in opposition to the Federalist Party and dominated American politics for 20 years until the 1820s when it faded away into the political dust bin.

Calvin Tracy (1805-1889) was a Professor of Mathematics at Michigan Agricultural College (Michigan State). In fact he was the FIRST professor chosen for the College which began in 1857. His first major book was *A New System of Arithmetic* (brief title) written in 1840. He also wrote *The Commercial and Mechanical Arithmetic* in 1855.

Reverend William Tracy (1807-1878) was a native of Norwich, Connecticut and a missionary to India beginning in 1846. He stayed there for over 40 years. A graduate of Williams College, he was the President of a theological seminary at Thirumangalam and was known as the Father of Pasumalai in Madurai India. He held a Doctor of Divinity degree from the University of Western Pennsylvania (University of Pittsburgh).

Charles H. Tracy (1833-1911) was a recipient of the Medal of Honor for two acts of bravery during the American Civil War. The first was at the *Battle of Spotsylvania Court House* in Virginia on May 12, 1864. The second was for bravery at the *Third Battle of Petersburg* in Virginia on April 2, 1865.

Direct Descendants of Thomas Tracy's son, John (1642-1702)
Dr. Elisha Tracy (1712-1783) was a physician in Norwich. He was among the first doctors to inoculate against smallpox for which he was heavily fined under a Connecticut law that forbid inoculations. His 20-year old son, *Phineas Lyman Tracy* (1755-1775) was killed at Roxbury, Massachusetts during the siege of Boston in the Revolutionary War. Dr. Elisha Tracy also had a foster son, *Dr. Philip Turner* (1740-1815) who was a noted surgeon from Norwich and New York. He was surgeon-general of the northern

states during the Revolutionary War. The Turner Paper Collection is housed at the *David M. Rubenstein Rare Book & Manuscript Library*, Duke University. Dr. Turner also trained Dr. Ebenezer Tracy (see below under Thomas Tracy, Jr.).

Uriah Tracy (1755-1807) was a graduate of Yale and a Federalist U.S. Representative from Connecticut, 1793-96. He was also a U.S. Senator from Connecticut, 1796-1807. *Wikipedia* notes that he has the distinction of being the first member of Congress interred in the Congressional Cemetery. His descendants include the mathematician Curtis Tracy McMullen and the author Jeanie Gould. He was the author of *Scipio's Reflections on Monroe's View of the Conduct of the Executive on the Foreign Affairs of the United States: Connected with a Mission to the French Republic in the Years 1794, '95, '96.* It was published in 1798. For some years the book had been erroneously credited to Alexander Hamilton

Henry Brown Tracy (1805-1878) was for many years the President of the Merchants National Bank of Norwich, Connecticut. Early in his career he was connected to the Yantic Manufacturing Company of Norwich. The mill burned down about 1865 and was replaced by the Yantic Woolen Company Mill.

Charles Tracy (1810-1885) was a graduate of Yale and a New York lawyer and counsel for numerous charitable societies in New York City. In 1855 he published a fascinating diary he kept during a summer excursion to Mount Desert Island, Maine: *The Tracy Log Book 1855: A Month in Summer.* His daughter, Francis, listed below, married John Pierpont Morgan. Like several of my contemporary cousins, Charles was a staunch Episcopalian.

Brigadier General Edward Dorr Tracy (1833-1863) was born in Macon, Georgia. He was a graduate of the University of Georgia, deacon of the First Presbyterian Church, and delegate to the 1860 Democratic National

Convention. He was living in Huntsville, Alabama when he joined the Confederacy in 1861. He was made Brigadier General in 1862. He was killed in action on May 1, 1863 at Port Gibson, Mississippi.

Reverend Charles Chapin Tracy (1838-1917) was a missionary, philanthropist, and educator. He graduated from William College. He was the first President of Anatolia College in Marsovan, Turkey. I wish I had known this when my wife, Patsy, and I served in the Peace Corps in Turkey, 1965-67. It would have been a good talking point with our Turkish colleagues and friends.

Frances Louise Tracy (1842-1924) was the daughter of New York lawyer Charles Tracy (1810-1885) noted above. She was the second wife of John Pierpont Morgan and the mother of all four of his children. The J. P. Morgan family records link Frances to Lt. Thomas Tracy. The records also attempt to link her to Stanway. Her pedigree is ostensibly traced back to Tassilo the Roman, circa 550.

Francis Gallatin Tracy (1863-1931) was the President of the Pecos Irrigation Company in Carlsbad, New Mexico. He testified in 1902 in the early hearings on statehood which was achieved in 1912. He grew the first crop of peaches in the state and experimented with raising cotton. He was a member of the Rotary Club of Carlsbad. I included him in the list because of current family ties to New Mexico and because he was a fellow Rotarian, serving above self.

Dr. John Clayton Tracy (1869-1955) was a Professor of Civil Engineering and Head of the Department of Civil Engineering, Sheffield Scientific School, Yale University. He received his Ph.D. and C.E. from Yale. He was the author of numerous books including: *Surveying: Theory and Practice*, 1947 and *Plane Surveying: A Text-Book and Pocket Manual*. His ancestor Thomas Tracy would have been very proud to know that a descendant had his surveying skills!

Henry Chester Tracy (1876-1958) was a biologist who wrote novels, operas, librettos, plays, poems, and articles for scientific journals. Some of his work was performed at Carnegie Hall and the Metropolitan Opera to great acclaim. His works include *The Two Gentlemen of Verona*, *Towards the Open: A Preface to Scientific Humanism*, and *Significance of White Markings in Birds of the Order Passeriformes*. He was born in Pennsylvania. He graduated from the University of California where he also briefly taught.

Direct Descendants of Thomas' son, Jonathan Tracy (1646-1711) – My Ancestor
Brigadier General Elisha Leffingwell Tracy (1800-1862) was a Confederate Brigadier General who was a veteran of the Mexican War and Commander of Fort Walker in Louisiana and the 1st Brigade of the Louisiana State Troops in 1861. He was born in Norwich, Connecticut. I don't know the story behind his becoming a Confederate officer. One possible reason is that he married a woman from New Orleans, Eliza Early, in 1825. He became a wealthy broker and had a strong interest in the military. He joined the New Orleans volunteer militia early in his career and made Brigadier General by 1852. He died of illness on October 16, 1862 in Chatawa Station, Mississippi.

Frederick Palmer Tracy (1815-1860), better known as F. P. Tracy, was born in Connecticut. He became a Methodist minister before going into the law profession. He was very active in Republican politics. He moved to San Francisco, California in 1849 and was admitted to the Bar in 1851. He was known nationally as a writer and lecturer on theology and abolitionism. He became a member of the New England Historic Genealogical Society on May 17, 1858. He believed that his family line could be traced to the Tracys of Stanway. His genealogical research on the Tracy family lines influenced Reuben Walworth, Frances Manwaring Caulkins, and other genealogists.

Cyrus Mason Tracy, Jr. (1824-1891), brother of Frederick Palmer Tracy was a noted botanist and historian of Essex County, Massachusetts. He was the author of Studies of the Essex Flora in 1858 and co-author of *Standard*

History of Essex County, Massachusetts. He was a founder of the "Exploring Circle" of Lynn, Massachusetts which morphed into the Trustees of the Free Public Forest.

Colonial Amasa Jonathan Tracy (1829-1908). According to *Wikipedia*, Amasa Tracy is best known for his four years as an officer in the Union Army during the Civil War. He enlisted as a 1st Lieutenant, fought in numerous battles, and was promoted to Colonel. He was awarded the Medal of Honor in April 2, 1865 for his gallantry commanding the Old Vermont Brigade in a charge of Rebel lines at Petersburg, Virginia. He was severely wounded at the Battle of Cedar Creek in the Shenandoah Valley on October 19, 1864. Following the war he went home to Middlebury, Vermont. There he was a Postmaster, manufacturer of carriages, and a U.S. Customs Agent.

Five Tracy Brothers: Five very interesting descendants of Jonathan Tracy are brothers Moses, Caleb Ensign, Joseph F., Lorenzo D., and Silas Horace Tracy. They are sons of Caleb B. Tracy (1786-1870) and nephews of my 2nd Great Grandfather, Joseph Tracy (1793-1855). The five brothers all left their home in Ellisburg, New York and traveled along the Oregon Trail at different times. Three ended up in Oregon and two in Utah. Three were Mormon and two were not. Two years ago in 2014 I wrote about their travels. If anyone is interested, I'd be glad to share that description.

Joseph F. Tracy (1820-1874) and *Silas Horace* (1830-1881). These were two of the brothers listed above. They traveled together with their wives and children. They left Kanesville, Iowa (Council Bluffs) on June 10, 1852 with the Joseph Outhouse Company. There were 230 individuals and 50 wagons in the Company. When it arrived at Utah on September 6, 1852, only 137 individuals remained alive. The wife of Silas Horace Tracy, Nancy Naomi Alexander Tracy, kept a fascinating diary of the trek to Utah: *Tracy, Nancy Naomi Alexander, Reminiscences and Diary, 1896 May – 1899, July, 37-42*. It is available online at

http://documents.htracyhall.org/pdf/IRH-Genealogy/Materials%20Added%20
April%202014/Nancy%20Naomi%20Alexander%20Tracy.pdf.

Direct Descendants of Thomas Tracy's son, Solomon (1650-1732)
Dr. Ebenezer Tracy (1762-1856) was a physician in Middletown, Connecticut
for more than 60 years. He was an itinerant doctor visiting his patients on
horseback. He is described as *"a gentlemen of great smoothness of manners."* He
was trained by Dr. Philip Turner who also Ebenezer's cousin Dr. Elisha
Tracy noted above.

Tracy Family Expansion in the 1700s
Frances Manwaring Caulkins wrote in 1845 and 1865 that in the 1700s
many descendants of the original settlers of Norwich founded numerous other communities. She mentions several Tracys in this context. For
example, Andrew Tracy and his son, Peleg, were among the first settlers
under the Indian Delaware Purchase that became Susquehanna County,
Pennsylvania. The above mentioned Dr. Elisha Tracy, along with Perez,
Jared, Philemon, and Benjamin Tracy were among the original grantees
of the Vermont town of Turnersburgh (now Chelsea, Orange County) in
1781. In 1767 several residents of Norwich, Connecticut settled Norwich,
Massachusetts which was renamed Huntington in 1855. The first Minister
of the Congregational Church in the community was Rev. Stephen Tracy,
a descendant of Stephen Tracy, Jr.

Good luck in researching and finding your roots! If you find errors in
this narrative or feel compelled to add information, please do and let me
know! Thanks for accompanying me on my journey through time.

As you blaze your own trail through your family genealogy, I offer a
final thought from Laurence Overmire (b. 1957), contemporary American
poet, author, actor, educator, peace activist, civil rights, human rights, animal rights advocate, environmentalist, and genealogist.

"Over the course of the millennia, all these multitudes of ancestors, gen-eration upon generation, have come down to this moment in time—to give birth to you. There has never been, nor will ever be, another like you. You have been given a tremendous responsibility. You carry the hopes and dreams of all those who have gone before. Hopes and dreams for a better world. What will you do with your time on this Earth? How will you contribute to the ongoing story of humankind?"

#luvurlineage!!

ABBREVIATED ANNOTATED BIBLIOGRAPHY

Stephen Tracy, Jr. (1596-1655)

Robert Charles Anderson, *The Great Migration Begins: Immigrants to New England 1620-1633, II G-O* (Boston, MA: Great Migration Study Project, New England Historic Genealogical Society, 1995), 1120. Anderson makes a reference to Stephen Tracie's (sic) land near Iland Creeke (sic).

Robert Charles Anderson, *Pilgrim Village Families Sketch: Stephen Tracy*. Retrieved August 11, 2013 from http://www.americanancestors. org/pilgrim-families-stephen-tracy/. Anderson gives a sketch of the life of Stephen Tracy.

Robert Charles Anderson, "Stephen Tracy", The Great Migration Begins: Immigrants to New England 1620-1633, I-III. (Online database: *AmericanAncestors.org,* New England Historic Genealogical Society, 2010), (Originally published as: New England Historic Genealogical Society. Robert Charles Anderson, *The Great Migration Begins: Immigrants to New England 1620-1633, Volumes I-III,* 3 vols., 1995), 373-374, 1832-1834. Anderson provides a biography of Stephen Tracy. In this publication Anderson notes that Stephen returned to England permanently, *"perhaps as early as 1643, and certainly by 1654."* It was later documented that Stephen was living in Duxbury as late as 1652. The author also mentions a grant of land to Stephen Tracy on November 2, 1640 *"at the North River."* His son-in-law George Partrich (sic) [Partridge] was granted 30 acres with some meadow next to Stephen's property.

Robert Charles Anderson, *The Great Migration Directory: Immigrants to New England 1620–1640 A Concise Compendium* (Boston: New England Historic Genealogical Society, 2015), 340; *U.S. and Canada, Passenger and Immigration Lists Index, 1500s–1900s,* online at Ancestry.com. Anderson provides the following entry for Stephen Tracy: *"Tracy, Stephen: Leiden, Holland; 1623 on*

Anne; Plymouth, Duxbury; returned permanently to England by 1654 [GMB 1832-34; PM 463-65; Abandoning 294]."

Robert Charles Anderson (Ed.), "Focus on Great Migration Towns." *The Great Migration Newsletter*, v. 14, No. 3 (July-September, 2005): 439. The origin of the town of Duxbury is described.

Robert Charles Anderson (Ed.), "Focus on The Jury System." *The Great Migration Newsletter*, v. II, No. 2 (April-June, 2002): 11. This article mentions Steephen (sic) Tracy as a member of the Plymouth Colony Grand Jury at the court of March 7, 1636/7.

"*Anne*," Retrieved September 14, 2106 from www.packrat-pro.com/ships/anne.htm. This website notes that the Anne left London with her Master, William Pierce, arriving at "Plymouth June or July of 1623, carrying many family members left behind from the *Mayflower* and the *Fortune*. It shows that Stephen arrived with his wife, Tryphosa and child, Sarah. His family probably did not accompany him.

Sarah Y. Bailey, *The Story of Jones River in Pilgrim Plymouth 1620-1726 which in the Latter Year became Kingston, Massachusetts* (Kingston, MA: Kingston Branch of the Alliance of Unitarian Women, 1920), 8-9, 11, 37. Bailey discusses the 1624 and 1627 land grants in Duxbury and the Jones River Settlement. She mentions that Stephen Tracy was a Say Maker in Leiden.

Jeremy Dupertuis Bangs, *Strangers and Pilgrims, Travellers (sic) and Sojourners: Leiden and the Foundations of Plymouth Plantation* (Plymouth, MA: General Society of Mayflower Descendants, 2009), 271, 289, 689, 715, 719, 726. Dr. Bangs, Director and founder of the Leiden American Pilgrim Museum in Leiden, writes a very scholarly work on the Pilgrims in Holland. He documents the marriage of Stephen and Tryphosa, discusses the Mayflower Compact, the debt to the Merchants, and the Pawtuxet origin of Duxbury.

Charles Edward Banks, *Topographical Dictionary of 2885 English Emigrants to New England 1620-1650* (Philadelphia, PA: Elijah Ellsworth Brownell, B. E. E., 1937), 58, 123-24. Banks cites the *Mayflower Descendant* 10/143 that Stephen came from Yarmouth, arriving on the *Anne*. Banks does not mention that Thomas Tracy's first destination was Watertown, Massachusetts.

Charles Edward Banks, *The English Ancestry and Homes of the Pilgrim Fathers Who Came to Plymouth on the "Mayflower" in 1620, the "Fortune" in 1621, and the "Anne" and the "Little James" in 1623* (Baltimore, MD: Genealogical Publications Co., Inc., 1964), ccxli, 123, 164. Banks notes that Stephen Tracy, Jr. was one of 32 individuals who went to Leiden, Holland from Great Yarmouth, England. Banks gives a very brief biography of Stephen. He notes that William Palmer of Plymouth mentions Stephen in his will of 1637.

Charles Edward Banks, *The Planters of the Commonwealth: A Study of the Emigrants and Emigration in Colonial Times: To Which are Added Lists of Passengers to Boston and to the Bay Colony; the Ships Which Brought Them; Their English Homes, and the Places of Their Settlement in Massachusetts 1620-1640* (Baltimore, MD: Genealogical Publishing Co., 1967), 54. Banks reproduces a passenger list by Abigail Warren showing *Stephen Tracy, Mrs. Stephen Tracy, and …. Tracy from Yarmouth arriving on the Anne*. This, as noted elsewhere is in dispute.

Francis Baylies, *An Historical Memoir of the Colony of New Plymouth. From the Flight of the Pilgrims into Holland in the Year 1606, to the Union of That Colony with Massachusetts in 1692* (Boston, MA: Wiggin & Lunt, 1866), 261, 263, 277, 309. The author gives details of the land granted to Stephen Tracy in 1623 & 1627 and mention him as recipient of land as an "old comer" in 1640. Stephen is also mentioned as one of the "*principal men of the colony.*"

George Ernest Bowman (Ed.), "Plymouth Colony Vital Records" *The Mayflower Descendant: An Illustrated Quarterly Magazine of Pilgrim Genealogy,*

History and Biography, no. 13 & 14 (1911):184. The marriage of Sarah Tracy and Georg Partrich (sic) is shown as November 1638.

George Ernest Bowman (Ed.), "Plymouth Colony Deeds: Stephen Tracy's Power of Attorney" *The Mayflower Descendant: An Illustrated Quarterly Magazine of Pilgrim Genealogy, History and Biography,* X (1908), 143-144. This is a complete copy of Stephen Tracy's Power of Attorney given to John Winslow. It is dated March 20, 1654/56.

Gershom Bradford, *Historic Duxbury in Plymouth Colony* (Boston, MA: G. Bradford, 1920), 11-12. Bradford lists Stephen Tracy as being one of the Duxbury freemen in 1646.

William Bradford, *History of Plymouth Plantation 1620-1647,* I (Boston, MA: The Massachusetts Historical Society, 1912), 316, 348-349. Governor Bradford lists the amount of acreage granted to Stephen Tracy (3) on the South Side of Plymouth in the division of land in 1623.

William Bradford, *Governor William Bradford's Letter Book* (Reprinted from the Mayflower Descendant) (Boston, MA: The Massachusetts Society of Mayflower Descendants, 1906), 39-40. Bradford documents that Stephen Trasie (sic) was one of those who participated in the purchase of Plymouth from the Merchant Company of Adventurers.

William Bradford & Worthington Chauncey Ford, *History of Plymouth Plantation 1620-1647,* II (Boston, MA: The Massachusetts Historical Society, 1912), 28-31. The authors list Stephen Trasie (sic) as one of the signers of the agreement to purchase Plymouth from the Merchants arranged by Allerton.

British Farthings, 17th Century Tokens: Yarmouth-04 in Norfolk. Retrieved April 23, 2016 from http://www.britishfarthings.com/Tokens/17th-Century/Norfolk/Yarmouth-04.html. This site lists the farthings created and used by Stephen Tracy, Sr. in Great Yarmouth.

Walter H. Burgess, *John Robinson Pastor of the Pilgrim Fathers: A Study of His Life and Times* (London, England: Williams and Norgate, 1920), 108-109, 157-158, 273-274. Burgess describes the location of the Pilgrim homes in Holland in the Zevenhuysen Ward, including Stephen and Tryphosa Tracy. The author describes a letter from Rev. Robinson regarding the *Anne* that carried Stephen.

William T. Davis (Ed.), *Bradford's History of Plymouth Plantation 1606-1646* (New York, NY: Barnes & Noble, Inc., 1908), 38-39, 44. This provides a description of living conditions of the Puritans in Holland.

William T. Davis, *Genealogical Register of Plymouth Families* (Baltimore, MD: Genealogical Publishing Co., Inc., 1975), 266. Davis notes that Stephen Tracy, his wife and child, arrived at Plymouth on the Anne in 1623. It also lists his children who were born afterwards.

William T. Davis, *History of the Town of Plymouth, with a Sketch of the Origin and Growth of Separatism* (Philadelphia, PA: J. A. Lewis & Co., 1885), 11, 31, 34, 46. In addition to giving a history of Separatism, the book makes numerous references to Stephen and Tryphosa Lee Tracy in the Plymouth Colony.

Patricia Scott Deetz, Christopher Fennell, & J. Eric Deetz, *William Tubs of Plymouth and Duxburrow: His Network of Relations in Plymouth (1635-1636) and Duxburrow (1636-1685?)*, The *Plymouth Colony Archive Project*, retrieved November 27, 2007 from http://www.histarch.illinois.edu/plymouth/Tubsnet.htm. The authors note that Stephen Tracy was among 12 men to receive *"land with meadow north of the Jones River"* in 1623.

"Emily Fuller Drew Collection MC16 Folder 4.6 Duxbury", 4-5. This document is also under the heading "Bradford and Freeman Notes on Island Creek." This document is a copy of a paper loaned to Ms. Drew by *"Mr. Henry A. Fish of Duxbury who probably copied and revised an article written in or about 1814 by a Mr. Bradford which had already been edited by Deacon Arnold*

Freeman of Island Creek." The document is housed at the Kingston Public Library, Kingston, MA. In the document is a paragraph on the location of the Duxbury property of Stephen Tracy north of that of Joseph Rogers. It also mentions the heritance of the land by John Tracy who sold it to Thomas Loring in 1702.

Thomas Bradford Drew, *The Ancient Estate of Governor William Bradford* (Boston, MA: Thos. P. Smith Printing Co., 1897), 5, 15-17, 34-35. Drew describes the location of Stephen Tracy as a neighbor of William Bradford at Jones River (Kingston, Massachusetts). The author also provides the will of Gov. Bradford with a bequest to his son, John, whose widow married Thomas Tracy.

Email from Susan Aprill, Archivist, Kingston Public Library, Kingston, Massachusetts, April 25, 2016. Ms. April responded to an email I sent on April 23 requesting information Stephen Tracy who lived near Governor Bradford at Jones River before 1636. She referred me to *The Story of Jones River* and promised to check other sources.

Email from Susan Aprill, Archivist, Kingston Public Library, Kingston, Massachusetts, May 13, 2016. Ms. Aprill attached two PDF files to an email taken from the Library's Vertical Files section on Land Division. She also sent a scanned paper of a copy of a paper by a Mr. Bradford given to the Library by Emily Fuller Drew.

Email from Charles Butcher, July 8, 2012. Mr. Butcher responded to my email requesting assistance regarding the story of Sir John Tracy of Stanhoe. He noted that there is a mention of Sir. John in Blomefield's History and the Visitation of Norfolk of 1664. He promised to look for the grave slab and refer my inquiry to local historian Gilliam Beckett.

Email from Lamont (Monty) R. Healy, May 6, 2016. Monty Healy replied to my email inquiry originally sent to Susan April.

Email from Lamont (Monty) R. Healy, May 11, 2016. Mr. Healy replied to my request for more information on the location of Stephen Tracy's property in Duxbury.

Email from Lamont (Monty) R. Healy, May 18, 2016." Mr. Healy gave me the definition of an acre and a "*lot*" as used by the Pilgrims.

Emails from Joanne Penn, August 20-23, 2013. Ms. Penn noted that there is a widespread error that Stephen Tracy, Sr. was the son of Christopher Tracy. He was the son of Roger and Margaret Tracy. She also noted that "*it is perfectly possible that Thomas and Stephen were related.*"

Emails from Carolyn Ravenscroft, April 27, 2016 & April 28, 2016. Ms. Ravenscroft, Archivist & Historian, Duxbury Rural & Historical Society, responded to an inquiry regarding material on Stephen Tracy in the Society. She referred me to Monty Healy. I sent her a copy of a PDF summary of the life of Stephen Tracy written June 14, 2013.

Email from Kimberly Stella, Administrative Assistant, Imaging and Rights, The Morgan Library and Museum, September 16, 2013. The email included the invoice for copies of the *Pedigree of Tracy of Toddington Co., Gloucester and Norwich, Connecticut: Autograph Manuscript and Typeset, 1904* by Wharton Dickinson.

Email from Tom Thompson, Archivist, Norfolk Record Office, Norwich, England, October 3, 2012. Mr. Thompson responded to an email request from me originally sent to Hannah Verge regarding records from St. Peter Mancroft Church in Norwich where a Thomas Tracy was alleged to have missed services in 1632. Meredith B. Colket, Jr. speculated that this might have been Thomas Tracy of Connecticut.

Email from Martin B. Tracy to Joanne Penn, August 21, 2013. In this email I provide genealogist Joanne Penn some references for background material to assist in her work on finding information on the family of Stephen Tracy, Jr.

Email from Carolyn Vega, Assistant Curator, Literary and Historical Manuscripts, The Morgan Library & Museum August 19, 2013. Ms. Vega mentioned that Francis Morgan's pedigree can be traced back to Tassilo the Roman, ca. 550. Ms. Vega also noted that she did not see any reference to Stephen Tracy in the pedigree typescript by Wharton Dickinson.

Email from Hannah Verge, Archivist, Norfolk Record Office, Norwich, England, July 12, 2012. Ms. Verge verified that Sir John Tracy lived in Stanhoe.

"England, Marriages, 1538-1973," index, *FamilySearch* (https://familysearch.org/pal:MM9.1.1/NXBB-S2K: accessed 21 Nov 2012), Stephen Trass (sic) and Agnes Erdley, 20 Feb 1586; citing reference item 16-26, FHL microfilm 1526327. This documents the marriage between Stephen Tracy, Sr. and Agnes Erdley, parents of Stephen Tracy, Jr.

"England, Birth and Christenings, 1538-1975," *FamilySearch* (https://familysearch.org/pal:/MM9.1.1MD-C2Z: accessed 03 Apr 2013), Stephen Trace (sic), 28 Dec 1596. This notes that Stephen Tracy christened in Yarmouth, Norfolk, England Dec 1596 is the son of Stephen Trace (sic).

Marilou West Ficklin, "*Leyden Pilgrims & The Holy Discipline*." Retrieved April 25, 2016 from www.westerly-journeys.com/pilgrims/pilganci.html. Ficklin explores the background of Tryphosa Lee who married Stephen Tracy, Jr. She notes that the Tracy's lived in Leiden with Thomas Brewer, the Willits, and the Fairfields.

Jillian Galle, "Servants and Masters in the Plymouth Colony, Appendices I, II, and III on Plymouth Laws, Court Orders, and Describing Statistics." *The Plymouth Colony Archive Project*. Retrieved January 8, 2016 from www.histarch.illinois.edu/plymouth/galleapp.html. This document notes that Stephen Tracy hired John Price for four months beginning in June 1638.

Esther Griswold French & Robert Lewis French (Eds.), *The Griswold Family: The First Five Generations in America* (Wethersfield, CT: The Griswold Family Association, 1990), 15-16, 26-27. The editors dispute the claim that the wife of Francis Griswold was a daughter of Thomas Tracy and suggest that she may have been the daughter of Stephen and Tryphosa Tracy. They mention the places Thomas lived, overlooking his residency in Watertown.

Timothy George, *John Robinson and the English Separatist Tradition* (Macon, GA: Mercer University Press, 2005), 73. George notes that Stephen Tracy received a land grant at Namassakeeset in Duxbury.

John A. Goodwin, *The Pilgrim Republic: An Historical Review of the Colony of New Plymouth with Sketches of the Rise of Other New England Settlements, the History of Congregationalism and the Creeds of the Period* (Boston, MA: Houghton Mifflin Company, 1920), 243,245, 295,299, 477. Goodwin mentions Stephen Tracy and family in the land division of 1624 and the cattle division of 1627. Goodwin also notes that Stephen, Triphosa (sic), and Sarah Tracy were all first comers. Rebecca was born in the colony.

Great Migration Begins: Immigrants to New England 1620-1633, Volumes I-III (The) (Online database: NewEnglandAncestors.org, New England Historic Genealogical Society, 2002), (Org. Pub. New England Historic Genealogical Society. Robert Charles Anderson, *The Great Migration Begins: Immigrants to New England 1620-1633, Volumes I-III*, 3 vols., 1995). Retrieved January 1, 2009 from newenglandancestors.org. Anderson gives a description of Stephen Tracy.

Thomas F. Harrington, *Dr. Samuel Fuller, of the Mayflower (1620), the Pioneer Physician* (Baltimore, MD: The Fiedenwald Co., 1903), 2-3. Harrington notes that Dr. Fuller married Bridget Lee.

Mitchell C. Harrison, *Prominent and Progressive Americans: An Encyclopedia of Contemporaneous Biography*, Volume I (New York: New York Tribune, 1902), 25. Harrison notes that Norwich was named by William Backus in 1659. Backus, one of the original 35 settlers of Norwich was from Norwich, Norfolk, England.

Lamont (Monty) R. Healy Registered Land Surveyor, Duxbury, Massachusetts "Letter to Martin Tracy, May 4, 2016." Mr. Healy enclosed a copy of part of Bertram H. White's Plan as part of the Plymouth 2nd Division that Monty is reviewing.

Lamont (Monty) R. Healy, "Letter to Martin B. Tracy, May 6, 2016." Monty encloses his worksheets based on deed and probate information regarding the location of Stephen Tracy's property.

Lamont R. Healy, *Duxbury History Timeline: Duxbury's Settlers, Their Land and Who Came Later* (Author, March 3, 2014), 2 pages. Healy provides a definition of a rod and acre. He also provides information on the land divisions of 1623, 1627, 1710, and 1712.

Lamont R. Healy, "Stephen Tracey (sic) and the Loring Family." *Duxbury Clipper*, Wednesday, October 1, 2014. Duxbury, Massachusetts. Healy includes a map showing the location of Stephen Tracy's land grant in Duxbury.

Lamont R. Healy, "The Kingston Nook – No Man's Land." *Duxbury Clipper*, undated. Duxbury, Massachusetts, 15-16. Healy discusses the boundaries of Duxbury and notes the land grant to Stephen Tracy.

Leon Clark Hills, *Cape Cod Series, 1 History and Genealogy of the Mayflower Planters and First Comers to Ye Olde Colonie* (Baltimore: Genealogical Publishing Co., Inc., 1981), 64-65. Hills provides a brief biography and documents Stephen Tracy as one of the purchasers of Dartmouth, MA.

James E. Homans (Ed), *The Cyclopaedia of American Biography*, v. VIII (New York: The Press Association Compilers, Inc., 1918), 243. Homans discusses Benjamin Franklin Tracy, Secretary of the Navy.

John Camden Hotten, *The Original Lists of Persons of Quality: Emigrants; Religious Exiles; Political Rebels; Serving Men Sold for a Term of Years; Apprentices; Children Stole; Maidens Pressed; and Other Who Went from Great Britain to the American Plantations 1600-1700* (London, England: Author, 1874) (Reprinted New York, NY: Empire State Book Co., 1972), xxx. Stephen Tracy is listed as having arrived on the *Ann* (sic).

E. J. V. Huiginn, *The Graves of Miles Standish and Other Pilgrims* (Booneville, NY: Herald and Tourist Steam Printing House, 1892), 178. The author notes that among the most important settlers of Plymouth after Standish and Brewster was Stephen Tracy.

Hamilton D. Hurd, *History of Plymouth County, Massachusetts with Biographical Sketches of Many of Its Pioneers and Prominent Men* (Philadelphia, PA: J. W. Lewis & Co., 1884), 101, 234, 252-253, 357. Hurd describes paths to and through Stephen Tracy's property in Duxbury, near that of William Bradford. Hurd also lists Stephen Tracy as included in the first list of freemen in 1633

"Items From the City Records at Leyden." *The New England Historical and Genealogical Register* 15 (1861): 30. This article notes that "*Stephen Tracy m. 2 Jan. 1621, Trifisa (sic) ------*." The marriage took place in Leiden, Holland.

Donald Lines Jacobus, *The Waterman Family: Descendants of Robert Waterman of Marshfield, Massachusetts Through Seven Generations*, 1 (New Haven, CT: E. F. Waterman, 1939), 21-28, 688-698. The author notes that Stephen Tracy had a daughter named Mary who was of the right age to have been the wife of Francis Griswold. Jacobus also notes that Thomas Tracy was probably related to Stephen Tracy of Norfolk. The author also repudiates the theory that Mary Mason was the first wife of Thomas.

Caleb Johnson, "Plymouth Colony Division of Cattle, 1627." *The Plymouth Colony Archive Project*. Retrieved January 8, 2016 from www.histarch.illinois .edu/Plymouth/cattlediv.html. Johnson provides details on the division of livestock in 1627.

Tim Lambert, "A Brief History of Norwich: Norwich in the 16th Century." Retrieved December 4, 2015 from www.localhistories.rg/norwich.html. Lambert traces the history of Norwich from when it was a small Anglo-Saxon settlement through the middle ages and each subsequent century. He mentions the Dutch weavers who brought the canaries with them in 1565.

John T. Landis, *Mayflower Descendants and Their Marriages for Two Generations After the Landing Including a Short History of the Church of the Pilgrim Founders of New England* (Washington, DC: Bureau of Military and Civic Achievement, 1922), 14. There is a citation that erroneously shows that William Bradford married a *"Mrs. _____ Wiswall."*

Jason K. Lee, *The Theology of John Smyth: Puritan, Separatist, Baptist, Mennonite* (Macon, GA: Mercer University Press, 2003), 71. Lee notes of the followers of Rev. John Robinson that *"Most of them had come from Norfolk where Robinson had been a minister before his move to Scrooby."* He took about 100 followers to Leiden.

Louis Lehmann, *Ups and Downs in the Life of Reverend Stephen Tracy: First Minister of the First Congregational Church in Norwich, Massachusetts* (March 28, 2011). Retrieved October 24, 2016 from http://freepages.family.rootsweb. ancestry.com/~genealogyaddict/stephentracy.htm. The author provides a detailed description of the life of Rev. Stephen Tracy who was a minister in Partridgeville, Berkshire, Massachusetts and in Norwich, Massachusetts.

Leyden Archives, *Leyden Documents Relating to the Pilgrim Fathers, Permission to Reside at Leyden and Betrothal Records; Together with Parallel Documents from the Amsterdam Archives. Facsimile, Transcript, Translation and Annotations by Dr. D. Plooij of Leyden and Dr. J. Rendel Harris of Manchester. 74 Phototypic Plates. Under the Auspices of the Netherland America Institute. Call Number F68. L68*, Betrothal Book B. Fol. 112 recto (Leyden, Holland: E. J. Brill, 1920), XLII. This document shows the betrothal of Stephen Tracy and Tryphosa Lee. It is housed at the Nashville Public Library, Nashville, TN. It is also available online at: https://familysearch.org/search/catal og/202042?availability=Family%20History%20Library. The document also records the betrothal of Bridget Lee to Samuel Fuller (page XXX). It is suspected that Bridget Lee was a sister of Tryphosa Lee.

Barbara MacAllan, "The Great Yarmouth Company of Migrant Families." *The New England Historical and Genealogical Register* 154 (2000): 215-217 (Boston, MA: New England Historic Genealogical Society, July 1859), 235-237. (Online database:*AmericanAncestors.org*, New England Historic Genealogical Society, 2001-2013. MacAllan discusses the inhabitants of Great Yarmouth who immigrated to New England.

"Mary & John," Retrieved July 17, 2105 from www.packrat-pro.com/ ships/maryjohn2.htm. This website shows that one of these ships carried Henry Travers and William Trace/Tracey (sic). Nothing is known of the fate of this William Tracy.

John Mason & Paul Royster (Ed.), *A Brief History of the Pequot War (1736)*. Electronic Texts in American Studies. Paper 42. http:// digitalcommons.unl.edu/etas/42.

G. E. McCracken, "President Grant's Ancestry: Aftermath." *The American Genealogist*, 52 (1976): 88-90. McCracken notes that Tryphosa did not come with Stephen Tracy on the Anne and provides background of Stephen Tracy, Jr. and his father, Stephen Tracy, Sr.

Susan Hardman Moore, *Pilgrims: New World Settlers & The Call of Home* (New Haven, CT: Yale University Press, 2007), Appendix 2, 180-181. The author includes Stephen Tracy as a New England settler who returned home, 1640-1660. She shows him as returning to Yarmouth, Norfolk.

Samuel Eliot Morison, *The Story of the "Old Colony' of New Plymouth, 1620-1692* (New York, NY: Knopf, 1956), 96-97. Morison provides a description of early life in Plymouth and mentions Stephen. He notes the dismay of many of the Plymouth arrivals regarding food and living conditions.

John Graham Mosely, "Stephen Tracy", *Society of Colonial Wars in the Commonwealth of Massachusetts*, Publication No. 8 (Boston, MA: Printed for the Society, 1906), 219-221. The author provides a biographical sketch of Stephen Tracy, including his origin and appointments in Plymouth and Duxbury.

Norfolk Family History Society, *Transcript of Great Yarmouth St. Nicholas Register of Marriages. Entry from Church of England Marriages from 1558 to 1599.* Stephen Trase (sic). Retrieved March 6, 2013 from http://norfolkfhs.ourarchives.ino/bin/aps_detail.php?id=3254194.   The entry records *"Married 20.02.1586."* This is probably the marriage record of Stephen Tracy and Agnes Erdley.

"Norfolk Token Project". Retrieved May 31, 2016 from https://norfolktokenproject.wordpress.com/tokens/. The website has information and photos on Stephen Tracy's trade tokens.

Norfolk [England] and Norwich [England] Archaeological Society, *A Calendar of the Freeman of Great Yarmouth, 1429-1800* (Norwich, England: Goose and Son, 1910), 53. There is a Stephen Trace (sic) listed as a Freemen of Yarmouth in 1606 who could have been Stephen Tracy, Sr.

Norwich, Norfolk Lists from the Reformation to the Present Time (Norwich, England: Matchett, Stevenson, and Matchett, Market-Place, 1837), 194.

This book lists Stephen Tracey (sic) as a Great Yarmouth merchant with his own farthing token.

N. Grier Parke, II. Donald Lines Jacobus (Ed.), *The Ancestry of Lorenzo Ackley & His Wife Emma Arabella Bosworth* (Woodstock, VT: The Elm Tree Press, 1960), 37-38. Parke and Jacobus provide a concise, accurate summary of the families of Stephen Tracy, Sr. and Stephen Tracy, Jr.

Joanne Penn, Professional Genealogist, Norfolk, England. *Tracy Family History*, July 11, 2012. This is a research document prepared by Joanne Penn, a professional genealogist associated with the Norfolk Record Office, Norfolk, England. She examined the East Ruston parish records to find the family lineage of Stephen Tracy, Sr. (1558-1630) and Stephen Tracy (1596-1654) that came to Plymouth on the *Anne* in 1623. Ms. Penn's website is: http://www.norfolkfamilysearch.co.uk/home.htm.

"Pilgrim Hall Museum, Passengers on the Anne and the Little James." Retrieved December 1, 2007 from http://www.pilgrimhall.org/ FortuneAnneLittleJames.htm. This website provides a list of passengers on the *Anne,* including Stephen, Tryphosa, and Sarah Tracey (sic). It notes that it is more likely that Tryphosa and Sarah came on the Jacob.

"Pilgrim's History in a Nutshell (The)," Retrieved January 13, 2008 from http://www.pigrimarchives.nl.html/pilgrims/top_html/history. html. This brief article discusses John Robinson's move to Leiden, the residence of William Brewster, and the departure of the Pilgrims.

Plimoth Plantation and the New England Historic Genealogical Society, *A Genealogical Profile of Stephen Tracy.* Retrieved May 17, 2016 from http://www.plimoth.org/sites/default/files/media/pdf/tracy_stephen. pdf. This brief profile gives a sketch of Stephen Tracy and family.

"Plymouth Colony Division of Cattle, 1627." *The Plymouth Colony Archive Project.* Retrieved January 8, 2016 from www.histarch.illinois.edu/

plymouth/galleapp.html. This document notes the awards to the Stephen Tracy family in the Division of Cattle.

David Pulsifer (Ed.), *Records of the Colony of New Plymouth in New England Printed by Order of the Legislature of the Commonwealth of Massachusetts, Deeds, &c. v. I.* 1620-1651

(Boston, MA: The Press of William White, 1861), 6, 12, 25, 78, 135. Pulsifer provides the locations of Stephen Tracy's properties.

David Pulsifer (Ed.), *Records of the Colony of New Plymouth in New England Printed by Order of the Legislature of the Commonwealth of Massachusetts, Laws* 1623-1682 (Boston, MA: The Press of William White, 1861), 9, 12. Pulsifer documents that Stephen and his family participated in the Division of Cattle in 1627.

"Rare Coins and Tokens: Dedicated to Serving Collectors Worldwide." Yarmouth, Stephen Tracey (sic) Farthing token. Retrieved September 17, 2016 from http://www.rarecoinsandtokens.co.uk/~millenni/index. php?main_page=product_info&products_id=3175. This website shows that this token was sold July 2016. It includes a description and photograph of the token.

Alvan Talcott & Jacquelyn L. Ricker, *Families of Early Guilford, Connecticut* (Baltimore: Genealogical Publishing Co., Inc., 1984), 530. The authors note the marriage of Thomas Tracy's son, Jonathan, to Mary Griswold.

Daniel Ricketson, *The History of New Bedford, Bristol County, Massachusetts* (New Bedford: Author, 1858), 26-29. Ricketson documents that Stephen Tracy was one of the 58 purchasers of Dartmouth, MA.

James Savage, *A Genealogical Dictionary of the First Settlers of New England Showing Three Generations of Those Who Came Before May, 1692 on the Basis of Farmer's Register,* IV (Baltimore, MD: Genealogical Publishing Company,

1965), 320-321. Savage provides a brief description of Stephen and Thomas Tracy and their children. There are 4 volumes in total.

James Sheppard, *Governor William Bradford, and His Son, Major William Bradford* (New Britain, CT: Author, 1900), 79. Sheppard addresses the name of Gov. Bradford's second wife and erroneously records her name as widow Wiswall who may have been a daughter of Thomas Fitch of Norwalk.

Nathanial B. Shurtleff (Ed.), *Records of the Colony of New Plymouth in New England Printed by Order of the Legislature of the Commonwealth of Massachusetts, Court Orders: I. 1633-1640* (Boston, MA: Press of William White, 1855), multiple pages. Shurtleff documents various appointments, land allocation, and court related events for Stephen Tracy. It is very comprehensive, including proof of being a purchaser of Dartmouth, MA on page 177.

Nathanial B. Shurtleff (Ed.), *Records of the Colony of New Plymouth in New England Printed by Order of the Legislature of the Commonwealth of Massachusetts, Judicial Acts, 1636-1692* (Boston, MA: Press of William White, 1857), 4, 9, 17, 20, 25. Shurtleff cites Stephen Tracy's service on juries.

Nathanial B. Shurtleff (Ed.), *Records of the Colony of New Plymouth in New England Printed by Order of the Legislature of the Commonwealth of Massachusetts, Miscellaneous Records, 1633-1689* (Boston, MA: Press of William White, 1857), 174. Shurtleff notes that Steephen Tracye (sic) is a Freemen of Duxburry.

Nathanial B. Shurtleff (Ed.), *Records of Plymouth Colony: Births, Marriages, Deaths, Burials and Other Records, 1633-1689* (Baltimore, MD: Genealogical Publishing Co., Inc., 1976), 173-175. Shurtleff cites a record of Steephen Tracye (sic) as a Freemen of Duxbury, MA in 1643.

Ian Smith, "The Early Emigrants." *World Family*. Retrieved March 25, 2016 from www.oldcity.org.uk/worldfamily/about/emigrants.php. This online newsletter from Norfolk County, England discusses the reasons for the migration from Norfolk to New England in the 1600s.

William C. Smith, *A History of Chatham, Massachusetts Formerly the Constablewick or Village of Monomoit with Maps and Illustrations and Numerous Genealogical Notes* (Hyannis, MA: F. B. & F. P. Goss, Publishers, 1900), 54. Smith notes that Stephen Tracy received one whole share of the purchase of Dartmouth, MA on March 7, 1652.

Ashbel Steele, *Chief of the Pilgrims: Or the Life and Time of William Brewster Ruling Elder of the Pilgrim Company that Founded New Plymouth, the Parent Colony of New England, in 1620* (Freeport, NY: Books for Libraries Press, 1857), 353, 410. Steele discusses Stephen's move to Duxbury and provides of list of passengers on the *Anne*.

Henry R. Stiles, *The Histories and Genealogies of Ancient Windsor, Connecticut; Including East Windsor, South Windsor, Bloomfield, Windsor Locks, and Ellington 1635-1891, I. History* (Hartford, CT: Press of the Case, Lockwood & Brainard Company, 1891). The author discusses the trading company in Plymouth and the settlement of Windsor.

Eugene Aubrey Stratton, *Plymouth Colony: Its History & People 1620-1691* (Salt Lake City: Ancestry Publishing, 1986), 419, 429, 435. Stratton shows that Stephen Tracy was of 53 who signed the agreement to purchase Plymouth from the Company of Merchant Adventures and the allocation of livestock in the Division of Cattle.

James Thacher, *History of the Town of Plymouth, From Its First Settlement in 1620, to the Present Time: With a Concise History of the Aborigines of New England, and Their Wars with the English, &c* (Boston, MA: Marsh, Capen & Lyon, 1835), 163. Thacher describes the bounds of the Plymouth Colony, including a reference to Stephen Tracy's property.

Clarence Almon Torrey, *New England Marriages Prior to 1700* (Baltimore, MD: Genealogical Publishing Co., Inc., 1985), 751. Torrey lists the marriage of Stephen Tracy to Tryphosa Lee January 2, 1620/1 in Leyden (sic), Holland.

Michael Tepper, *New World Immigrants: A Consolidation of Shop Passenger Lists and Associated Data from Periodical Literature*, I (Baltimore, MD: Genealogical Publishing Co., Inc., 1980), 10-12. Tepper records that Stephen, Tryphosa and Sarah Tracy arrived on the *Anne* in late July, 1623. Note that it more likely that Stephen came by himself. His wife and child probably came later on the *Jacob*.

James Thatcher, *History of the Town of Plymouth from its First Settlement in 1620, To the Present Time: With a Concise History of the Aborigines of New England, and Their Wars with the English, &c* (Boston, MA: Marsh, Capen & Lyon, 1835), 163. Thatcher gives a description of Stephen Tracy's property in Plymouth.

Town of Dartmouth, Massachusetts, "A Brief History." Retrieved November 30, 2015 from http://www.town.dartmouth.ma.us/about-our-town/pages/brief-history. This is a brief history of Dartmouth, the Quaker community whose property was originally purchased by 34 proprietors from Plymouth, including Stephen Tracy.

Town of Duxbury, "Bay Farm Conservation Area." Retrieved September 20, 2016 from http://www.town.duxbury.ma.us/public_documents/DuxburyMA_Conservation/ConAreas/bayfarm?textPage=1. This city website describes the present-day conservation area and briefly mentions the Loring family. It notes that the original owners were Stephen Tracy and, later, John Tracy.

Evert E. Tracy, *Tracy Genealogy: Ancestors and Descendants of Lieutenant Thomas Tracy of Norwich, Connecticut 1660* (Joel, Munsell's Sons Publishers,

Albany, NY, 1898), 239-240. The author gives a brief biography of Stephen Tracy in the appendix.

Sherman Weld Tracy, *The Tracy Genealogy: Being Some of the Descendants of Stephen Tracy of Plymouth Colony, 1623* (Rutland, VT: The Tuttle Publishing Company, 1936), 19-25. Weld covers the lineage of Stephen Tracy beginning with his parents. He reproduces a chart on the family compiled by Phillimore & Company., Ltd. Weld reprints the power of attorney (will) that Stephen gave to John Winslow (1597-1674) before Stephen returned to England where he died. Weld also discusses the issue of whether or not Stephen came with his family on the *Anne*. He also refers to the 1627 Division of Cattle. His depiction of Stephen Tracy is much more accurate than that of Thomas Tracy.

"Stephen Tracy Family, MA." *Seattle Genealogical Society Bulletin,* v. 8, no. 8 *(April, 1958)*: 539. This briefly lists Stephen, his wife, Tryphosa, and daughter Sarah and her husband, George Partridge.

Stephen and Tryphosa (Lee) Tracy: Early Plymouth Colony Settlers, Circa 1623. Retrieved November 28, 2007 from http://ntgen.tripod.com/bw/tracy_s.html. This is a concise overview of Stephen Tracy noting his arrival, residence, appointments, family, and exerts from his power of attorney.

"Stephen Tracy Marriage Certificate." Recorded as "Stephen Tracey (sic), bachelor, sayworker, England; Tryphosa Lee, spinster, England." Retrieved January 13, 2008 from http://www.pilgrimarchives.nl/html/pilgrims/regestenen/1049.htm. This is a copy of Stephen's marriage certificate.

Declan Tracey (sic), "Trade Tokens of the Seventeenth Century." Retrieved April 24, 2016 from http://www.traceyclann.com/files/Irish%20Tracey%20Arms.htm. This website shows a photograph of the Trade Token of Stephen Tracy, Sr. and explains the letter on the token.

Chrystopher Trayes (sic), "England, Births and Christenings, 1538-1975," index, *FamilySearch* (https://familysearch.org/pal:?MM9.1.1/J7NF-ZJF: accessed 05 Feb 2013), Chrystophor Trayes, 01 Mar 1659; citing Yarmouth, Norfolk, England, reference; FHL microfilm 1526327. This man is apparently a brother of Stephen Tracy, Jr.

Roland G. Usher, *The Pilgrims and Their History* (New York, NY: The McMillan Company, 1920), 35, 302-303. Stephen Tracy, wife and child, are listed as members of Rev. John Robinson's Congregation in Leiden. Usher also discusses the hardships of living in Leiden.

Robert S. Wakefield, "The Adventurous Tryphosa (Lee) Tracy. *The American Genealogist*, v. 51, No. 1, January, 1975): 71-73. Wakefield provides information on both Stephen and Tryphosa Tracy in Holland and England. He notes that Tryphosa came to Plymouth with her daughter, Sarah on the *Jacob* in 1625 and that her daughter, Jane died before the trip.

Lyman Horace Weeks (Ed), Griswolds of Connecticut. *Genealogy: A Journal of American Ancestry, Volumes One and Two* (New York: William M. Clemens, Publisher), 1912, 124. Weeks notes the marriage of Thomas Tracy's son, Jonathan, to Mary Griswold.

Dorothy Wentworth, *Settlement and Growth of Duxbury 1628-1870* (Duxbury, MA: The Duxbury Rural and Historical Society, 1972). Wentworth gives a very brief sketch of Stephen Tracy. She describes his land north of Rogers grant in Duxbury and that John Tracy lived on it for nearly fifty years before selling it to Thomas Loring, a boat builder from Boston. The tract became known as the Bay farm.

Henry Whittemore, *The Heroes of the American Revolution and Their Descendants: Battle of Long Island* (New York, NY: The Heroes of the Revolution Publishing Co., 1897), 85-89. Whittemore inexplicably suggests that Stephen Tracy was a direct descendant of Richard of Stanway through his grandson Samuel.

Henry Whittemore, *The Signers of the Mayflower Compact and Their Descendants* (New York, NY: Mayflower Publishing Co., 1899), 3-5. Whittemore mentions that Stephen Tracy was associated with William Bradford at Leiden, Holland.

George C. Williamson, *Trade Tokens Issued in the Seventeenth Century in England, Wales, and Ireland, by Corporations, Merchants, Tradesmen, Etc.*, II (London, England: Elliot Stock, 1891), 881. Williamson lists the trade token of Stephen Tracy, Sr. as recently having been sold.

George Findlay Willison, *Saints and Strangers, Being the Lives of the Pilgrim Fathers & Their Families, with Their Friends & Foes; & an account of Their Posthumous Wanderings in Limbo, Their Final Resurrection & Rise to Glory, & the Strange Pilgrimages of Plymouth Rock* (New York: Reynal & Hitchock, 1945), 448. Wilson notes that Stephen Tracy *"removed to Dartmouth circa 1652"* and returned to England 1654.

Justin Winsor, *History of the Town of Duxbury, Massachusetts with Genealogical Registers* (Boston, MA: Crosby & Nichols, 1849), 13, 17, 81, 326. Winsor describes the bounds between Duxbury and Plymouth near Stephen Tracy's property and that Stephen Tracy served as constable of Duxbury. He gives a brief summary of Tracy family members. Winsor incorrectly lists Lt. Thomas Tracy as son of Stephen Tracy. He also mentions that Miles Standish was a resident of Duxbury.

Samuel Woodward, *The Norfolk Topographer's Manual: Being a Catalogue of the Books and Engravings Hitherto Published in Relation to the County. Appendix I. Original Drawings, Engravings, Etchings and Deeds Inserted in a Copy of Blomefield's History of Norfolk* (London, England: Nichols and Son, 1812), 211. Woodward lists Stephen Tracy as having a farthing Trade Token in Yarmouth.

Alexander Young, *Chronicles of The Pilgrim Fathers of the Colony of Plymouth, From 1602 to 1625* (Boston, MA: Charles C. Little and James Brown, 1971), 352. Young's passenger list of the *Anne* only lists Stephen Tracy, which is probably accurate.

Lt. Thomas Tracy (1610-1685)

Matilda O. Abbey, *Genealogy of the Family of Lt. Thomas Tracy of Norwich, Conn: Compiled from the Genealogical Works of the Hydes and Tracy's by Chancellor Reuben H. Walworth and Other Reliable Sources* (Milwaukee, WI, 1888), 14-15, 36-37, 126. Abbey cites information copied from the Norwich town records of births, marriages, and deaths. She covers these dates for the children of Lt. Thomas Tracy. She also includes a map of the first house lots in Norwich in 1660. She notes only that Thomas Tracy came from England. Abbey erroneously puts Salem as his first destination, instead of Watertown. Abbey also describes F. P. Tracy's background and research.

Sherman Walcott Adams & Henry R. Stiles, *The History of Ancient Wethersfield, Connecticut Comprising the Present Towns of Wethersfield, Rocky Hill, and Newington; And of Glastonbury Prior to Its Incorporation in 1693, From Date of Earliest Settlement Until the Present Time* (New York, NY: The Grafton Press, 1904), 31, 71, 72, 149, 165, 306. Adams and Stiles discuss the Pequot massacre at Mystic. They list Thomas Tracy as one of the 26 participants from Wethersfield. They cite his place of origin as Tewkesbury, England. They erroneously say that his first place of residency was Salem, instead of Watertown.

Ralph W. Allen, "Frederick Palmer Tracy", *Memorial Biographies of The New England Historic Genealogical Society*, v. IV, 1860-1862 (1885): 125-133. Allen provides a detailed biography of F. P. Tracy whose research on genealogy apparently influenced Reuben Walworth's belief that Thomas Tracy was born in Tewksbury, England. Allen fails to mention that Thomas' first destination was Watertown.

Americana (American Historical Magazine) XVI, January, 1922 – December, 1922, ccxlii (New York, NY: American Historical Society). The entry for Tracy includes an explanation of the origin of the name, a notation of Stephen Tracy who came to Plymouth in 1623, and a notation on Thomas Tracy who is depicted as the son or nephew of Peter Tracy of the Manor of Stanway, Gloucestershire, England.

Ancestry.com. *New London County, Connecticut: A Modern History* [database on-line]. Provo, UT, USA: The Generations Network, Inc., 2002. Original data: Benjamin Tinkham Marshall, ed. *A Modern History of New London County Connecticut.* New York City, NY, USA: Lewis Historical Publishing Company, 1922. This collection of data from Benjamin Tinkham Marshall provides a more detailed description of the allocation of land Thomas received as compensation for his giving up part of the Indian Burying Grounds.

Ancestry.com. *U.S. and Canada, Passenger and Immigration Lists Index, 1500s-1900s* [database on-line]. (Provo, UT: Ancestry.com Operations, Inc. 2010. This index was originally compiled by William P. Filby (cited below). It is now available on Ancestry.com. It is compiled from thousands of different records from original passenger lists to personal diaries. It contains the names of over 4,838,000 individuals and is update annually. The index for Thomas Tracy records that he arrived in Massachusetts in 1636. The source is Meredith B. Colket, Jr.

Robert Charles Anderson, *The Great Migration Directory: Immigrants to New England 1620-1640 A Concise Compendium* (Boston, MA: New England Historic Genealogical Society, 2015), 340. Anderson provides the following entry for Thomas Tracy: *"Tracy, Thomas: Unknown; 1636; Watertown, Salem, Wethersfield, Saybrook, Norwich [STR 1:33, 101; TAG 41:41:250-52 (clue); Granberry 334-35; NEHGR 61:93; Moore Anc 506-13; Waterman 1:69-95]."*

Robert Charles Anderson (Ed.), "Focus on Massachusetts Bay Freemen." *The Great Migration Newsletter,* v. 10, No. 1 (April-June, 2001): 303. Anderson notes that the criteria to be a freemen changed often, depending on time and place.

Robert Charles Anderson (Ed.), "Focus on Massachusetts Bay Freemen." *The Great Migration Newsletter,* v. 10, No. 1 (April-June, 2001): 303. Anderson discusses the fluid definition of freemen.

Robert Charles Anderson (Ed.), "Focus on Watertown." *The Great Migration Newsletter*, v. 11, No. 3 (July-September, 2002): 343-346. This is an excellent overview of Watertown and each of the divisions of grants of land. In December, 1635 foreigners were excluded from grants because of too many inhabitants. Foreigners could purchase land.

Robert Charles Anderson (Ed.), "Focus on the Trainband." *The Great Migration Newsletter*, v. 13, No. 4 (October-December, 2004): 27-32. Anderson discusses the military operation of New England. All able-bodied men between 16 and 60 were required to participate in the trainbands.

Robert Charles Anderson (Ed.), "Focus on Watertown." *The Great Migration Newsletter*, v. 14, No. 3 (July-September, 2005): 19. Anderson highlights the restriction of land purchase in Watertown on November 30, 1635.

Robert Charles Anderson (Ed.), "When Did the Great Migration End?" *The Great Migration Newsletter*, v. 14, No. 4 (October-December, 2005): 445-446. Anderson concludes that 1639 was the last year of the Great Migration due to circumstances related to the dissolution of Parliament in May of 1640 and the subsequent English Civil War (1642-1651).

Robert Charles Anderson (Ed.), "Focus on the West Country." *The Great Migration Newsletter*, v. 24, No. 2 (April-June, 2015): 11. Anderson notes that there were 145 known immigrants from Norfolk during the Great Migration. He defines East Anglia as Essex, Suffolk, and Norfolk. Norfolk had many unknown immigrants.

Robert Charles Anderson (Ed.), "Focus on the Brownist." *The Great Migration Newsletter*, v. 25, No.1 (January-March, 2016): 3-5. Anderson describes the role of Robert Browne in the development of the Separatists in England.

Virginia Dejohn Anderson, *New England's Generation: The Great Migration and the Formation of Society and Cultures in the Seventeenth Century* (Cambridge, England: Cambridge University Press, 1991), various pages. The author describes a study of 693 immigrants from England to the New England Colonies on seven ships in the period 1635-1638. The author discusses the reasons for immigration from East Anglia, including Norfolk and their goals in the new world. She notes that most settlers in TGM were *"middling"* families, not wealthy.

Charles M. Andrews & Frances G. Davenport, *Guide to the Manuscript Materials for the History of the United States to 1783, in the British Museum, in Minor London Archives, and in the Libraries of Oxford and Cambridge* (Washington, DC: Carnegie Institution of Washington, 1908), 16. The authors note that Thomas Tracy and Thomas Leffingwell petitioned the General Court for 400 acres of land from Uncas and his son Owaneco that lay east of the Showatuckket (Shattuck) River outside the bounds of Norwich. Copies (?) of this and the deed to purchase Mohegan/Norwich are in the British Museum.

Edward Arber (Ed.), *The Story of the Pilgrim Fathers, 1606-1623 A.D.; as Told by Themselves, Their Friends, and Their Enemies* (London, England: Ward and Downey, 1897), 388. Arber notes that Stephen received three acres of land in Plymouth.

Bernard Bailyn, *The Barbarous Years, The Peopling of British North America: The Conflict of Civilizations, 1600-1675* (New York, NY: Alfred A. Knopf, 2012), 352ff, 426. Professor Bailyn discusses the overshadowing of the Plymouth Colony by the Massachusetts Bay Company and the resulting relative obscurity of the Plymouth Colony. He notes that almost all of the original people of Watertown were from East Anglia.

Charles Edward Banks, *Topographical Dictionary of 2885 English Emigrants to New England 1620-1650* (Philadelphia, PA: Elijah Ellsworth Brownell, B. E. E., 1937), 58, 123-24. Banks cites Caulkins that Thomas

Tracy lived in Salem, Wethersfield & Norwich. He makes no mention of Watertown or Saybrook.

John Warner Barber, *Connecticut Historical Collections, Containing a General Collection of Interesting Facts, Traditions, Biographical Sketches, Anecdotes, &c. Relating to the History and Antiquities of Every Town in Connecticut, with Geographical Descriptions. Illustrated by 190 Engravings,* 2nd edition (New Haven, CT: Durrie & Pack and J. W. Barber, 1837), 297, 299-300. Barber relates the report that Thomas Tracy was one of three men appointed to survey 300 acres of land for Owaneco near the Shetucket River. In April 1673, Thomas was also one of several men on the committee to build a new meeting house in Norwich.

John Bennet, *The History of Tewkesbury* (Tewkesbury, England: The Author, 1830), 437-438. Bennet provides a brief pedigree of the family of Tracy in Tewkesbury and Stanway, including the marriage of Henrietta Tracy, daughter and only surviving child of Henry, to Charles Hanbury, Esq. of Pontypool, Monmouth, England. He adopted the name hyphenated name Hanbury-Tracy.

George Madison Bodge, *Soldiers of King Phillip's War; being a Critical Account of that War, with a Concise History of New England 1620-1675* (Baltimore, MD: Genealogical Publishing Co., 1976). Bodge provides a notation of the officers who were appointed on August 14, 1673 to be prepared to defend in case of a Dutch attack on the Connecticut Colony if the regular soldiers were not available. Thomas Tracy was one of those appointed.

Boxted Village Website, *The Great Migration to America.* Retrieved July 4, 2016 from https://boxted.org.uk/history/migration-to-america/. This is a short online posting about the migration from East Anglia to the Massachusetts Bay Colony and Watertown. It references Groton, England where John Winthrop lived and Rev. George Phillips who sailed on the *Arabella* from Yarmouth, Isle of Wight. About 700 people came, with about 200 dying on route.

Kimberly G. Burgess & Katherine A. Spilde, *Indian Gaming and Community Building: A History of the Intergovernmental Relations of the Mohegan Tribe of Connecticut.* The Harvard Project on American Economic Development (Cambridge, MA: Malcolm Center for Social Policy, John F. Kennedy School of Government, Harvard University, April 2004), 3-4. The authors note that Thomas Tracy was one of the three Colonists to rescue Uncas. They also discuss the process by which the settlers at Saybrook obtained Norwich. Major Mason obtained a deed from Uncas in 1659, surrendered it to the Colony of Connecticut in 1660. The Mohegan argued for years that Mason meant to give it back. In 1721 between 4,000 and 5,000 acres were set aside and designated for the Mohegan. Caulkins also discusses this.

Frances Manwaring Caulkins, *History of New London, Connecticut, From the First Survey of the Coast in 1612, to 1652* (New London, CT: Author, 1852), 161-162. Caulkins list the appointment of Thomas Tracy, Matthew Griswold, and James Morgan to try and rectify the bounds of New London in May, 1661. Thomas was also appointed to a new boundary commission in October, 1663.

F. (Frances) M. (Manwaring) Caulkins, *History of Norwich, Connecticut, From Its Settlement in 1660, to January 1845* (Norwich, CT: Thomas Robinson, 1845), 112-113. Ms. Caulkins made a brief mention of Thomas Tracy as a "ship-carpenter" being received at Salem. She includes a great deal of information on his son, John. There is no reference to Thomas' place of birth.

Frances Manwaring Caulkins, *History of Norwich, Connecticut: From its Possession by the Indians, to the Year 1866* (Norwich, CT: Author, 1866), 189, 200. In this second edition of her book, Caulkins references the Hyde Genealogy by Reuben Walworth. Unlike the first edition Caulkins says that Thomas was from Tewksbury, Gloucestershire, England. Presumably, this is based on the Walworth book.

Frances Manwaring Caulkins, *History of Norwich, Connecticut: From its Possession by the Indians, to the Year 1866 Also A Brief Sketch of the Life of the Author, to Which is Added An Appendix Containing Notes and Sketches, Continuing the History to the Close of the Year 1873* (Hartford, CT: The Friends of the Author, 1874), multiple pages. Caulkins provides extensive discussion of Thomas Tracy with numerous references. On page 200 she repeats the Tracy lineage from the 1866 edition that Thomas was from Tewksbury.

Edward M. Chapman, "The Founders. An Address for the Two Hundred and Fifty Anniversary of the First Church in Old Saybrook, July 1, 1896", *The First Church of Christ (Congregational) Old Saybrook, Conn. The Celebration of the Two Hundred and Fiftieth Anniversary, Wednesday, July 1, 1896. Historical Review and Addresses* (Middletown, CT: J. S. Stewart, 1896), 83-88. Rev. Chapman mentions the ordination of John Fitch by Thomas Hooker. He also relates the rescue of Uncas at Shattuck's Point, but does not include Thomas Tracy. He does mention Thomas as an honorable member of the Church.

F. W. Chapman, *The Chapman Family or the Descendants of Robert Chapman One of the First Settlers of Say-Brook, Conn., with Genealogical Notes* (Hartford, CT: Printed by Case, Tiffany and Company, 1854), 34, 345. Chapman cites court records of sale of Thomas' 40 acres and several parcels of land in the Oyster River Quarter. He also mentions Thomas' appointment to explore Narragansett country for potential plantations.

Amos Sheffield Chesebrough, "History of the First Church of Old Saybrook", *The First Church of Christ (Congregational) Old Saybrook, Conn. The Celebration of the Two Hundred and Fiftieth Anniversary, Wednesday, July 1, 1896. Historical Review and Addresses* (Middletown, CT: J. S. Stewart, 1896), 9-10. This text mentions Thomas Tracy as a member of the congregation in 1646.

Harriet Chapman Chesebrough *Glimpses of Saybrook in Colonial Days* (Saybrook, CT: Celebration 3 ½, 1984), 28-30, 89. Chesebrough notes the purchase of land from Attawanhood by Thomas Tracy and Francis Griswold in 1659. She also mentions that Thomas escaped the fort with his three little children. And that Thomas Tracy's first wife is buried in The Ancient Cemetery at Saybrook Point (now Cypress Cemetery).

John Christoffersen, "Mohegans Restore Ancient Burial Ground." *The Washington Post*, June 22, 2007. Retrieved July 23, 216 from http://www.washingtonpost.com/wp-dyn/content/article/2007/06/22/AR2007062200231_pf.html. Christoffersen discusses the history of the restoration of the Mohegan Burying Ground in Norwich that was originally a part of Thomas Tracy's land.

G. E. Cockayne (Ed.), *The Complete Baronetage, I, 1611-1625* (Exeter, England: William Pollard & Co. Ltd., 1900), 2. Cockayne gives the peerage of the Tracy family and mentions the marriage of the daughter of Sir John Tracy, Catharine to Butts Bacon.

Meredith B. Colket, Jr., *Founders of Early American Families: Emigrants from Europe 1607-1657* (Revised) (Cleveland, OH: The General Court of the Order of Founders and Patriots of America, 1985), 317-18, 366. Colket supports Hunt's supposition that Thomas of Connecticut is the same Thomas who skipped out of attending church in Norwich County, England. Colket is the source for the U.S. and Canada, Passenger and Immigration List Index for listing Thomas Tracy's arrival in Massachusetts in 1636.

William Richard Cutter (Ed.), *Genealogical and Family History of the State of Connecticut: A Record of the Achievements of Her People in the Making of a Commonwealth and the Founding of a Nation*, II (New York, NY: Lewis Historical Publishing Company, 1911), 849-851. Cutter provides a pedigree that shows Lt. Thomas Tracy as the son or nephew of Sir Paul Tracy of Tewkesbury.

William Richard Cutter (Ed.), *New England Families Genealogical and Memorial: A Record of the Achievements of Her People in the Making of Commonwealths and the Founding of a Nation*, v. IV (New York, NY: Lewis Historical Publishing Company, 1914), 2127. This later volume repeats the information in Vol. II noted above.

Bruce C. Daniels, *The Connecticut Town: Growth and Development, 1635-1790* (Middletown, CT: Wesleyan University Press, 1979), 9-11, 65-66. Daniels discusses the development of the River Towns (Windsor, Weathersfield, and Hartford). He also mentions the trek along the Connecticut Path, the Fundamental Orders of 1639, the Code of 1650, and the fact that the right to vote was based on property ownership.

Debrett Ancestry Research, *The Origins of Thomas Tracy of Connecticut: Reports of Debretts Ancestry in England* (Salt Lake City, UT: O. Tracy, 1992). This research examined questions about the origin of Thomas Tracy. No definitive answers were given. The research was conducted at the request of Mrs. Edward A. Williams in February 1986.

John W. De Forest, *History of the Indians of Connecticut from the Earliest Known Period to 1850* (Hartford, CT: Wm. Jas. Hamersley, 1851), 214. Deforest notes that Thomas Tracy was probably involved in the rescue of Uncas at Shantok Point.

Nancy Backus Detrick, "Corrections to the Thomas Tracy and Francis Griswold Lines," *Hear-Saye, Quarterly Newsletter of the Saybrook Colony Founders Association*, v. 9, No. 2 (Spring 1989): 7-8. Detrick notes that Thomas Tracy of Saybrook and Norwich was most likely born in Norfolk, England. She disputes claims that the first wife of Lt. Thomas Tracy was Mary Mason. She also records that Thomas Tracy did not have a daughter named Mary and that it is unlikely that Francis Griswold's first wife was Mary Tracy. She cites Waterman and Jacobus as supporting this. She also suggests that

E. T. Nash in *Fifty Puritan Ancestors* may have referred to Mary Tracy daughter of Stephen Tracy of Plymouth as the wife of Francis Griswold.

She provides a list of Thomas Tracy's children. Nash is not considered to be a very trustworthy source by leading genealogists.

Tracy Campbell Dickson, *Some of the Descendants of Lieutenant Thomas Tracy of Norwich, Connecticut* (Philadelphia, PA: John C. Winston Company, 1936), 10, 12, 172. Dickson lists some of the activities of Thomas Tracy in Wethersfield, Saybrook, and Norwich. The book includes a description of the siege of Shattuck's Point on the Thames River in 1645.

Wharton Dickinson, *Pedigree of Tracy of Toddington Co., Gloucester and Norwich, Connecticut: autograph manuscript and typescripts, 1904 Dec. 10 / compiled by Wharton Dickinson.* This report is available from the Morgan Library and Museum – Pierpont Morgan Library. As the title suggests, Dickinson believed Lt. Thomas Tracy and, therefore, Francis Louise Tracy Morgan, to be descendants of the Stanway Tracy family.

Thomas Bradford Drew, *The Ancient Estate of Governor William Bradford* (Boston, MA: Thos. P. Smith Printing Co., 1897), 15-17. Drew provides the will of Gov. Bradford that includes a bequest to his son, John, whose widow married Thomas Tracy.

Email from Tracy Allen, October 25, 2016 to Martin & Patsy Tracy conveying the message from the Bancroft Library that v. 2:1 and 2:2 are not on the shelf.

Email from Tracy Allen, October 31, 2016 to Martin & Patsy Tracy with identification of the whole set of Tracy Family Papers, circa 1800-1888, as follows: BANC MSS Z-Z 107 v. 1; BANC MSS Z-Z 107 v. 2:1; BANC MSS Z-Z 107 v. 2:2; BANC MSS Z-Z 107 v. 3.

Email from Tracy Allen, November 24, 2016 to Martin & Patsy Tracy with information he found in volumes 1 and 3. He photographed the documents and put them in a cloud for me to access.

Email from Tracy Allen, Ph.D., Author's 1st Cousin, December 10, 2016. Dr. Allen reported on his examination of BANC MSS Z-Z 107 v. 2:1 and BANC MSS Z-Z 2:2 in the "Tracy Family Papers, Circa 1800-1888" in the Bancroft Library, University of California, Berkeley. He also reviewed the papers on subsequent visits and sent photographs to the author of pertinent sections.

Email from Bancroft Library, Circulation Services, October 25, 2016 to Tracy Allen with the notification that the documents: *"BANC MSS Z-Z 107 v. 2:1 and v. 2:2, are not on the shelf. We will continue to search for them."*

Email from J. H. Torrance Downes, Trustee, Cyprus Cemetery, Old Saybrook, Connecticut, July 26, 2016. Mr. Downes noted that the first marked grave in the "Ancient Cemetery" of Saybrook was not until 1685. There were, therefore, 50 years of unmarked graves. He referred my request to Susan Sangster who could find no reference to Thomas Tracy's wife.

Email from Diane Hoyt, Administrative Assistant, Old Saybrook Historical Society, October 21, 2015. Ms. Hoyt informed the author that all records for Old Saybrook were destroyed in the fire of 1647. She also provided information on The Ancient and Cypress Cemeteries. [While the records were burned, the town recorder had some records that he took to Norwich.]

Email from Diane Hoyt, Administrative Assistant, Old Saybrook Historical Society, August 26, 2016. Ms. Hoyt reported on the completion of exhaustive research of Harriet Chesebrough's Journal that was published as *Glimpses of Old Saybrook*. Notes in the journal said that there is no proof of the name of Thomas Tracy's wife. Notes show that he was listed on the Saybrook proprietor's list in 1650, so he was in Saybrook at the time of the burning of Fort Saybrook.

Email from Diane Hoyt, Administrative Assistant, Old Saybrook Historical Society, August 19, 2016. Ms. Hoyt noted that the burials in the "Ancient Cemetery" of Saybrook were moved to Cypress Cemetery. She said that she was reviewing *Glimpses of Old Saybrook*, as I had requested.

Email from Diane Hoyt, Administrative Assistant, Old Saybrook Historical Society, August 26, 2016. Ms. Hoyt informed me that she and her staff had "finished 6 hours of reading and researching everything we have on Thomas Tracy." She confirmed that Harriet Chesebrough's journal had notes saying that there *"is no proof regarding the name of his [Thomas's] first wife."* Ms. Hoyt also confirmed that Thomas was on the list of Saybrook proprietors in 1650, proving that he was living there after Fort Saybrook burned.

Email from Lorna K. Kirwan, Collections Manager, The Bancroft Library, University of California, Berkeley, CA, October 12, 2016. Ms. Kirwan responded to my email of October 10 in which I made an inquiry regarding the *"Tracy Family Papers, Circa 1800-1888."* She estimated the cost of reproducing the papers at $300.

Email from Louise Leake, Genealogist, The Society of the Founders of Norwich, June 14, 2016. Ms. Leake provided me with information on Thomas Tracy decedents in Norwich in 1795 taken from the Genealogy of Williams Family. The map of 1795 shows the location of the Tracy & Coit Store, as well as the locations of several other Tracys.

Email from Ellen O'Herlihy, Acton Public Library, Acton, Connecticut, August 2, 2016. Ms. O'Herlihy responded to my inquiry regarding questions I had on the original manuscript of *Glimpses of Saybrook in Colonial Days* that was originally presented to the Acton Library and in 1943 was transferred to the Old Saybrook Town Hall

Email from Maurice Klapwald, Assistant Manager, Interlibrary, Document & Research Services, The New York Public Library,

Email from Joanne Penn, Professional Genealogist, Norfolk, England August 21, 2013. Ms. Penn replied to my email of August 20, 2013 in which I inquired about the possibility of her researching the birth place of Thomas Tracy. I was particularly interested in a Thomas Tracy born in 1613 in Lessingham, Norfolk, England. She responded noting the extreme difficulty in finding any existing evidence. She noted that typically when a person emigrated they were left out of wills and related family materials. I did not follow-up given the small chances of finding any primary records.

Email from David J. Russo, Chair, Watertown (Massachusetts) Historical Commission, May 17, 2016. Mr. Russo gave me references to two histories of Watertown neither of which had any information on Thomas Tracy.

Email from Susan Sangster, Record Keeper, Cyprus Cemetery, Old Saybrook, Connecticut, July 26, 2016. Ms. Sangster verified that there is no one named Tracy buried in the Cyprus Cemetery and that there are no records of unmarked graves.

Email from Kimberly Stella, Administrative Assistant, Imaging and Rights, The Morgan Library & Museum, September 16, 2013. This email regarded the invoice for photographs of pages from the *Pedigree of Tracy of Toddington Co., Gloucester and Norwich, Connecticut: Autograph Manuscripts and Typescripts, 1904* by Wharton Dickinson. I did not place an order due to the high cost to purchase a copy.

Email from Martin B. Tracy, June 23, 2016 to The New York Public Library with an inquiry regarding the H. Minot Pitman paper collection.

Email from Martin B. Tracy, August 5, 2016 to Diane Hoyt with three specific questions on the manuscript of *Glimpses of Saybrook in Colonial Days.*

Email from Hannah Verge, Archivist, Norfolk Record Office, Norwich, England, October 3, 2012. Ms. Verge explained the difficulties of finding any records of Thomas Tracy who may have immigrated to New England.

Email from Kathleen Wieland, Genealogy Librarian, Otis Library, Norwich, Connecticut June 8, 2016. Ms. Wieland noted that the Otis Library collection does include a specific file on the Tracy family. It holds works by Dwight Tracy and Evert Evertsen Tracy and the *History of Norwich* by Frances Manwaring Caulkins.

Email from Kathleen Wieland, Genealogy Librarian, Otis Library, Norwich, Connecticut June 10, 2016. Email exchanged between Ms. Wieland and an email I sent her on June 8, 2016.

William P. Filby (Ed.), *Passenger and Immigration Lists Index, 1500-1900s* (Farmington Hills, MI: Gale Research, 2012.) Original index to immigration passenger lists. See Ancestry.com citation for current source.

First Congregational Church. Franklin, Connecticut, *The Celebration of the One Hundred and Fiftieth Anniversary of the Primitive Organization of the Congregational Church and Society, in Franklin, Connecticut* (New Haven, CT; Tuttle, Morehouse & Taylor, Printers, October 14, 1868), 48. This document provides a complete list of the Thirty-Five Original Proprietors who settled Norwich in 1660. It also includes a poem by Stedman entitled "*The Inland City.*"

Convers Francis, *An Historical Sketch of Watertown, in Massachusetts, from the First Settlement of the Town to the Close of Its Second Century* (Cambridge, MA: E. W. Metcalf and Company, 1830), 26-27. Francis notes the scarcity of land in Watertown with the requirement to live half a mile from the meeting house. He also mentions Wethersfield.

Genealogical and Biographical Record of New London County, Connecticut Containing Biographical Sketches of Prominent and Representative Citizens and

Genealogical Records of Many of the Early Settled Families (Chicago, IL: J. H. Beers & Co., 1903), 38-40. The record for Winslow Williams includes a note that Thomas Tracy was with Thomas Leffingwell when Uncas was relieved of the siege at Shattuck's Point in 1645. The article also assumes that Thomas Tracy was from Tewkesbury, England and that his first wife's name was Mary.

General Society of Colonial Wars, *Second Supplement to the General Register of the Society of Colonial Wars* (New York: Author, 1911), 403. This document lists the military appointments of Thomas Tracy.

Gilman C. Gates, *Saybrook at the Mouth of the Connecticut: The First One Hundred Years* (Orange, CT: Press of the Wilson H. Lee Co., 1935), 141, 164, 210-214, 227-228. Gates discusses Thomas Tracy's involvement in the survey and division of the Saybrook *"outlands"* into quarters in 1648. Thomas chose the Oyster River Quarter to live after the fort burned. Gates also relates that Thomas was asked to come back in 1684 to settle a boundary dispute. The author includes a copy of the 1685 patent reconfirming the original nine-square mile patent.

Daniel Coit Gilman, *A Historical Discourse Delivered in Norwich, Connecticut, September 7, 1859 at the Bi-Centennial Celebration of the Settlement of That Town* (Boston, MA: Geo. C. Rand Avery, City Printers, 1859), 5-6, 14, 18, 25. Gilman describes the landscape of Norwich when settled and location of Thomas' home lots. He also describes the journey from Saybrook to Norwich pass the Chair of Uncas.

William Gogswell (Ed.), "First Settlement of Norwich, CT." *The New England Historical and*

Genealogical Register 1 (1847): 314-317. This issue of the *Register* contains a section with the names of the 35 original settlers of Norwich, including two from Marshfield, John Bradford and Thomas Waterman. It also includes the Patent of the Town of Norwich, A. D., 1685 signed by Robert Treat, Governor. All the names are inscribed on the Uncas monument in Norwich.

David L. Greene, Ph.D. "Lt. Thomas Tracy of Saybrook and Norwich: His (Unknown) Origin and (Unknown) Wife," *Hear-Saye, Quarterly Newsletter of the Saybrook Colony Founders Association*, v. XI, No. 3, Issue 39 (Fall 1996): 540-542. Greene was the Editor of *The American Genealogist*. Greene disputes two previous articles in Hear-Saye, published in 1995 and 1996 that state that Lt. Thomas Tracy was from Gloucestershire County, England. He notes that the origin and wife of Thomas Tracy are unknown, but that he was indisputably not the son or grandson of Sir Paul Tracy or that he was connected to the Tracys of Toddington *"or any other gentry family."* He cites Jacobus and Hunt that Thomas Tracy most likely came from Norfolk.

Esther Griswold French & Robert Lewis French (Eds.), *The Griswold Family: The First Five Generations in America* (Wethersfield, CT: The Griswold Family Association, 1990), 15-16, 26-27. The editors dispute the claim that the wife of Francis Griswold was a daughter of Thomas Tracy and suggest that she may have been the daughter of Stephen and Tryphosa Tracy. They mention the places Thomas lived, overlooking his residency in Watertown.

Thomas Fuller, *The History of the Worthies of England, Vol. I* (London, England: Printed for Thomas Tegg, 1740), 552, 558. Fuller gives the history of the proverb: *"The Tracies have always the wind in their faces."*

Marion W. Hall (Ed.), *Preston in Review* (Norwich, CT: Franklin Impressions, Inc., 1971). Sponsored by the Preston Historical Society, Inc., the book mentions Thomas Tracy and his sons as early settlers.

Dwight Craig Haven, *Haven Family Genealogical Research Papers, 1880-1933 (bulk 1929-1933), Mss col NYGB 18232*. New York Public Library, Manuscript & Archives Room 328. Box 1 contains letters between Dwight Tracy, M.D., D.D.S. and Dwight C. Haven. In a letter dated June 21, 1905

Dr. Dwight Tracy mentions Henry Reed Tracy of Roxbury, Massachusetts. Other material includes survey letters sent by Dwight Tracy to Haven family members.

Pliny LeRoy Harwood, *History of Eastern Connecticut Embracing the Counties of Tolland, Windham, Middlesex and New London*, v. 1 (Chicago, IL: The Pioneer Historical Publishing Company, 1932), 152, 155, 161. Harwood includes a reprint of The Norwich Deed of the nine-mile square and mentions that Thomas Tracy and others surveyed land for Owaneco.

R. R. Hinman, *A Catalogue of the Names of the First Puritan Settlers of the Colony of Connecticut with the Time of Their Arrival in the Colony and Their Standing in Society, Together with Their Place of Residence, As Far as Can be Discovered by the Records, No 1* (Hartford, CT: E. Gleason, 1846), 28, 49, 61, 80, 111, 165. Hinman mentions the appointment of Thomas Tracy to survey the bounds of New London, CT, his jury duty, his appointment as ensign in case of war with the Dutch, and that Thomas was one of the first settlers of Wethersfield. This book is not to be confused with the book listed next which has a similar title.

Royal R. Hinman, *A Catalogue of the Names of the Early Puritan Settlers of the Colony of Connecticut with the Time of Their Arrival in the Colony, Their Standing in Society, Place of Residence, Condition in Life, Where From, Business, &C., As Far as is Found on Record* (Hartford, CT: Press of Case, Tiffany and Company, 1852), 88, 164, 452. In this book, Hinman refers to Thomas Tracy participation in laying out land for the Indian Robin. He also refers to the theft of a sack from Thomas by Robert Beadle. Another reference is to Thomas's appointment as a property appraiser for William Waller and John Clark, Jr.

Historical Society (The), Watertown Massachusetts, *Watertown Records Comprising the First and Second Books of Town Proceedings with the Land Grants and Possessions Also the Proprietors' Book and the First Book and Supplement of Births Deaths and Marriages* (Watertown, MA: The Author: Press of Fred

G. Barker, 1894), 2-3. The historic records show that in 1635 no foreigner could hold land with the consent of the freemen. And only freemen could participate in making decisions related to civil affairs.

G. H. Hollister, *The History of Connecticut from the First Settlement of the Colony*, 1 (Harford, CT: L. Stebbins & Co., 1858), 199-201, 349, 500-508. Hollister covers the history of Saybrook, including the proprietor, Thomas Tracy. It includes a roll of Deputies to the General Court to which Thomas was appointed 23 times, beginning in 1662.

John G. Hunt, "Fiction Versus Possibility in the Tracy Genealogy," *The American Genealogist*, v. 41 (October 1965): 250-252. This brief article supports the contention of Donald Lines Jacobus in the Waterman Family, v. 1, 1939, pages 691-94 that Thomas Tracy of New England was not directly related to the Tracy family of Stanway House, England. Hunt disputes the findings of Dr. Dwight Tracy, M.D., D.D.S. that Lt. Thomas Tracy was the son of William Tracy of Stanway. Hunt suggests that Lt. Thomas Tracy may have been of Norwich, Norfolk, England.

Leslie Stephen & Sidney Lee (Eds.), *The Dictionary of National Biography Founded in 1882 by George Smith. From the Earliest Times to 1900, Vol. XIX, Stow-Tytler (Oxford, England: Oxford University Press, 1917), 1067-1070.* This dictionary includes a biography of Richard Tracy of Toddington and his descendants to Paul Tracy. It also includes a section on William de Tracy, one of the five assassins of Thomas Becket. There is no reference to a Thomas Tracy born in the family in 1610.

Albert Leffingwell & Charles Wesley Leffingwell, *The Leffingwell Record: A Genealogy of the Descendants of Lieut. Thomas Leffingwell One of the Founders of Norwich* (Aurora, NY: Leffingwell Publishing Company, 1897), 17, 33, 214-217. This book contains 174 references to the Tracy family, demonstrating the close connection between the two families.

Mattie Liston-Griswold Hunt, *Tracy Genealogy: Ancestors and Descendants of Thomas Tracy of Lenox, Massachusetts* (Kalamazoo, MI: Doubleday, 1900), 23. Hunt notes that during King Philip's War in 1675, Thomas was appointed Commissary and Quartermaster along with John Bradford.

Hamilton D. Hurd, *History of New London County, Connecticut with Biographical Sketches of Many of Its Pioneers and Prominent Men* (Philadelphia, PA: J. W. Lewis, 1882), 248, 264, 330, 535, 596. Hurd gives a description of Thomas Tracy's plot in Norwich and his farm east of the Shetucket River, his appointments to the legislature, and his survey work in Lisbon. Hurd also mentions that John Bradford and his wife Martha Bourne Bradford were neighbors of Thomas Tracy. The widow Martha became Thomas' second wife.

Donald Lines Jacobus, *The Waterman Family: Descendants of Robert Waterman of Marshfield, Massachusetts Through Seven Generations*, 1 (New Haven, CT: E. F. Waterman, 1939): 21-28, 616-629, 691-698. Jacobus covers the relationship of Thomas Waterman to both Thomas Tracy and Stephen Tracy. He notes that Stephan was from East Ruston, Norfolk, England and states that "*Lieut. Thomas Tracy, born perhaps in Norfolk, England.*" The book has an outline of the families of both Tracys. Jacobus also cites the record for Thomas in Salem, Massachusetts recorded "*2 Mar. 1636-7, vpon a Certificate from duers of watter Towne.*" Citing Sidney Perley's *The History of Salem* (1924) Jacobus says that Thomas was granted five acres of land. He notes that "*We do not know who Tracy's vouchers in Watertown were, nor do we find him mentioned in Watertown records.*" Jacobus also notes that Thomas Tracy was probably related to Stephen Tracy of Norfolk.

"Joshua's Tract Conservation and Historic Trust." (2015, March 4). In *Wikipedia, The Free Encyclopedia*. Retrieved 20:44, September 4, 2016, from https://en.wikipedia.org/w/index.php?title=Joshua%27s_Tract_Conservation_and_Historic_Trust&oldid=649788813.

Sam Libby, "Norwich Plan Yields to Burial Ground." *The New York Times*, March 8, 1998. Retrieved July 23, 2016 from http://www.nytimes. com/1998/03/08/nyregion/norwich-plan-yields-to-burial-ground.html.

Ellen Masters "The Fate of the Tracys." *Notes and Queries: A Medium of Intercommunication for Literary Men, General Readers, Etc.* Tenth Series, v. IV (July-December, 1905): 335. Masters briefly discusses the history of Sir William de Tracy and the proverb regarding the wind in the face of the Tracys. She also alludes to two pedigrees, one in the Library of the British Museum, the other in the possession of her half-brother.

George Norbury Mackenzie & Nelson Osgood Rhoades (Eds.), *Colonial Families of the United States of America in Which is Given the History and Armorial Bearings of Colonial Families who Settled in the American Colonies from the Time of the Settlement of Jamestown, 13th May 1607, to the Battle of Lexington, 19th April, 1775, Volume V* (Baltimore, MD: Genealogical Publishing, Co., Inc., 1912), 291-293. In this volume, the authors include a section on Henry Tracy of Toddington. They mention Thomas Tracy as having been born in Tewkesbury, England. The also mention that he came to Salem then to Wethersfield, Saybrook, and Norwich. The authors make no reference to his first destination in the Colonies as being Watertown. Two other significant errors are the claims that Francis Griswold married Mary Tracy, daughter of Lt. Thomas Tracy and that the wife of Lt. Tracy was the widow Mason.

Charles William Manwaring, *A Digest of Early Connecticut Probate Records, Vol. 1, Hartford District, 1635-1700* (Hartford, CT: R. S. Peck & Co., 1904), 55-56. This record cites a dispute between John Goodrich and Mary, wife of Thomas Tracy. This is a reference to Mary Foote Stoddard Goodrich Tracy. The widow Goodrich married Thomas in 1683.

Benjamin Tinkham Marshall (Ed.), *A Modern History of New London County, Connecticut, Volume 1* (New York, NY: Lewis Historical Publishing Company, 1922), 123-127, 160-161. This book reprints the Deed of

Norwich. It also provides a list of original settlers to Norwich, and a description of the location of Thomas Tracy's home-lot.

Puella F. Hull Mason, *Lineage of the Tracy Family with Notes of the Lord, Garrett, Russell, and other Intermarrying Families* (S.I. : s.n., 1895). Mason cites *Burke's Passage*, Browning's *Hyde Genealogy*, and Caulkins *History of Norwich* as her sources to connect Thomas Tracy to Stanway, son of Nathaniel.

Massachusetts Historical Society, *Collections of the Massachusetts Historical Society*, 4th Series, v. II (Boston, MA: Printed for the Society, 1865), 426-427. This book includes a description of Ensign Tracy bearing a letter from John Mason to John Winthrop, Jr. on July, 1669.

John Matthews & Louis R. Sosnow (Ed.), *Complete American Armoury and Blue Book* (New York, NY: Heraldic Pub. Co., 1965), 76. Editor Sosnow combines Matthews' original editions of 1903, 1907, and 1911-13. Matthews describes Thomas Tracy of Salem, Massachusetts as a grandson of Richard Tracy of Stanway.

Anne Mazlish (Ed.), *The Tracy Log Book 1855: A Month in Summer* (Bar Harbor, ME: Acadia Publishing Co., 1997). This log book is based on Charles Tracy's Diary on Mount Desert Island near Bar Harbor, Maine.

Mrs. Edward J. Merkle, et al, *Lineages of the National Society of the Sons and Daughters of the Pilgrims 1929-1952, v. II* (Baltimore, MD: Genealogical Publishing Co., Inc., 1988), 67. Merkle discusses a Mrs. J. L. Edwards of Barberton, Ohio who lists her 10th great grandmother as the wife of Lt. Thomas Tracy. Mrs. Edwards incorrectly writes that Thomas Tracy's wife was the widow of Edward Mason.

Mohegan Tribe (The), "Heritage: Uncas, Sachem and Statesman". Retrieved September 3, 2016 from http://mohegan.nsn.us/heritage/our-history/sachem-uncas. This website includes a description of the origin of the Mohegan Tribe as a breakaway group from the Pequot.

"Names of the First Settlers of Norwich, in 1660." *New England Historical and Genealogical Register*, 1 (October, 1847): 315. This lists all 35 of the original founders of Norwich. It also provides a copy of The Patent of the Town of Norwich in 1685.

"Names of the First Settlers of Norwich, in 1660." Retrieved June 9, 2016 from http:www. dunhamwilcox.net/ct/Norwich-ct-settlers.htm. This is another source for a list of the original proprietors of Norwich.

The National Cyclopaedia of American Biography Being the History of the United States as Illustrated in the Lives and Founders, Builders and Defenders of the Republic, and of the Men and Women Who Are Doing the Work and Molding the Thought of the Present Time, v. XXXIV (New York, NY: James T. White & Company, 1947), 220. This volume has a biography of Henry Holton Conland, the man who commissioned H. Minot Pitman to do the research on the origin of Thomas Tracy in 1938.

New England Historic and Genealogical Society, "Corresponding Members." *The New England Historical and Genealogical Register* 12 (October, 1858):368. This record lists Frederick Palmer Tracy as a corresponding member from San Francisco.

New England Historic and Genealogical Society, "Active Members, From the Formation of the Society in 1844, to March 1, 1858." *The New England Historical and Genealogical Register* 12 (April, 1858):189. This record lists Frederick Palmer Tracy as an active member of NEHGS.

The New International Encyclopedia, 2nd Edition, v. V (New York, NY: Dodd, Mead & Company, 1917), 767. This entry describes the sale of Saybrook to Connecticut and the establishment of the Connecticut Commonwealth and a democratic constitution.

Chas. A. Northrop, "The First Church of Norwich." *The First Church of Christ (Congregational) Old Saybrook, Conn. The Celebration of the Two Hundred and Fiftieth Anniversary, Wednesday, July 1, 1896. Historical Review and Addresses* (Middletown, CT: J. S. Stewart, 1896), 88-97. Rev. Northrop discusses the role of Thomas Tracy as an original proprietor of Norwich from Saybrook. He also describes the role of the Norwich Church as a "*hot-bed*" of spiritual and ecclesiastical freedom. In addition, Northrop describes the purchase of the nine-mile square.

Michael Leroy Oberg, *Uncas: First of the Mohegans* (Ithaca, NY: Cornell University Press, 2003), 199. Oberg relates the story that following King Philip's war, Uncas was ordered by Connecticut magistrates to pay one hundred acres of land to Thomas Tracy as damages after one of the Chief's sons killed several pigs belonging to Tracy.

James C. Odiorne, "A Complete List of the Ministers of Boston of All Denominations, from 1630 to 1842, Arranged in the Order of Their Settlement." *The New England Historical and Genealogical Register* 1 (October, 1847): 320. This list shows Frederick Palmer Tracy as minister of the 5th Methodist Church in Boston from June 1836 to 1837.

"Original House Lots, Norwich, Connecticut." *The Connecticut Nutmegger.* v. 20 (1987): 437. This is a drawing of the locations of the houses in Norwich. Thomas Tracy's home is next to those of Bradford, Adgate, S. Huntington, Olmstead, and Backus.

Arthur L. Peale, *Memorials and Pilgrimages in the Mohegan Country* (Norwich, CT: The Bulletin Co., 1930), 21-22, 39. Peale reports on a speech by Edwin A. Tracy who mentions that Thomas Tracy and Uncas were close friends. The pamphlet also includes the names on the Memorial to Major John Mason.

Brainerd T. Peck, "Pre-American Origins, Proven, Disproved, Questionable", *The Connecticut Nutmegger,* v. 6 (1973): 206. Peck wrote a brief summary of the discussion of the origin of Lt. Thomas Tracy up to that point. He drew on the analysis of Pitman and Jacobus and dismissed the Walworth and subsequent claims. He cites Donald Lines Jacobus from his work: *The Waterman Family*.

Mary E. Perkins, *Old Houses of the Antient Town of Norwich, 1660-1800: With Maps, Illustrations, Portraits and Genealogies* (Norwich, CT: Press of the Bulletin Co., 1895). Perkins makes 28 references to Thomas Tracy, many related to the location of his property in Norwich. She makes 267 references to the Tracy family of Norwich. Perkins includes a chapter on the genealogy of Thomas Tracy, repeating the theory that links Thomas to English aristocracy.

Sidney Perley, *A History of Salem, Massachusetts, Vol. 1, 1626-1637* (Salem, MA: The Author, 1924-28), 426. In a footnote the author observes that Thomas Tracy, a ship carpenter from Watertown, was received as an inhabitant of Salem and given five acres of land.

H. Minot Pitman genealogical research files, cs/ 2932-ca, Bx. 14, Folder 10, (Henry Conland File) "Report on Lt. Thomas Tracy", Feb 1938. The New York Public Library. This excellent research of primary documents raises questions as to the origin of Thomas Tracy. It neither supports nor refutes the claim that he was a son of the Tracy family of Stanway.

Preston Historical Society, Inc., *Preston: Early Homes and Families* (Norwich, CT: Franklin Impressions, Inc., 1998). This book lists the homes of 16 Tracy families in Preston.

David Pulsifer (Ed.), *Records of the Colony of New Plymouth in New England Printed by Order of the Legislature of the Commonwealth of Massachusetts, Deeds, &c. Vol. I. 1620-1651*

(Boston, MA: The Press of William White, 1861), 6, 12, 25, 78, 135. Pulsifer gives the locations of Stephen Tracy's properties and the laying out of land for William Coller at Morton's Hole.

David Pulsifer (Ed), *Records of the Colony of New Plymouth in New England Printed by Order of the Legislature of the Commonwealth of Massachusetts, Vol. II. 1653-1679* (Boston, MA: The Press of William White, 1859), 247-248. Pulsifer documents the incident when some Narragansett Indians fired eight bullets into an English home in Norwich in 1660 and that Thomas Tracye (sic) was one the men asked to bring them to justice.

P. H. Reaney, *The Origin of English Surnames* (New York, NY: Barnes & Noble, Inc., 1967), 70. Reaney lists the surname Tracy's origin from Tracy-Bocage, Calvados, France.

Paul C. Reed, *Research Report (#38083 – Seto)*, Lineages, Inc., Salt Lake City, Utah August 2, 1993. This four page unpublished summary report prepared for Bonnie Aloma Seto on Thomas Tracy sites the re-search by Donald Lines Jacobus that the genealogy published by Charles Stedman Ripley in 1895 was apparently flawed. The Thomas Tracy of Stanway, Gloucestershire, England referred to by Ripley never married. Lt. Thomas Tracy of Norwich, Connecticut was not a descendant of the Tracy family of Stanway and Tewkesbury, England. *"The origin of Thomas TRACY, the New England immigrant, is probably to be found in co. Norfolk, England….."*

"Residence and View on the Estate of Winslow Tracy Williams, Esq., Yantic." *New England Magazine. An Illustrated Monthly. New Series, XL, March, 1909 – August, 1909*: 438-439.This article shows a photograph of the estate of Winslow Tracy Williams. It also mentions that Edwin A. Tracy was the treasurer and general manager of the Norwich Nickel and Brass Company.

Charles Stedman Ripley, *The Ancestors of Lieutenant Thomas Tracy of Norwich, Connecticut* (Boston, MA: Mudge & Son, 1895), 16-20. Ripley claims that Thomas Tracy was the grandson of Richard Tracy of Stanway, England. Donald Lines Jacobus and John G. Hunt, among others, have presented convincing arguments that Thomas was not of this family line.

Eloise M. Roberts, *Some Colonial Families: Avery, Brewster, Mills, Morgan, Smith, Starr, Stewart, Tracy* (Avard, OK: Author, 1926). Roberts cites the dubious description of Thomas Tracy compiled by Evert E. Tracy, M.D.

James Savage, *A Genealogical Dictionary of the First Settlers of New England Showing Three Generations of Those Who Came Before May, 1692 on the Basis of Farmer's Register*, IV (Baltimore, MD: Genealogical Publishing Company, 1965), 320-321. Savage provides a brief description of Stephen and Thomas Tracy and their children. There are 4 volumes in total.

Mark Sanner, "The Founders of Saybrook Colony 1635-1660". Retrieved July 4, 2016 from http://www.ctgenweb.org/county/comiddlesex/Old%20 Saybrook/SCFA%20founders.html. Sanner lists the founders of the Saybrook Colony, including Thomas Tracy,

Bonnie Aloma Seto, *A Genealogy of the Tracy & Booth Families* (Salt Lake City, UT: Lineages, Inc., March 6, 1995). This report compiled for Bonnie Seto by Lineages, Inc., consists of pedigree charts and a booklet on the Tracy and Booth families.

Society of Colonial Wars in the State of Connecticut, 1941. *Register of Pedigrees and Services of Ancestors* (Author, Hartford, CT: 1941), various pages. The book has eight pedigrees based on ancestry traced to Thomas Tracy. One shows his birthplace as Tewkesbury, England. All have his wife as Mary _____ Mason.

"Society of Founders of Norwich," Retrieved March 28, 2015 from http://www.leffingwellhousemuseum.or/society-of-the-founders-of-Norwich/. This site lists Thomas Tracy as one of the 35 original settlers, along with John Tracy, John Bradford, and Bradford wife's nephew, Thomas Waterman.

William B. Stanley, *Bill Stanley Books Presents the Norwich Historical Society's The 9-Mile Square* (Norwich, CT: The Norwich Historical Society, 2005). Stanly provides a photographic history of Norwich.

Elaine F. Staplins, "Saybrook Colony: A Talk Given to CSG Members, September 21, 1991." *The Connecticut Nutmegger*, v. 24 (December, 1991):445. Staplins erroneously notes that Thomas Tracy's "first" place was Salem. She also mistakenly identifies his wife as the widow Mason.

Edmund Clarence Stedman, *The Inland City: A Poem and a Letter* (Norwich, CT: The Academy Press, 1906). Stedman includes the *Inland City* poem he wrote in this book. There is a bio on Stedman on *Wikipedia*.

John W. Stedman, *The Norwich Jubilee. A Report of the Celebration at Norwich, Connecticut, on the Two Hundredth Anniversary of the Settlement of the Town, September 7th and 8th, 1859* (Norwich, CT: John W. Stedman, 1859), 111, 198 ff., 299. This document provides a list of the deputies from Norwich to the General Court and Representatives in the General Assembly, 1662-1704. The author cites Chancellor Walworth and Judge F. P. Tracy, a renowned speaker and family genealogist from San Francisco, CA. Walworth attended the Jubilee, F. P. Tracy did not.

John Swett, *Public Education in California: Its Origin and Development, with Personal Reminiscences of Half a Century* (New York, NY: American Book Company, 1911). The author provides a lengthy footnote on his father-in-law, Frederick Palmer Tracy, including the observation that Tracy's genealogical manuscript was a thousand pages.

Alvan Talcott & Jacquelyn L. Ricker, 1984, *Families of Early Guilford, Connecticut* (Baltimore, MD: Genealogical Publishing Co., Inc., 1966), 530. The authors note that *Francis Griswold, son of Edward and Margaret, was born 1629 and died October 1671. He married Mary Tracy.* Like some others, they may have mistakenly believed that Lt. Thomas Tracy had a daughter named Mary. He did not.

Edward Livingston Taylor, "Monuments to Historical Indian Chiefs," *Ohio History: The Scholarly Journal of the Ohio Historical Society*, *1*, July 11, 1902, 1-29." Retrieved April 29, 2016 from http://publications.ohiohistory.org/ohj/browse/displaypages.php?display[]=0011&display[]=1&display[]=29. Taylor provides a detailed description and analysis of sachem Uncas. He mentions Thomas Tracy on page 6 as one of three men who rescued Uncas.

Roger Thompson, *Mobility and Migration: East Anglian Founders of New England, 1629-1640* (Amherst, MA: The University of Massachusetts Press, 1994), multiple pages. Prof. Thompson discusses the movement of East Anglian extended families to the colonies and the great majority of planters who left from Great Yarmouth who went to Salem.

Roger Thompson, *Divided We Stand: Watertown, Massachusetts 1630-1680* (Amherst, MA: University of Massachusetts Press, 2001), 11-19. Prof. Thompson provides an in-depth discussion of the immigrants who settled Watertown. Most were from East Anglia and especially Norfolk.

Clarence Almon Torrey, *New England Marriages Prior to 1700* (Baltimore, MD: Genealogical Publishing Co., Inc., 1985), 751. Torrey lists the marriage of Thomas Tracy to (1) unknown ca 1641 in Wethersfield, (2) Martha Bourne Bradford, and (3) Mary Foote Stardard Goodrich. He also had a fourth wife, Martha Bourne Bradford.

Town of Yarmouth, "Yarmouth's History". Retrieved September 5, 2016 from http://www.yarmouth.ma.us/index.aspx?nid=833. This is a paragraph that explains the origin of the town of Yarmouth, Massachusetts.

Town Records of Salem, Massachusetts, 1, 3 vols. (Salem, MA: The Essex Institute, 1868): 33, 40. This document contains the record of Thomas Trace (sic) arriving from Watertown to Salem and being offered five acres if he paid for them.

"Stephen Trace (sic)". Retrieved February 7, 2013 from http://www.
freereg.org.uk.cgi/SearchResults.pl?RecordType=Baptisms&Record
ID=247481. This record from the U.K. Parish Registers shows a Stephen
Trace (sic) baptised at St. Mary Church in East Ruston, Norfolk on April
7, 1558. It correctly shows his mother's name as Margaret, but erroneously
shows his father's name as "*Ctopher.*" Baptismal records in the Norfolk
Record Office irrefutably show that the parents of Stephen Tracy of East
Ruston in 1558 were Roger and Margaret Trace (sic).

Thomas Trace (sic), "England, Births and Christenings, 1538-
1975," index, *FamilySearch* (https://familysearch.org/pal:?MM9.1.1/J796-
VQC:accessed 03 Apr 2013), Thomas Trace, 18 Jan 1613. This Thomas
Tracy has been suggested as being the Lt. Thomas Tracy of Connecticut.
It is unlikely.

Dwight Tracy, "The Progeny of the Saxon Kings in America:
Unbroken Line of Descent from Egbert, First King of All England,
800-938, to William Tracy of Hayles Abbey Who Came to America in
1620 – Royal Lineage Sustained Through Thomas Tracy of Connecticut,
1636 – Illustrated with Eighteen Rare Reproductions from Antient
Documents." *The Connecticut Magazine*, 11 (1907): 217-245. As the title
suggests, Dr. Tracy, M.D., D.D.S. argues that Thomas Tracy was of royal
descent as a son of the William Tracy of Stanway who immigrated to
Virginia in 1620. He includes a purported signature of Thomas Tracy in
the book.

Dwight Tracy, "Tracy, Mason," *The New England Historical and Genealogical
Register* 61 (1907): 93. In this brief note, Dr. Tracy refutes the fact that Mary
Mason, the widow of Edward Mason was as the first wife of Thomas Tracy.
He correctly points out that the widow never remarried.

Dwight Tracy, "Recently Discovered English Ancestry of Governor
William Tracy of Virginia, 1620, and of His Only Son, Lieutenant Thomas

Tracy of Salem, Massachusetts and Norwich, Connecticut." *The Journal of American History*, MCMVIII. The premise by a usually more reliable historian as noted in the title has been debunked by several highly-respected historians in recent years.

Evert E. Tracy, *Tracy Genealogy: Ancestors and Descendants of Lieutenant Thomas Tracy of Norwich, Connecticut 1660* (Joel, Munsell's Sons Publishers, Albany, NY, 1898), 3-5, 20-23, 233-235. Tracy includes a brief biographical description of Thomas Tracy and family. He supports the claim that Thomas Tracy was born in Gloucestershire, England based on information from F. P. Tracy and Charles Stedman Ripley. The author also gives a brief biography of Frederick Palmer Tracy.

Helon Henry Tracy Genealogy and Temple Records (MSS 6792). L. Tom Perry Special Collections, Harold B. Lee Library, Brigham Young University, Provo, UT. This hand written collection includes a diary by Helon Henry Tracy that outlines his ancestry. He shows Thomas Tracy as having been born in Tewkesbury, England.

John Tracy (Sir), *Norfolk Family History Society*. Retrieved March 3, 2013 from http://norfolkfhs.ourarchives.info/bin/aps_detail.php?id=3972618. This records the date of death of Sir John Tracy as ??.03.1663 and his burial in the south aisle of the All Saints Anglican Church in Stanhoe, Norfolk.

John Kent Tracy, *A Short Memoir, Critically Illustrating the Histories of the Noble Families of Tracy, and Courtenay, Exhibiting Likewise, the Ancient Usage, or Variation, of Coat Armour, in That of Tracy* (Canterbury, England, 1796). Reprinted by Eighteen Century Collections Online (ECCO). John Tracy of Brompton, Gillingham, Kent details the evolution of the Tracy family line dating to William de Tracy (d. 1136), illegitimate son of Henry I who married the daughter of Turgis de Traci (sic). William took the name of his wife.

Martin Booth Tracy, *New England Colonial Ancestors of James Albert Tracy, Sr. (Born 1972 in Wood County, WV) Descendant of Lt. Thomas Tracy (1610-1685) & Stephen Tracy (1595-1655)* (Murray, KY: Author, January 2009). This is a compilation of brief biographies of 14 New England ancestors of the author.

Martin Booth Tracy, "Lt. Thomas Tracy (1610-1685) of Norwich, Connecticut." *The Connecticut Nutmegger* (forthcoming). This is an extensively documented narrative on Lt. Thomas Tracy's origin and life.

Nathaniel Brackett Tracy, *Historical Address before the Fourth Annual Reunion of the Tracy Family at Gouldsboro, Maine, August 19, 1989* (Auburn, ME: Palmer Print & Stamp Works, 1900), 13. N. B. Tracy, as he is better known, also bought into the notion that Thomas Tracy was the son of Nathaniel of Tewksbury based on the writings of Judge F. P. Tracy.

Ruby Tracy, Past President, Tracy Reunion Association. "Lt. Thomas Tracy". Retrieved July 12, 2012 from http://www.myfamily.com/group/tracy/discussions/131869284. The posting is dated July, 2001. The website retired September 30, 2014. Ruby Tracy supports the theory that Lt. Thomas Tracy was from Gloucestershire, England. She cites Hyde, Browning, and Burke as evidence.

Sherman Weld Tracy, *The Tracy Genealogy: Being Some of the Descendants of Stephen Tracy of Plymouth Colony, 1623. Also Ancestral Sketches and Chart* (Rutland, VT: The Tuttle Publishing Company, Inc., 1936), 15-18. While the focus is on Stephen Tracy, Weld outlines the purported lineage of Thomas Tracy as being from Toddington. This, of course, has been shown to be not likely.

"Tracy Family Papers (MS 816)". Manuscripts and Archives, Yale University Library. These papers provide biographical histories of several prominent Tracys.

Tracy Family: Cyrus Tracy, Frederick Palmer Tracy, Frank Tracy Swett, John Swett. *Tracy Family Papers, Circa 1800-1888.* BANC MSS Z-Z 107, v.2:1 and v.2:2.These papers include a notebook by Cyrus Tracy, letters addressed to F.P. and Mrs. Emily Tracy and from Mary Tracy to John Swett, a printed article on grape growing in Contra Costa County, a *"Tracy Family Genealogy"* probably completed around 1848. The papers are housed at the Bancroft Library, University of California, Berkeley.

"Tracy", Inquiry from F.P.T. of San Francisco. *The Historical Magazine and Notes and Queries Concerning the Antiquities, History and Biography of America,* v. II (New York, NY: C. Benjamin Richardson, 1858), 91. This is a letter from Frederick Palmer Tracy asking for information on the name of the first wife of Thomas Tracy. He mentions that Thomas was from Gloucestershire, England.

Benjamin Trumbull, *A Complete History of Connecticut Civil and Ecclesiastical: From the Emigration of its First Planters from England, in the Year 1630, to the Year 1764; and to the Close of the Indian Wars,* v. 1 (New London, CT: H. D. Utley, 1898), 84. Thomas Tracy is listed as a principle planter of Saybrook.

J. Hammond Trumbull, *The Public Records of the Colony of Connecticut Prior to the Union with New Haven Colony, May 1665; Transcribed and Published, (In Accordance with a Resolution of the General Assembly,)Under the supervision of the Secretary of State, with Occasional Notes, and an Appendix,* v. 1 (Hartford, CT: Brown and Parsons, 1850). Trumbull makes multiple references to Thomas Tracy serving on juries and election as Deputy to the General Court.

J. Hammond Trumbull, *The Public Records of the Colony of Connecticut, From 1665 to 1679; With the Journal of the Council of War, 1675-1678; Transcribed and Edited, in Accordance with a Resolution of the General Assembly, with Notes and an Appendix,* 2 (Hartford, CT: F. A. Brown, 1852), 49, 56, 70, 74, 87, 90, 96, 126, 136, 170-71, 189, 286, 294, 386, 523. Trumbull records the engagement of Thomas with the General Court, Court of Election, and Council.

J. Hammond Trumbull (Ed.), *The Memorial History of Hartford County, Connecticut 1633-1884, Vol. II, Town Histories* (Boston, MA: Edward L. Osgood Publisher, 1886), 435, 437. Trumbull mentions Thomas Tracy as one of the 26 militia from Wethersfield during the Pequot War. He also mentions him as an early settler of Wethersfield.

William Henry Upton, *Upton Family Records: Being Genealogical Collections for an Upton Family History* (London, England: Mitchell and Hughes, 1893), 159-160. Upton provides a pedigree of the Tracy of Stanway family. He chides Walworth for not providing any authority to support the claim that Thomas was a member of the Stanway family.

Roland G. Usher, *The Pilgrims and Their History* (New York, NY: The McMillan Company, 1920), 170. Usher discusses the relatively obscurity of the Plymouth Colony in the shadow of the Massachusetts Bay Company.

Vital Records of Norwich 1659-1848, Part I (Hartford, CT: Society of Colonial Wars in the State of Connecticut, 1913), 7. The records list *"Thomas Tracy deceased 7 November 1685."*

Vital Records of Norwich 1659-1848, Part I (Hartford, CT: Society of Colonial Wars in the State of Connecticut, 1913), IX. The records note that "Norwich was settled in 1659, under the name Mohegan, and received its present name in 1662."

(Robert) Wace, *Roman de Rou: The Conquest of England from Wace's Poem* translated by Alexander Malet (London, England: Bell and Daldy, 1860), 197. This is a verse by Wace written in the Norman language. It is a Normandy epic poem. The poem has a footnote referring to a Tracy family and castle in the commune of Caen in the prefecture of Calvados.

Reuben H. Walworth, *Hyde Genealogy or the Descendants, in the Female as well as in the Male Lines from William Hyde, of Norwich with Their Places of*

Residence, and Dates of Birth, Marriages, &C., and Other Particulars of Them and Their Families and Ancestry, I, 1 (Albany, NY: J. Munsell, 1864), vii-viii, 26. Walworth claims that Thomas Tracy of Connecticut was a son of Nathaniel Tracy of Tewksbury. He cites Burke's Peerage, 1856 and F. P. Tracy as sources.

Reuben H. Walworth, *Hyde Genealogy or the Descendants, in the Female as well as in the Male Lines from William Hyde, of Norwich with Their Places of Residence, and Dates of Birth, Marriages, &C., and Other Particulars of Them and Their Families and Ancestry*, II, 2 (Albany, NY: J. Munsell, 1864), 1175-1178. The second volume of *Hyde Genealogy* includes the descent of Lt. Thomas Tracy beginning with the 8th generation from King Egbert. Thomas is shown as the 20th generation, son of Nathaniel Tracy of Tewksbury.

David Jay Webber, "Major William Bradford's Second Wife: Was She the Widow of Francis Griswold?" *The New England Historical and Genealogical Register,* 155 (July, 2001): 245-250. Webber dispels the myth that the widow of Francis Griswold was the daughter of Thomas Tracy or Thomas Fitch, as well as the myth that she was the widow of a Wiswall. He contends she was most likely the widow of Francis Griswold.

Harriette Hyde Wells, *Several Ancestral Lines of Moses Hyde and His Wife Sarah Dana, Married at Ashford, Conn., June 5, 1757 with A Full Genealogical History of their Descendants to the End of the Nineteenth Century, Covering Three Hundred Years and Embracing Ten Generations* (Albany, NY: Joel, Munshell's Sons, 1904), 39. Wells notes the amount of land and cash that Thomas left in his will.

Henry Whittemore, *History of Middlesex County Connecticut with Biographical Sketches of Its Prominent Men* (New York, NY: J. B. Beers & Co., 1884), 334, 451, 537. Whittemore lists the original proprietors of Saybrook, including Thomas Tracy. There is a reference to the request of Thomas in 1684 to resolve a boundary dispute and his involvement in the surveying of the four quarters of the *"outlands"* and the Potapaug Quarter at Lyme. He notes that there were 48 proprietors in Saybrook and Lyme in 1648.

"Will of Joshua Uncas." *The New England Historical and Genealogical Register 13* (July, 1859): 235-237. (Online database: *AmericanAncestors.org*, New England Historic Genealogical Society, 2001-2013). Joshua Uncas, son of Uncas wrote his will on February 29, 1675. In it he left a sizable tract of land to 13 men, including Thomas, John Mason, and Thomas Leffingwell. The land was to be divided equally among them.

J. P. C. Winship, *Historical Brighton, Volume Two: An Illustrated History of Brighton and Its Citizens* (Boston, MA: George A. Warren, Publisher, 1902), 43. Winship briefly mentions Thomas Tracy as an ancestor of a citizen of Brighton. Thomas is identified as having come to Salem from Stanway. Like so many others, there is no mention that Watertown was Thomas' first destination.

Justin Winsor, *History of the Town of Duxbury, Massachusetts, with Genealogical Registers* (Boston, MA: Crosby & Nichols, 1849), 229. Winsor shows the marriage of Martha Bourne to John Bradford (1) and to Thomas Tracy (2).

"Yale Indian Papers Project, Committee Report Concerning Uncas' Complaints." Retrieved July 30, 2016 from http://yipp.yale.edu/annotated-transcription/digcoll3863. This brief article notes that Thomas Tracy and Francis Griswold were asked to warn the Indians of Quinebaug not to hunt within the land of Uncas.

PURITAN-PILGRIM-SEPARATIST-NON-SEPARATIST & PLYMOUTH BACKGROUND

"A New Insight into the Early Settlement of Plymouth Plantation." *The Plymouth Colony Archive Project*. Retrieved January 8, 2016 from www.histarch.illinois.edu/plymouth/galleapp.html. This document provides concise background information on the settlement at Plymouth.

Robert Charles Anderson (Ed.), *The Great Migration Newsletter*. GreatMigration.org. New England Historic Genealogical Society. Multiple issues. Anderson edits this wonderful resource for all things related to the Great Migration.

Robert Charles Anderson (Ed.), "Migration from County Essex." *Great Migration Newsletter*, v. 5, No. 1 (January-March, 1994):129. This article describes the pattern of immigration from East Anglia.

Animals and Livestock of Early Plymouth. Retrieved August 15, 2013 from http://mayflowerhistory.com/livestock. The article notes that the first cattle arrived on the *Anne*.

Robert Ashton, "Memoir of Rev. John Robinson." *Collections of the Massachusetts Historical Society, Vol. 1 of the Fourth Series* (Boston, MA: Published by the Society, 1852), 111-164. Ashton provides an overview of Rev. John Robinson, including references to his ministry in Norwich, England.

J. Jason Boroughs, "A New Insight into the Early Settlement of Plymouth Plantation." *The Plymouth Colony Archive Project*, April 1997. Retrieved January 8, 2016 from www.histarch.illinois.edu/plymouth/jbthesis.html. Boroughs' undergraduate thesis at the University of Virginia provides an interesting overview of the colonization of New England.

J. M. Bumsted, "Revivalism and Separatism in New England: The First Society of Norwich, Connecticut, as a Case Study." *The William and Mary Quarterly*, v. 24, No. 4 (October 1967): 588-612. Bumsted includes a discussion of the half-way covenant and Rev. Fitch.

Nick Bunker, *Making Haste From Babylon: The Mayflower Pilgrims and Their World. A New History* (New York, NY: Alford A. Knopf, 2010), 126, 132-34, 172-73, 213-15, 219, 252, 332, 338, 388, 402-03. Bunker is an excellent resource for a background on the development of the Pilgrims and distinguishing Separatists from Non-Separatists. He discusses the desire of Puritans to be more virtuous and do more public service. He mentions the need to expand and the concern it created for Gov. Bradford.

Jo Ann Butler, *Rebel Puritan: A Scandalous Life* (Ann Arbor, MI: Neverest Press, 2010). Butler wrote an interesting novel of the life and times during the early 1660s in New England.

Jo Ann Butler, *The Reputed Wife: A Scandalous Life* (Ann Arbor, MI: Neverest Press, 2013). Butler wrote a sequel to the first book.

Doris Palmer Buys, "Who Were the Parents of Lieut. Thomas Tracy born 1610, Gloucestershire, England, Died Norwich, CT. 7 Nov 1685, Second Husband of Mary Mason, Widow of Edward (or John) Mason, by Whom He Had Seven Children." *Hear-Saye, Quarterly Newsletter of the Saybrook Colony Founders Association*, v. XI, No. 1 (Spring 1996): 517. Buys' inquiry is answered by Dr. David L. Greene in the Fall issue of *Hear-Saye*.

William T. Davis (Ed.), *Bradford's History of Plymouth Plantation 1606-1646* (New York, NY: Barnes & Noble, Inc., 1908), 38-39, 44. Davis provides an excellent description of living conditions of the Puritans in Holland.

William T. Davis, *Genealogical Register of Plymouth Families* (Baltimore, MD: Genealogical Publishing Co., INC., 1975), 266. Davis notes the arrival of Stephen Tracy on the *Ann* (sic) in 1623 with his wife Tryphosa and daughter Sarah. After arrival he had Rebecca, Ruth, Mary, and John. Note that Tryphosa probably was not with him on the *Anne*. She and Sarah probably arrived on the *Jacob*.

William T. Davis, *History of the Town of Plymouth with a Sketch of the Origin and Growth of Separatism* (Philadelphia, PA: J. W. Lewis & Co., 1885), 11, 30-34, 40, 46. Davis notes that Stephen Tracy was a say-maker; he participated in the division of lands in 1624, and was granted 50 acres. He also notes that Stephen was on the list of freemen in 1633.

Patricia Scott Deetz & J. Eric Deetz, *Population of Plymouth Town, Colony & County, 1620-1690*. Retrieved November 27, 2007 from http// etext.virginia.edu/users/deetz/Plymouth/townpop.html. This brief article discusses each of the first five ships to arrive at Plymouth and the 1623 Division of Land.

Henry Martyn Dexter & Morton Dexter, *The England and Holland of the Pilgrims* (Boston, MA: Houghton, Mifflin and Company, 1905), 490. The authors briefly discuss the makeup of the English in Holland, including "*S. Tracy.*"

Christopher Fennel, "The Duties and Rights of Freemen." *The Plymouth Colony Archive Project*. Retrieved September 18, 2016 from http://www. histarch.illinois.edu/plymouth/ccflaw.html. Fennel describes the duties and rights of a freeman in Plymouth.

Louise Greene, *The Development of Religious Liberty in Connecticut* (Boston, MA: Houghton, Mifflin and Company, 1905). Greene gives an excellent description of the development of Congregationalism, especially in Watertown and Wethersfield which, along with Boston and Salem set the type for the 35 churches founded in New England before 1640.

Dwight B. Heath (Ed.), *Mourt's Relation: A Journal of the Pilgrims at Plymouth* (Bedford, MA: Applewood Books, 1963). Heath edits a version of a journal originally written in 1622.

Frank R. Holmes, *Directory of the Ancestral Heads of New England Families 1620-1700* (Baltimore, MD: Genealogical Publishing Co., Inc., 1964), ccxli. Holmes discusses the Tracy family line in the United Kingdom as apparently being descended from Sire de Tracie, an illegitimate son of William the Conqueror who fought in the Battle of Hastings during the Norman Conquest in 1066.

"Mary Queen of Scots: How Her Death Gave Rise to the Pilgrim Fathers," *Self Culture: A Magazine of Knowledge with Departments Devoted to the Interests of the Home University League*, v. III, No. 2 (May, 1896): 137-141. This article provides information and insights on the impact of the death of Queen Mary on William Brewster, the hamlet of Scrooby, John Robinson, and the Separatists.

Edmund S. Morgan, *The Puritan Family: Religious and Domestic Relations in Seventeenth-Century New England* (New York, NY: Harper & Row, 1944, 1966). Morgan provides seven essays of Puritan beliefs and life in New England.

Forrest Morgan (Ed), *Connecticut as a Colony and as a State, or One of the Original Thirteen* (Hartford, CT: The Publishing Society of Connecticut, 1904), 279. Morgan suggests that Uncas sold the nine-square mile to fund his fight against the Narragansets. He also provides an excellent description of the attack at Mystic.

Daniel Neal, *The History of the Puritans; or Protestant Nonconformists from the Reformation in 1517, to the Revolution in 1688* (London, England: Printed for Thomas Tegg and Son, 1837), 419ff, 689. Neal provides a description of the Puritans (Brownists) of England. He notes the high concentration of them in Norfolk and Suffolk.

"Pilgrims in a Nutshell (The)." Retrieved January 1, 2008 from http://www.pilgrimarchives.nl/html/pilgrims/top_html/history.html. This is a brief summary of the Pilgrims in Leiden, Holland.

"Population of Plymouth Town, Colony & County, 1620-1690." *The Plymouth Colony Archive Project*. Retrieved January 8, 2016 from www.histarch.illinois.edu/plymouth/galleapp.html. This document covers the arrival of the *Anne* and the *Little James* and the 1623 Division of Land.

"Separatists, Puritan," *Dictionary of American History*. Retrieved March 4, 2016 from http://www.encyclopedia.com/doc/1G2-3401803807.html. This entry in the Dictionary briefly defines Separatism and Puritanism.

"The Puritan Scene". Retrieved October 4, 1015 from www.christianchronicler.com/history1/puritan.scene.htm. The article defines types of Puritanism and Separatism in 1600s England.

Walter Rye, *An Address from the Gentry of Norfolk and Norwich to General Monck in 1660: Facsimile of a Manuscript in the Norwich Public Library* (Norwich, England: Jarrold & Sons Ltd., 1913), 62. Rye refers to Sir Tracy of Stanhoe who signed the letter to General Monck protesting government interference and heavy taxes.

Henry Whittemore, *The Heroes of the American Revolution and Their Descendants: Battle of Long Island* (Brooklyn, NY: The Heroes of the Revolution Publishing Co., 1897), 85. Whittemore discusses the Tracy family line in the United Kingdom as apparently having descended from Sire de Tracie, an illegitimate son of William the Conqueror who fought in the Battle of Hastings during the Norman Conquest in 1066.

WORKS OF PEDIGREE AND HERALDRY OF THE TRACYS OF TEWKESBURY, TODDINGTON, & STANWAY, GLOUCESTERSHIRE, ENGLAND

James Bennett, *The History of Tewkesbury* (Tewkesbury, England: Author, 1830). Bennett gives a very clear, concise description of the pedigree of the ancient family of Tracy.

John Britton, *Graphic Illustrations with Historical and Descriptive Accounts of Toddington, Gloucestershire, The Seat of Lord Sudeley* (London, England: The Author, 1840), Chapter V. Britton provides a detailed chart of the Tracy family that morphed into the Sudeley family.

Charles H. Browning, *Americans of Royal Descent: A Collection of Genealogies of American Families whose Lineage is Traced to the Legitimate Issue of Kings* (Philadelphia, PA: Porter & Coates, 1883), 220. Browning lists the Tracy family lineage of Stanway, including Nathaniel as father of Thomas. He shows a pedigree going back to the Saxon King Ethelred.

John Bernard Burke, *A Genealogical and Heraldic Dictionary of the Peerage and Baronetage of the British Empire, 14th edition* (London: Colburn and Co., Publisher, 1852), 952-53. Burke outlines the lineage of the ancient family of Tracy dating back to the Saxon Kings and William the Conqueror.

John Bernard Burke, *A Genealogical History of the Dormant, Absent, Forfeited, and Extinct Peerages of the British Empire* (London, England: Harrison, 1866), 536-37. Burke provides an outline of the lineage of Viscount Tracy of Rathcoole up to Henrietta Susanna Tracy who married Charles Hanbury.

John Burke & John Bernard Burke, *A Genealogical and Heraldic History of the Extinct and Dormant Baronetcies of England, Ireland, and Scotland*, Second

Edition (London, England: Printed for Scott, Webster, and Geary, 1841), 530-532. The Burkes include the extinct linage of Sir John Tracy of Toddington through Henry Leigh Tracy, 8th Viscount whose death in 1797 ended the male line of this family. His daughter Henrietta married Charles Hanbury.

Henry Chitting, et al., *The Visitation of the County of Gloucester: Taken In the Year 1623* (London, England: Harleian Society, 1885), 165-167. Chitting gives a chart on the Tracy family of Toddington and Stanway.

"Family Tree of the Tracys of Stanway and of the Charterises of Amisfield, Earls of Wemyss." This chart was obtained by the author from the Gloucestershire Record Office. It has detailed information on the Tracy pedigree. There is no mention of a Thomas Tracy born about 1610.

Edward Kimber & John Almon, *The Peerage of Ireland: A Genealogical and Historical Account of All the Peers of that Kingdom, Their Descents, Collateral Branches, Births, Marriages, and Issue* (London, England: Printed for J. Almon, 1768), 43-47. The Tracy peerages in this book begin with an explanation of the Tracy family in Normandy who arrived in 1066 with William the Conqueror. It traces the line through Thomas-Charles the 5th Viscount Tracy.

Audrey Locke, *The Hanbury Family*, v. 1 (London, England: Arthur L. Humphreys, 1916). Locke provides an accurate family chart of the Family of Hanbury-Tracy of Stanway. It begins with Charles Hanbury-Tracy, 1st Lord and his wife the Hon. Henrietta Susanna Tracy, the last of the Tracy line.

Cuyler Reynolds, *Genealogical and Family History of Southern New York and the Hudson River Valley: A Record of the Achievements of Her People in the Making of a Commonwealth and the Building of a Nation*, Volume III (New York, NY: Lewis Historical Publishing Company, 1914), 1414-1416. Reynolds reviews the ancient lineage of the Tracy family, including the residents of Toddington and Stanway. He makes a grievous error in identifying the Pilgrim Stephen Tracy as a grandson of Richard Tracy of Stanway. Baptismal records prove that Stephen was born in Norfolk County.

MISCELLANEOUS RESOURCES

Peter Ackroyd, *Tudors: The History of England from Henry VIII to Elizabeth I* (New York, NY: Thomas Dunne Books, 2013). An excellent overview of the development of Puritanism in England as a backdrop to the reign of Kings and Queens from Henry VIII to Elizabeth I.

G. Albemarle, G. Monck, W. Rye & H. Le Strange, *An Address from the Gentry of Norfolk and Norwich to General Monck in 1660: Facsimile of a Manuscript in the Norwich Public Library* (Norwich, England: Jarrold & Sons, Ltd., 1913), 62. There is a one sentence mention of Sir John Tracy of Stanhoe in this book.

S. T. Bindoff (Ed.), "Tracy, Richard (by 1501-69), of Stanway, Glos." *The History of Parliament: The House of Commons 1509-1558*. Retrieved July 6, 2012 from http://www.historyofparliamentonline.org/volume/1509-1558/member/tracy-richard-1501-69. Bindoff provides a thorough description of the life of Richard Tracy of Stanway.

Biographical Directory of the State of New York 1900 (New York, NY: Biographical Directory Company, 1900), 498-499. This directory highlights several well-known Tracys in the state of New York, including Benjamin Franklin Tracy, Evart Tracy, Howard Crosby Tracy, Dr. Ira Otis Tracy, Jeremiah Evarts Tracy, Osgood Vose Tracy, and Roger Sherman Tracy. These distinguished men were descendants of Stephen Tracy of Plymouth & Duxbury, except for Dr. Ira Otis and Osgood Vose Tracy. Dr. Ira Otis Tracy was a descendant of Lt. Thomas Tracy through Thomas Tracy, Jr. Osgood Vose Tracy descended from Thomas Tracy's son, John.

Email from Jo Ann Butler, September 5, 2014. Ms. Butler responded to my inquiry on the Puritan lifestyle she portrays in her novels, as well as to a specific question on the Gardner family.

Catharine Davies "A Protestant Gentleman and the English Reformation: The Career and Attitudes of Richard Tracy, 1501-1569. In Margaret Aston, *Broken Idols of the English Reformation* (Cambridge, England: Cambridge University Press, 2016), 121-134. Davies provides an insightful discussion of the role of Richard Tracy of Stanway during the Reformation.

Evens, W., Malkin, M., Miah, M., Nikolov, I., Welshimer, K., Tebb, S., Tracy, P. D., & Tracy, M. B. (2003). Russian-American Summer University: A Collaboration between Samara Oblast, Russia & Southern Illinois University Carbondale, Illinois. In Y. Asamoah, L. M. Healy & M. C. Hokenstad (eds.) *Models of international collaboration in social work education* (Alexandria, VA: Council on Social Work Education, 2003):125-132.

C. L'Estrange Ewen, *A History of Surnames of the British Isles: A Concise Account of Their Origin, Evolution, Etymology and Legal Status* (London, England: Kegan Paul, Trench, Trubner & Co., Ltd., 1931), 81, 169, 243-44. Ewen lists Tracy as among the surnames from place-names in France and Normandy.

Charles A. Flagg, *A Guide to Massachusetts Local History: Being a Bibliographic Index to the Literature of the Towns, Cities and Counties of the State, Including Books, Pamphlets, Articles in Periodicals and Collected Works, Books in Preparation, Historical Manuscripts, Newspaper Clippings, etc.* (Salem, MA: The Salem Press Company, 1907), 187-188. Flagg notes that the village of Namassakeeset was annexed to Duxbury in 1658.

Connecticut Historical Society, *The Law Papers: Correspondence and Documents during Jonathan Law's Governorship of the Colony of Connecticut 1741-1750, I (October 1741-July 1745).* (Hartford, CT: Author, 1907), 101-111. The "*Mason Controversy*" that divided the Mohegan tribe for years is discussed in these papers.

Charles Harding Firth, *Oliver Cromwell and the Rule of the Puritans in England* (London, England: Oxford University Press, 1953). An excellent source for a history of the English Civil War and the rise and fall of Oliver Cromwell and his Puritan supporters.

John Espy and Janet Elaine Gertz, *Guide to the Tracy Family Papers, MS 816* (New Haven, CT: Yale University Library Manuscripts and Archives, 2015), 3-7. These papers on the Tracy Family are housed in the Sterling Memorial Library at Yale. They include papers on ten members of the Tracy family. The most prominent are Uriah Tracy, Roger Sherman Tracy, Howard Crosby Tracy, and Evarts Tracy.

"Charles Hanbury-Tracy, 1st Baron Sudeley." Retrieved July 5, 2012 from https://en.wikipedia.org/wiki/Charles_Hanbury-Tracy,_1st_Baron_Sudeley. This article describes the life of the 1st Baron Sudeley who married Henrietta Susanna Tracy only child of and heiress of Henry Leigh Tracy, 8th (and last) Viscount Tracy.

"Merlin Hanbury-Tracy, 7th Baron Sudeley." Retrieved July 5, 2012 from https://en.wikipedia.org/wiki/Merlin_Hanbury-Tracy,_7th_Baron_Sudeley. This article describes Merlin Charles Sainthill Hanbury-Tracy, Conservative Party member. Twice married, he has no children.

David Howes, "The Tracey and Blaizie Conundrum." *The Norfolk Ancestor*, v. 7, Part 2 (June, 2010): 131-132. Howes wrote a piece for the *The Norfolk Ancestor* in which he raises the question of the relationship between the Tracey (sic) and Blaizie connection in Norfolk. This prompted a series of email exchanges between the Howes and myself to determine if there was an connection between our families. The conclusion was that it isn't likely. However, it did lead me to discover that one branch of the Tracy family that came to England might have originated in two villages near Paris.

Pete Kendall, "Hardware Store Owner Knew How to Get Along." *Cleburne [Texas]Times Review*, 26 January, 2009. Retrieved January 28, 2011 from http://www.cleburnetimesreview.com/news/local_news/hardware-store-owner-knew-how-to-get-along/article_e175bda5-aa36-5764-9e5f-f38c8d827d54.html.

Pete Kendall, "The Yankee Who Befriended Johnny Reb after Civil War." *Cleburne [Texas] Times Review,* 28 March 2011. Retrieved January 27, 2017 from http://www.cleburnetimesreview.com/archives/the-yankee-who-befriended-johnny-reb-after-civil-war/article_f94a5f2a-397c-582f-a4d3-cdfdfb68c828.html.

The National Cyclopaedia of American Biography Being the History of the United States as Illustrated in the Lives and Founders, Builders and Defenders of the Republic, and of the Men and Women Who Are Doing the Work and Molding the Thought of the Present Time, XV (New York, NY: James T. White & Company, 1916), 336. This volume includes a section on Howard Crosby Tracy, descendant of Stephen Tracy of Plymouth & Duxbury.

Julie Helen Otto, "Name Origins: Tryphena." *NEHGS, eNews, 11, No. 28, Whole #435* (July 15, 2009). Retrieved July 25, 2009 from an obsolete website. Otto explains the origin of the names Tryphena and Tryphosa.

"Saybrook Colony," Retrieved September 21, 2016 from https://en.wikipedia.org/wiki/Saybrook_Colony. This article provides a brief overview of the history of the Saybrook Colony.

"Baron Sudeley," Retrieved July 5, 2012 from https://en.wikipedia.org/wiki/Baron_Sudeley. This article gives a brief explanation of the third creation of the Baron Sudeley of Toddington in 1838 to Charles Hanbury-Tracy.

Cyrus Mason Tracy, Jr. *Studies of the Essex Flora: A Complete Enumeration of All Plants Found Growing Naturally Within the Limits of Lynn, Mass., and the Adjoining, Arranged According to the Natural System, with Copious Notes as to Localities and Habits* (Lynn, MA: Stevenson & Nichols, Printers, 1858), 15-16. The author gives a poetic perspective of the wonders of nature.

Cyrus Mason Tracy, Jr., William E. Graves & Henry M. Batchelder, *Standard History of Essex County, Massachusetts, Embracing A History of the*

County From Its First Settlement to the Present Time, with a History and Description of Its Towns and Cities (Boston, MA: C. F. Jewett & Company, 1878). The authors provide detailed descriptions of the early towns of Massachusetts.

"Tracy, Frederick Palmer", Quarterly Obituary, *The New England Historical and Genealogical Register* 15 (January, 1861) 90. This obituary provides a succinct summary of the life of F. P. Tracy.

John Kent Tracy, *A Short Memoir, Critically Illustrating the Histories of the Noble Families of Tracy, and Courtenay, Exhibiting Likewise, the Ancient Usage, or Variation, of Coat Armour, in that of Tracy* (Canterbury, England: Unknown, 1796). Reproduction from British Library. This book provides a detailed description of the origin of the Tracy family beginning in Tracy-Bocage, Calvados, France.

"Tracy Pedigree". *Willimantic [Connecticut] Journal*, XVIII, v. 49, No. 7 (December, 1865):199.

"Tracy, Richard (by 1501-69), of Stanway, Glos." Retrieved September 21, 2016 from http://www.historyofparliamentonline.org/volume/1509-1558/member/tracy-richard-1501-69. This article provides a good biography of Richard Tracy.

"Viscount Tracy," Retrieved July 5, 2012 from https://en.wikipedia.org/wiki/Viscount_Tracy. This brief article lists all the Viscount Tracys beginning with Sir John Tracy on January 12, 1643, previously member of the Parliament from Gloucestershire. He was made Baron Tracy of Rathcoole, Dublin County.

ACKNOWLEDGEMENTS

I haven't done anything interesting in the past nearly 54 years without the love and support of my wife, Patsy. She even encouraged me to take on the challenge of writing this narrative knowing full well she'd be subjected to listening to me for hours on end about each new discovery. Her input, as always, has been priceless. She is my muse! Of course, I'm indebted to Cousin Bonnie Alamo Seto Myers for getting me started on this quest so many years ago. And also to her mother, Cousin Muriel Bloxom Seto, who's shared gusto for family history and appreciation for historical accuracy has been an ongoing inspiration. My son, Morgan, the provider of many otherwise unattainable books and tricks of online searches, continues to support me in so many wonderful ways.

Cousin Thomas Tracy Allen were kind enough to take time from his busy schedule to examine two of the three volume collection *"Tracy Family Papers, Circa 1800-1888,"* housed at the Bancroft Library, University of California, Berkeley. It turned out to me a much more onerous task than expected. However, it was worth it given that the papers do apparently include the missing genealogical record written by Frederick Palmer Tracy. Tracy and his equally talented wife, Teri, also went beyond the call of duty and volunteered to help edit this tome. I, of course, am the sole person responsible for any errors of fact or abuse of the English language.

I want to give a special shout out to Dr. Duane Bolin, Professor of History at Murray State University. I have greatly benefited from delving into his vast reservoir of knowledge of early American history through conversations and book loans! Thanks also to Constance Alexander, Murray, Kentucky poet, writer, and social activist extraordinaire who encouraged me to write despite having read my meager attempts at prose and poetry.

Outside of the Bluegrass state, I've greatly benefited from materials and leads on Stephen Tracy graciously and speedily provided by Carolyn Ravenscroft, Archivist & Historian, *Duxbury Rural & Historical Society*; Lamont (Monty) R. Healy, Land Surveyor, Duxbury, MA; David J. Russo of the *Watertown Historical Commission*; and Susan Aprill, Archivist, *Kingston Public Library*, Kingston, MA. Likewise I'm indebted to Louise Leake, Genealogist, *Society of the Founders of Norwich*; Kathy Wieland, Genealogy Librarian, *Otis Library, Norwich* with their assistance on the life and times of Thomas Tracy; and Diane Hoyt, Administrative Assistant, *Old Saybrook Historical Society* for her help with clarifying the status of early Saybrook records and manuscripts.

Appreciation also goes to J. H. Torrance Downes, Trustee and Susan Sangster Record Keeper of *Cyprus Cemetery in Saybrook* for the information they provided on the cemetery. I am very grateful for an email discussion I had with Jo Ann Butler, author of the novels Rebel Puritan and Reputed Wife. Another very helpful source is Lorna K. Kirwan, Circulation Manager, *Bancroft Library, University of California* for her help in tracking down the Tracy Family Papers in the Library.

A very patient and understanding Maurice Klapwald, Assistant Manager, Interlibrary, Document & Research Services, New York Public Library searched out and delivered a copy of the illusive and illuminating 1938 *Report on Lt. Tracy* by H. Minot Pitman to me. The report is safely housed in the New York Genealogical and Biographical Society Collection and available for the asking. Another item housed in the NYPL is a file on the Haven genealogy which includes materials on Dr. Dwight Tracy, M.D., D.D.S. I want to give thanks to fellow Tracy-Haven family genealogist William H. Havens for going to the library, making copies of material of interest to me and sharing it with me.

Thanks much to Cousin Sean C. Tracy for his helpful suggestions and the leads I picked up from his stellar research on Thomas Tracy. Cousin Richard Tracy gave me valuable and much appreciated feedback on a very early draft. I've had several valuable email exchanges with Cousin Coralee Griswold on family ancestry. An expression of gratitude is also due my nephew Tracy Karnavas who walked me through a math problem.

On the other side of the big pond in my ancestral land in "The Norfolk Broads" (an ancient and lovely network of rivers and lakes in Norfolk and Suffolk) I have been fortunate to benefit from the expertise of professional genealogist Joanne Penn, as well as from the abundant historic records in the Norfolk Record Office. I also want to acknowledge the help of local genealogists Charles Butcher and Gillian Beckett of Stanhoe, Norfolk for clarifying the identity of Sir John Tracy. And Hannah Verge, Archivist, Norfolk Record Office who confirmed their information on Sir John.

Then there are my ancestors, Stephen and Thomas Tracy. It would be unconscionable for me not to thank them for living their lives and leaving a legacy of their worldly experiences. The statistical odds of me being a product of their procreation is beyond imagining. It has been great fun to try and narrow the gap of the nearly four centuries that separate me from them. Knowing more about who they were, how they lived, and the mettle they showed in their role in laying the foundation for this great democracy I love makes me proud to carry their DNA.

As John Lennon so eloquently expressed it in *"My Life"*: *"Though I know I'll never lose affection / For people and things that went before / I know I'll often stop and think about them / In my life I love you more"*

ABOUT THE AUTHOR

Martin Booth Tracy, Ph.D. is a retired professor, administrator, and international consultant. He received a BA degree in history and political science from Murray State University, an AM in political science and doctorate in social work from the University of Illinois. He is a U.S Army veteran. He and his wife, Patsy, served in the Peace Corps in Turkey. He was a Professor at the University of Iowa, Southern Illinois University, and the University of Kentucky. He held senior research positions with the U.S. Social Security Administration's Office of International Policy in Washington, D. C. and with the International Social Security Association in Geneva, Switzerland. He was a long-time consultant and trainer with the International Labor Organization in Geneva and Budapest, Hungary. He was a Fulbright Senior Specialist in Social Work at the University of Bucharest, Romania. He is a Rotarian and local United Way Board member. He lives with his wife in his hometown of Murray, Kentucky where they retired after a 40-year absence. They are the proud parents of one son and grandparents of two wonderful granddaughters.